The Culture and Politics of Populist Masculinities

The Culture and Politics of Populist Masculinities

Edited by
Outi Hakola, Janne Salminen,
Juho Turpeinen, and Oscar Winberg

LEXINGTON BOOKS
Lanham • Boulder • New York • London

Published by Lexington Books
An imprint of The Rowman & Littlefield Publishing Group, Inc.
4501 Forbes Boulevard, Suite 200, Lanham, Maryland 20706
www.rowman.com

6 Tinworth Street, London SE11 5AL, United Kingdom

British Library Cataloguing in Publication Information Available

Library of Congress Cataloging-in-Publication Data

Names: Hakola, Outi, editor.
Title: The culture and politics of populist masculinities / edited by Outi Hakola, Janne
    Salminen, Juho Turpeinen, and Oscar Winberg.
Description: Lanham : Lexington Books, [2021] | Includes bibliographical references
    and index.
Identifiers: LCCN 2021002283 (print) | LCCN 2021002284 (ebook) |
    ISBN 9781793635259 (cloth) | ISBN 9781793635266 (epub)
    ISBN 9781793635273 (pbk)
Subjects: LCSH: Masculinity—Political aspects. | Populism. | Political culture.
Classification: LCC HQ1090 .C848 2021 (print) | LCC HQ1090 (ebook) |
    DDC 155.3/32—dc23
LC record available at https://lccn.loc.gov/2021002283
LC ebook record available at https://lccn.loc.gov/2021002284

Contents

Introduction

Outi Hakola, Janne Salminen, Juho Turpeinen, and Oscar Winberg

President Donald J. Trump stands between Secretary General of NATO Jens Stoltenberg and British Prime Minister Theresa May in a photograph from the opening ceremony of the July 2018 Brussels Summit of the North Atlantic Treaty Organization. Trump is smiling broadly, May grimaces as she holds her hands in front of her as if to measure something. The caption reads "His balls . . ." or "They're the biggest I've ever seen! How does he walk?!?"—an internet meme, one of many. As these memes comment and propagate current topics, they emphasize political and cultural human agency behind such images (e.g., Shifman 2013). In the above example, the meme supports President Trump's position as a masculine leader. "Big balls" become metonymic for leadership, the ability to make decisions and take chances, and for virility and vitality. When this connection is made in contrast to other leaders, the meme offers an interpretative frame where a feminine leader, like May, is forced to admit Trump's "alpha male" masculinity. Here, this contemporary form of popular culture is utilized to legitimize Trump's political leadership and to idealize the masculinity of the leader. Politics and popular culture intertwine and issues of gender and populism are contested and negotiated in both. In this book, we turn critical attention to these kinds of intersections of politics, (popular) culture, and gender. In particular, we explore the intimate connection of populism and masculinity.

Populist political movements have dominated political discussions in the twenty-first century. Much has been said about the ways in which populist movements construct their political agendas and how they appeal to audiences. The role that popular culture—that is, what is popular in everyday life—plays in supporting, challenging, and portraying these movements, especially from the perspective of gender, has received comparatively less attention. In this book, we focus on gender, because it appears to be one of the central cultural discussions that make populist movements so divisive. Some approaches to contemporary politics emphasize the equality of genders and co-existence of diverse sexualities, while others often idealize clear-cut and traditional gender roles. Feminism and/or gender equality, particularly, have become a battleground for many populist movements.

Cultural tensions that constellate around gender inform the support and opposition for populist movements, both within right-wing and left-wing populist movements (Meret and Siim 2013; Rosdil 1991). Many left-wing movements have seen gender equality as a way to include women, and women's rights have become an important tool for approaching "the people." In comparison, right-wing movements view these social changes as a threat to masculinity and to male leadership, even if some of these movements, for example, in the Nordic countries, utilize some ideals of gender equality. Ruth Wodak (2015, 22) has called this "pseudo-emancipatory *gender policies*," which acknowledges gender equality, while interpreting gender through essentialist biological traits that aim to justify and support heteronormative socio-cultural values. Thus, the value of women or gender equality can be accepted and supported to a point that does not threaten, and rather aims to restore, "traditional" gender order and power relations. However, a more extreme version of masculine right-wing populism rejects even this approach. Didem Unal (chapter 4 in this collection) argues that, in the Turkish context, the conservative political establishment includes a moderate "complementarity of genders" model, which is criticized as inadequate by feminists and as feminist by anti-gender and anti-feminist movements. Both the moderate and the more extreme version can be read as part of what Tuija Saresma (2018, 181–192) calls "gender populism," where the desire is to see gender, in terms of power, as a "natural" and hierarchical social order that needs to be preserved.

Regardless of how populist movements approach gender equality and feminist politics, performances and ideas of masculinity tie into their politics. While definitions and histories of populism vary, notions of masculinities have become closely associated with populism around the globe. The populist narratives of culturally required and idealized masculinity legitimize attempts to maintain men's dominant position in society. At the same time, discussions on the (assumed) crisis of masculinity attract supporters by offering conservative gender views as an alternative to progressive gender politics. With this collection, we aim to bring these fears and ideals related to masculine practices in populist movements to the forefront of academic debates.

In order to discuss the complex relationship between populist politics and gender politics, this edited collection takes a cultural studies approach. Such an approach brings forward two important notions—radical contextuality and the role of everyday life, media and popular culture. First, radical contextuality, as defined by Lawrence Grossberg (2010), means that all everyday, social and political phenomena are complex, open to alteration, and can be understood only in their cultural contexts. Although "cultural studies does not deny the importance of abstract or general categories" (Grossberg 2010, 28), and the contributors in this collection draw on and develop such conceptual tools, it is not the aim of this book to seek a universalist theory of populism and masculinity. Instead, we argue that it is vital to understand what populist masculinities and masculine populisms mean in their cultural contexts. The various and complex forms that populism and gender equality take in different countries make overall arguments hard to present (Mudde and Kaltwasser 2015). For these reasons, this collection has a comparative perspective. Different chapters investigate different cultural contexts in Asian, European, Latin American, and North American societies, ranging from right-wing to left-wing populism. The argument is that although global debates bring transnational elements to contemporary understandings of both masculinities and populism, local cultural contexts also shape these discussions.

Second, it is important to remember that political debates do not take place on their own. We recognize that politics is more than matters of state; it is a part of the very fabric of human social life, its expressions worth investigating in all their forms. We argue that the ways in which both populism and ideas of gender, and masculinity in particular, are presented in culture and everyday discussions on media and social media, for example, are tightly connected to politics. For example, recent decisions to cast women in action roles, such as casting Jodie Whittaker to play the role of Doctor Who in the legendary television series, have incited backlash from many (male) viewers. The debates on what kind of masculinities and femininities are culturally acceptable and desirable are directly linked to the debates highlighted by populist performances and self-definitions. Thus, political movements are influenced by popular culture as much as they influence popular culture.

POPULISM AND GENDERED UNDERSTANDINGS OF "THE PEOPLE"

A contested concept, "populism" can mean radically different things in both academic and public discussions. Once we add historical contexts into the mix, definitions become even more complicated. Various political movements have had different uses for populism over the years, and in different countries, populism takes unique forms. Researchers have recognized at least left and right-wing populism, nationalist and neoliberal populism, as well as classical populism and neopopulism. Most writers, both academic and non-academic, accept that populism can be part of any political movement.

Indeed, for Ernesto Laclau (2005), populism is thin in meaning and becomes meaningful only when filled with ideological content in a political context. A rather widely used basic conceptualization is the contradiction between "the people" and "the elite," where "the people" is assumed to be the "pure" voice of citizens and "the elite" is a corrupt power (Moffitt and Tormey 2014; Mudde and Kaltwasser 2015). In this understanding, populism supports the beliefs and concerns of ordinary people, however artificial the notion of "ordinary people" might be.

When populism is understood as supporting the beliefs and concerns of ordinary people, the performative aspects of this process are highlighted. A performative approach emphasizes populist political movements' style of interacting with "ordinary people." According to Benjamin Moffitt and Simon Tormey, the rise of the mediatized landscape has increased the importance of political style and turned attention to performance. For example, populist leaders speak for "the people" although "the people" is always a construction that does not really exist, and yet, as a speech act it can produce that "people" at the same time (Moffitt and Tormey 2014). Several researchers have noted that these constructions tend to include gendered values and expectations (Eksi and Wood 2019; Geva 2020; Kantola and Lombardo 2019). In some cases, "the people" are assumed to be men set against some other elements of society, such as elites (particularly feminists) or outsiders (such as women or immigrants). For example, in Katinka Linnamäki's analysis of Viktor Orbán's populism in Hungary, this inside–outside logic is performed in relation sports, especially football, as a home-away distinction (chapter 2 in this collection).

Like populism, gender can be understood as performative. Judith Butler (1990) influentially noted that gender, and as such masculinity, is not an essentialist category, but a culturally constructed and performed phenomenon. As such, what kind of masculinities are considered desirable or the norm, for example, by populist movements, depends on their context. As R. W. Connell (2005) has argued, there is no singular masculinity, but various masculinities. While (right-wing) populist movements often idealize masculine traits and practices, they utilize different forms of masculinity. For example, Kovala and Pöysä note that in the Finnish context, populist practices have inspired a change in the styles of political masculinities. Stiff and "aristocratic" political masculinities have transformed into a plurality of masculinities that include also working-class or "rugged" political images. These masculinities highlight the notion of "the people," as it includes an "anti-elite" attitude, yet maintains gendered power relations (Kovala and Pöysä 2018). In addition, gender hierarchies are tightly interwoven with intersectional questions of sexualities, social class, race, and ethnicities (Norocel et al. 2020). Populist performances create ideals of masculinity that are preferred in relation to given groups of people. Different chapters in this book bring forward these intersections between power, "the people," and populism.

Throughout this book, we try to answer the following questions: What kinds of masculinities do populist movements create through performances and representations? What kinds of masculinities do they idealize in public discourses? What are gender debates used for, and how does gendered politics define the possibilities to participate in public? Each researcher uses a different type of source material, method, and conceptual framework, and by bringing their findings together and into discussion with each other, we build a more comprehensive picture of the gendered politics and political cultures of populism.

MASCULINITIES OF POPULIST LEADERS AND MOVEMENTS

Masculinity has a substantial role in the public image and style of populism, including political leaders' ability to address and represent "the people" through symbolic repertoires. This style highlights the importance of personalized leadership, political identification, and political spectacles (Jansen 2011; Moffitt and Turney 2014). However, male leadership and populism should not be causally linked. More likely, underlying cultural values and beliefs (such as practices of gender populism) affect what is expected of leadership (Mudde and Kaltwasser 2014). It appears that many populist movements tend to rely on populist leaders who emphasize the role of a strong and charismatic leader. This leadership has been quite masculine, both on the right and the left, and such leaders as Boris Johnson (UK), Donald Trump (US), Pablo Iglesias Turrión (Spain), Jair Bolsonaro (Brazil), and Daniel Ortega (Nicaragua) have personified male populist leadership.

This book opens with a comparison between different types of masculine leadership, and between different approaches to populism. Nicholas Manganas (chapter 1) analyzes Spanish populism and how historical context shapes the form of populist masculinities. Recognizing the decline of the dominant political parties and moments in the 2000s, he explores the new populist movements and visions in Spanish politics. Focusing on the importance of masculinity in populist politics, Manganas explores how gender informs political performances in Spain. While the left call for "feminist masculinity," meaning a masculine leadership that could also accommodate women's role in society, the right embraces macho-images opposing "feminazis." Manganas argues that this visible contradiction in gender issues serves as a metaphorical battleground between two different conceptualizations of the nation. Thus, the way in which masculine leadership is defined in populism also provides a certain image of what the nation itself is assumed (or desired) to be; the leader becomes a representation of the nation.

Gender appears to add affective power to the connections between political performance of leadership and populist idea of the nation and its "people." For example, Betul Eksi and Elizabeth Wood argue that Vladimir Putin and Recep T. Erdoğan heightened masculine performances as part of their appeal to "the people" in three different ways. First, they establish legitimacy through transgressive actions that highlight their "outsider-yet-dominant status." Second, they use conservative, heteronormative, and masculine behavior to establish their power. Third, while in power they represent themselves as "fathers" of the nation, who are strong and capable of protecting "the people." This process also aims to emasculate and other their opponents, which highlights their own masculinity (Eksi and Wood 2019; see also Norocel 2013). Similar tendencies have been recognized in left-wing populism of Latin America where populist leaders assume roles of paternal figures who are stereotypically "wise, brave, strong, responsible, protective" (Kampwirth 2010).

Patriarchal notions may have made these roles accessible for male politicians, yet populist movements also include women leaders, such as Marine Le Pen in France and Pauline Hanson in Australia. Their leadership positions do not automatically contradict the idealized understanding of (masculine) head-of-the-family type of strong protector of the nation. In many cases, these women leaders do not represent feminism—instead, they present themselves in a maternal way (Mudde and Kaltwasser 2015). For example, Dorit Geva argues that Marine Le Pen symbolizes both feminized and masculinized characteristics. She represents herself both as a mother caring for her people and as a masculine figure with virility to defend "the people" against foreign and internal threats, such as elites or immigrants. Thus, women can participate in populist politics as long as they perform an appropriate mix of caring for the people and having the strength to protect them (Geva 2020). Scholarship tends to agree that political power remains equated with masculinity, and in the case of populism, this holds true for both left-wing and right-wing populism.

However, the top-down performance of a dominant outsider, paternalistic or maternalistic, is not the only way in which populist leaders position themselves in relation to "the people." In this collection, Katinka Linnamäki (chapter 2) argues that Hungary's Viktor Orbán is a "gendered performative signifier" of an illiberal turn that began to take place in Hungary in 2006. Based on an analysis of photographic images posted on Orbán's Facebook page, Linnamäki argues that since 2010, Orbán has positioned himself, utilizing the empty signifiers of "sport" and "football," as the core of the Hungarian people, conceptualizing hegemonic masculinity and "the people" of the Hungarian illiberal logic as "home," while casting femininities to the periphery and the others of the Hungarian "people," such as the European Union, as "away."

Furthermore, many populist leaders have adopted performances related to (aggressive) masculine behavior. For example, in Latin American populism, male leadership roles are often paired with "machismo" discourse (Mudde and Kaltwasser 2015). Indeed, according to Mudde and Kaltwasser (2017), masculine populist leaders tend to be associated with the "charismatic strongman," a performance that is useful when attacking elites, uniting "the people" against outsiders, and for transforming the populist leader into the father figure of the nation. The "strongman" traits, such as being virile, potentially violent, and using simple and coarse language, emphasize action and the ability to make decisions. For example, Donald Trump has intentionally created his public image as a strong "alpha" male using insults and vulgarity (Winberg 2017). Joshua D. Martin (chapter 3) argues that Trump used his reputation from popular culture and media debates to reach the White House, sounding populist themes around the southern border. From his campaign announcement, Trump portrayed a crisis on the border, most notoriously in his calls for a border wall, to build a populist and masculine image. Portraying opponents as weak in the face of a crisis, Trump performed a populist masculinity to establish a "strongman" image of himself. While Trump has claimed that strong masculinity functions as a stabilizing force, for many these tactics also appear controversial.

Whereas populist leadership, in many cases, idealizes masculine traits and treats them as an extension of the nation itself, masculinity and gender issues are emphasized differently in the agendas of populist movements. Earlier research has shown that gender politics in populist movements have tended to be divided among the line of left–right-wing populism. However, more intriguingly, gender politics tends to refer to women's rights, families and feminism, whereas men's position in society is often bypassed (Lange and Mügge 2015). This absence of men in discussions concerning gender politics frames men and masculinity as not having societal issues that could or should be solved, but as normal, as the dominant group, as something related to all politics.

Right-wing populism has also shown a dislike of feminism. In populist rhetoric, feminism is articulated as elitist, and as a result, many of these movements have traces of anti-feminism (Kantola and Lombardo 2019). Elżbieta Korolczuk and Agnieszka Graff (2018) argue that feminism and gender egalitarianism have not only been connected to elitism, but to colonization as well. Anti-genderism that emphasizes the rights of the family as a societal unit then becomes a form of conservative anti-colonialism. In chapter 4, Didem Unal brings this anti-genderism into focus in the contemporary Turkish context, arguing that anti-gender and anti-feminist movements draw on notions of "cultural authenticity" as they argue that Turkey as a nation is under attack from feminism and "gender ideology" that represent a secularized Western culture incompatible with traditional Islamic values. Moreover, these movements interpret feminism as anti-family and as deprivileging men as a social group and endangering their rights in the legal sphere.

However, anti-genderism and anti-feminism are not novel tools in masculine populism. Femininity, in particular, has been historically attributed to various actors in an effort to undermine them. Nicholas Blower (chapter 5) argues that when male conservationists in the United States attempted to challenge industrial development after the second world war, their critics rhetorically attacked them as not only elitist, but as weak, elderly, and "overly emotional"—and, as such, effeminate. Conservationists responded by articulating public lands as platforms for the performance of traditional masculinity, particularly in the form of physically demanding activities. Thus, both conservationists and their critics framed masculinity as a positive and femininity as a negative, as an "us" and "them," respectively, albeit in different ways.

Whereas elites are one of the main opponents of populism, several researchers argue that pluralism, meaning heterogeneous society, is another one (Mudde and Kaltwasser 2015). In pluralism, "the people" are threatened by "others," and particularly in right-wing and conservative populist rhetoric, the "people" is often set against outsiders, such as immigrants, in society (Moffiit and Tormey 2014). Gender plays a useful tool in this opposition. Several populist parties, particularly in Europe, promote gender equality as an essential national value when they address immigration, in particular Muslim immigrants (Akkerman 2015; Lange and Mügge 2015; Mayer, Ajanovic, and Sauer 2014; Meret and Siim 2013). In these contexts, women's rights are seen as an ideological weapon against the "Islamization" of Europe, even if the evolving women's rights and feminism of native (and non-muslim) citizens would be seen as threat to masculinity, family values, and "traditional" roles of men and women, and as such to society (Mudde and Kaltwasser 2015; Kantola and Lombardo 2019; Lange and Mügge 2015; Vieten 2016).

Left-wing populist parties both in Europe and in South America have shown a slightly different attitude toward gender politics. These parties have been more eager to grasp feminist politics in terms of empowerment and women's rights (Kantola and Lombardo 2019; Kampwirth 2010; Mudde and Kaltwasser 2015). On the left, populist movements tend to support women's rights, and, in fact, for some movements they have been an important part of approaching "the people." However, the same studies have also shown that this relationship tends to be complex. What feminism and women's rights mean in these movements can vary, and while gender equality can be named as an important political goal, the gendered practices within the movements tend to support a hegemonic masculine ethos, in which patriarchy is reinforced through political leadership and values related to it (Mudde and Kaltwasser 2015; Kantola and Lombardo 2019; Kampwirth 2010).

This tendency to hold on to clearly defined gender roles in which men and women have their own roles and positions has often led to situations where feminism might be pushed forward in some areas of politics while at the same time various political movements continue to normalize male leadership and men as the "core" of "the people." In many cases, when masculine leadership has created a parallelism between the populist leader of "the people" and the soul of the nation, and gendered agendas portray feminism as a threat from which the nation needs to be protected, the rhetoric of crisis takes center stage.

CULTURES AND CRISES OF MASCULINITY

Benjamin Moffitt (2015) argues that crisis is an integral, and useful, part of the ethos of populism. Populist movements often try to trigger a crisis because it allows populists to pit "the people" against the threatening other, and creates a need for strong leadership. In this way, populism tends to be driven by a perception and performance of crisis or threat that demands action and solutions (Taggart 2000). While different populist movements have identified their own threats, one commonly employed threat is the so-called crisis of masculinity. This crisis refers to the assumption that social change related to gender issues favors women, and consequently undervalues men and threatens their masculinity and position in society.

The crisis of masculinity is visible in the performances of populist leaders. These leaders, according to Eksi and Wood (2019, 737), play up "a male-dominated and conservative set of ideas that appear to restore an imagined and idealized gender order based on male dominance that will provide stability and 'greatness' to their nations." For example, by linking himself to these narrow gender constructs, Trump personifies a long-gestated angst white middle-class men have nurtured against socioeconomic changes in the United States (and other countries). Trump's "alpha-male" posturing seems to be aimed at people who feel feminism and other struggles toward equality have gone too far, and that some nostalgic vision for society needs to be reinstated. President Trump's consistently boorish attempts to construct his image as "alpha-male" generates a discourse in which he legitimizes a form of masculinity that promotes a patriarchal gender order. He aligns himself with a conservative hegemonic masculinity in which masculinity is seen as the biological destiny of men, and characteristics such as aggressiveness, physical toughness, heterosexuality, and competitiveness are part of a canonized gender narrative for men. This narrative legitimizes attempts to maintain men's dominant position in society.

Not only do many populist leaders present themselves as a solution to the (gender equality) threat, but these populist parties attempt to attract more supporters by offering conservative gender views as an alternative to progressive gender politics. These strategies address men who view themselves as having been "left behind" by society see, who themselves as victims of feminism and affirmative action (Faludi 1999; Kimmel 2017; Roose 2019). For example, Michael Butter (2019) argues that Trump is heroicized through memes, online videos and texts where different interpretations of his persona, including masculinity, are idealized and admired. These globally circulated forms of social media and popular culture create a transnational imagery of political heroism.

To fully understand these social media discourses, then, it is necessary to look beyond the masculine and masculinist performances and rhetoric of figures such as Trump, and attempt to understand the cultures, both local and transnational, that respond to such populism. Juho Turpeinen (chapter 6) draws on social media discourses to illustrate a discursive white masculinity that responds to and is subjectivized by Trumpian populism. Focusing on the case study of Trump's 2017 reduction of Bears Ears National Monument, campaigned for by Native Americans and designated by Barack Obama, Turpeinen conceptualizes the primogeniture of the white man—a constellation of ideological narratives including anti-statism, pastoralism, and liberalism—as a means of understanding this populist masculinity. Turpeinen's contribution also continues the discussion on the relationship between environmentalism and masculinity (Blower, chapter 5), arguing that Barack Obama's desire to combine conservation and social justice in terms of Indigenous land rights was seen as an elitist endeavor, while Trump's antiregulatory approach was welcomed, not only as policy, but as an identity politics in which "the people" was interpreted in white, masculine terms, against a black and effeminate "elite."

Social media is, of course, not the only platform of cultural production where populist masculinities can be studied. Already in the 1980s, Cathy Schwichtenberg (1987) recognized that the television show *The A-Team* reflected the working class' as well as the radical right's cultural ideals of masculinity in which being a "real man" is connected to national interests. In this book, Christian Jimenez (chapter 7) focuses on white male aggrievances in three Hollywood films from the 1990s: *Falling Down* (1993), *Forrest Gump* (1994), and *Fight Club* (1999). He argues that these films narrate experienced suffering (and aggression) by white men so that American values and way of life appear to be threatened by outside forces, particularly feminism. Each film deals with the fear of reducing status differently, ranging from oblivious to aggressive but always maintaining a sense of male victimhood. In this way, these classics formulate the tendencies and formulations of populism as we understand it in the contemporary political situation and expose the long roots of the phenomenon.

Swapna Gopinath (chapter 8) shows that similar cultural discussions are not limited to Hollywood films. She studies Keralan cinema, which has an important cultural function as an affordable and approachable form of entertainment in Indian society. She argues that since the 1990s, the turn to right-wing political positions is visible in cinema, particularly in the images of masculinity in Indian cinema. The hypermasculine, patriarchal, misogynous, and challenging authority type of a hero supports populist powers and their understanding of leadership. Thus, these cultural representations have been successfully used as a part of social and political transformations.

Tatu-Ilari Laukkanen (chapter 9) turns our gaze to Brazilian crime films. He argues than in two *Elite Squad* films from 2007 and 2010, the starting point is men in crisis in a situation where postcolonial and neoliberal policies as well as Latin American left-wing populist traditions threaten the economic position and male privilege of working and lower-middle-class men. Laukkanen argues that these crime narratives, while distributed years before the ascendancy of right-wing populist politician Jair Bolsonaro's administration, tap into the concerns and anxieties of patriarchal Brazilian society in a way that resonated with Bolsonaro's campaign and presidency. Primarily, the *Elite Squad* films performed masculinity and power in ways that connected postcolonial and global politico-economical trends to the working-class/middle-class male crisis.

Thus, performances of masculinity (and femininity) appear to be deeply rooted in populist discourses—at the level of these movements' agenda and their leadership, but also in the everyday cultural practices and gender-related experiences. However, these ideas are highly contested. While some popular culture representations support populist ideals of masculinity, other voices also tear these understandings apart. Thus, it is necessary to pay special attention to how things are presented, what assumptions and cultural values are related to representations of populism, and to the act of performing either for or against populism.

While many populist movements have wanted to highlight a hegemonic masculinity that sometimes even celebrates vulgar and sexist behavior, public debates have also started to question this understanding of masculinity, often referred to as "toxic masculinity." The concept of toxic masculinity initially rose from the Mythopoetic Men's movement. In its original context, toxic masculinity represented something that kept men specifically from connecting with "natural" masculinity within themselves, signaling an essentialist view of gender identities (Messner 1997). In the 2010s, and now in the 2020s, toxic masculinity refers to a role of dominant men that is considered traditional, yet limiting the ways in which men are allowed to express emotions and their identities, which then has an adverse impact on not only the men themselves but on people around them. In this context, the wording of "toxic" has also been used as a tool to show the limitations of the populist understanding of masculinity. It can challenge the ideals of a vulgar "strongman," revealing the potential harm done to the people and the state by such practices (e.g., Scott 2018).

Particularly among those who are aligned with right-wing populist movements, the conceptual politics of "toxic masculinity" has been seen as another feminist aggression against masculinity (e.g., McDaniel 2019; Shapiro 2019). The claim that toxic masculinity vilifies all men undercuts the possibility of multiple masculinities and maintain the idea that masculinity is exclusively about male-identified individuals. Conceptualizing gender as a rigid binary built on opposing stereotypes is relatively common in populist conservative thinking (Lakoff 2002). Thus, when feminist critiques are articulated as condemning all men, the focus shifts to the assumed emotional distress of men, which can increase the appeal of right-wing populists who utilize anger in their speech. Misogynist and openly sexist comments did not derail Donald Trump's presidential campaign in 2016, instead it arguably increased his appeal among his core supporters (Johnson 2017). As a counterforce to such developments, the reemergence of toxic masculinity as a concept to problematize noxious masculine behavior has propagated the concept of gender performances beyond academia. The rhetoric use of "toxic masculinity" has created a culture in which masculinity becomes more visible and is no longer the unquestioned norm.

For example, John Quinn (chapter 10) brings this debate to the level of aesthetics of masculinity and populism in Todd Phillips's film *JOKER* (2019). In his analysis, Quinn examines the titular character's dysfunctional mode of masculinity in relation to the super-gendered norms often present in conventional superhero films. He argues that the film underlines the entire superhero genre's problematic nature, which often represents ideal masculinity as strong, powerful, and heterosexually desirable. At the same time, the film makes a direct connection between the twisted masculinity of the Joker and populist movements in society. Quinn explores how problematic representations of masculinity are connected to populist movements and work both for and against these movements in contemporary discussions. This chapter suggests that even when populism tends to celebrate narratives about exaggerated forms of masculinity, these narratives can also reveal the noxious nature of rigid gender norms.

Janne Salminen (chapter 11) continues this discussion by looking into reactions to the recent *Star Wars* films. His chapter focuses on the sequel film trilogy released between 2015 and 2019. While Disney has diversified the casting of *Star Wars* characters, mainly including more women and non-white actors in central roles, the films have incited backlash from many (male) viewers. This backlash revolves around issues of diversity and how the franchise has supposedly abandoned its central narrative about white male heroes. These debates on what types of masculinities and femininities are culturally acceptable and discussions on populist performances and self-definitions are directly linked. Therefore, these cultural presentations that resist populist perceptions of gender can appear subversive, and as such, they can become tools for igniting intense political discussions on how gender is performed—in popular culture, society, and institutional politics.

CONCLUSION

In this book, we look into the question of populism in the contexts of popular culture studies and gender studies. We argue that in order to understand what could be defined as populism, we need to look at the culture that it inhabits. The effort is to understand what is popular, and how that popular is claimed, challenged, and reclaimed. We argue that popular culture, including such elements as film, television, and social media, influences culture and society by addressing popular beliefs, values, and experiences. Political movements do not emerge solely from the political field, they are also the products (and the producers) of popular everyday culture.

This edited collection is divided into two parts. The first part takes a closer look at the masculine practices of populist politicians and movements. The second part flips the perspective around, and focuses on the ideals of populist masculinities, and how these have been pushed forward in media debates, social media, and films. These two aspects, which inherently overlap, highlight the complex phenomenon of populism and gender issues in various (popular) culture contexts.

Together, all the chapters contribute to the on-going debates on masculinity and populism by developing two overarching arguments. First, the relationship between masculinity and populism is culturally contingent and the problems of populist masculinities as well as the appeal of masculine populism can only be made intelligible in the particular context in which populist politics constructs "the people" and appeals to it. This context can be mapped across the cultural field, but especially so within popular culture, where "the people" participates in the construction of populist identities even while staying outside of institutional politics.

Second, while neither masculinity nor populism are intrinsically problematic, the populist articulation of masculinity as the norm, or as superior to others, arises from a history of social hierarchy. These social hierarchies of a given cultural context—inflected by race, ethnicity, class, gender, sexuality, physical ability, and other forms of identity and experience—are the kindling for the fires of populist masculinities of the kind that could be described as exclusive, oppressive, or—as they now often are—"toxic." This very contingency leaves room for the possibility of an inclusive and pluralist populist masculinity. Such pluralist populist masculinity and masculine populism must, however, be based on the principles of equality. While democracy does not guarantee equality, it retains the hope of such a future, and is, finally, the only means by which we, the people, can decide for ourselves how we are to live together.

BIBLIOGRAPHY

Akkerman, Tjitske. 2015. "Gender and the Radical Right in Western Europe: A Comparative Analysis of Policy Agendas." *Patterns of Prejudice* 49 (1–2): 37–60.

Butler, Judit. 1990. *Gender Trouble. Feminism and the Subversion of Identity*. New York: Routledge.

Butter, Michael. 2019. "'This Beast in the Shape of a Man': Right-Wing Populism, White Masculinity, and the Transnational Heroization of Donald Trump." In *Heroism as a Global Phenomenon in Contemporary Culture*, edited by Barbara Korte, Simon Wendt, and Nicole Falkenhayner, 114–132. London and New York: Routledge.

Connell, R. W. 2005. *Masculinities: Second Edition*. Cambridge: Polity.

Eksi, Betul, and Elizabeth A. Wood. 2019. "Right-Wing Populism as Gendered Performance: Janus-Faced Masculinity in the Leadership of Vladimir Putin and Recep T. Erdogan." *Theory and Society* 48: 733–751. https://doi.org/10.1007/s 11186-019-09363-3.

Faludi, Susan. 1999. *Stiffed: The Betrayal of the American Man*. New York: William Morrow and Company.

Geva, Dorit. 2020. "Daughter, Mother, Captain: Marine Le Pen, Gender, and Populism in the French National Front." *Social Politics: International Studies in Gender, State & Society* 27 (1): 1–26. https://doi.org/10.1093/sp/jxy039.

Grossberg, Lawrence. 2010. *Cultural Studies in the Future Tense*. Durham and London: Duke University Press.

Jansen, Robert S. 2011. "Populist Mobilization: A New Theoretical Approach to Populism." *Sociological Theory* 29 (2): 75–96.

Johnson, Paul Elliot. 2017. "The Art of Masculine Victimhood: Donald Trump's Demagoguery." *Women's Studies in Communication* 40 (3): 229–250.

Kampwirth, Karen. 2010. "Introduction." In *Gender and Populism in Latin America: Passionate Politics*, edited by Karen Kampwirth, 1–24. University Park, PA: The Pennsylvania State University Press.

Kantola, Johanna, and Emanuela Lombardo. 2019. "Populism and Feminist Politics: The Cases of Finland and Spain." *European Journal of Political Research* 58: 1108–1128. https://doi.org/10.1111/1475-6765.12333.

Kimmel, Michael. 2017(2013). *Angry White Men: American Masculinity at the End of an Era.* New York: Nation Books.

Korolczuk, Elżbieta, and Agnieszka Graff. 2018. "Gender as 'Ebola from Brussels': The Anti-Colonial Frame and the Rise of Illiberal Populism." S*igns Journal of Women in Culture and Society* 43: 797–821.

Kovala, Urpo, and Jyrki Pöysä. 2018. "The 'Jytky' of the Finns Party: Or, How to Take Advantage of Masculinity in Populist Politics." In *Populism on the Loose*, edited by Urpo Kovala, Emilia Palonen, Maria Ruotsalainen, and Tuija Saresma, 161–175. Jyväskylä: Jyväskylän Yliopisto.

Laclau, Ernesto. 2005. "Populism: What's in the Name?" In *Populism and the Mirror of Democracy*, edited by Francisco Panizza, 32–49. London: Verso.

Lakoff, George. 2002. *Moral Politics: Second Edition.* Chicago: University of Chicago Press.

Lange, Sarah L. de, and Liza M. Mügge. 2015. "Gender and Right-Wing Populism in the Low Countries: Ideological Variations across Parties and Time." *Patterns of Prejudice* 49 (1–2): 61–80. https://doi.org/10.1080/0031322X.2015.1014199.

Mayer, Stefanie, Edma Ajanovic, and Birgit Sauer. 2014. "Intersections and Inconsistencies: Framing Gender in Right-Wing Populist Discourses in Austria." *NORA: Nordic Journal of Women's Studies* 22 (4): 250–266.

McDaniel, Rick. 2019. "Words Can be Toxic; Masculinity is Not." *Family Life.* https://www.familylife.com/articles/topics/life-issues/relationships/men/words-can-be-toxic-masculinity-is-not/.

Meret, Susi, and Birte Siim. 2013. "Gender, Populism and Politics of Belonging: Discourses of Right-Wing Populist Parties in Denmark, Norway and Austria." In *Negotiating Gender and Diversity in an Emergent European Public Sphere*, edited by Birte Siim, and Monika Mokre, 78–96. New York: Palgrave Macmillan.

Messner, Michael A. 1997. *Politics of Masculinities: Men in Movements.* Thousand Oaks: Sage Publications.

Moffitt, Benjamin. 2015. "How to Perform Crisis: A Model for Understanding the Key Role of Crisis in Contemporary Populism." *Government and Opposition* 50 (2): 189–217. https://doi.org/10.1017/gov.2014.13.

Moffitt, Benjamin, and Simon Tormey. 2014. "Rethinking Populism: Politics, Mediatisation and Political Style." *Political Studies* 62 (2): 381–397.

Mudde, Cas, and Rovira Kaltwasser. 2014. "Populism and Political Leadership." In *The Oxford Handbook of Political Leadership*, edited by R. A. W. Rhodes, and Paul't Hart. https://doi.org/10.1093/oxfordhb/9780199653881.013.016.

Mudde, Cas, and Cristóbal Rovira Kaltwasser. 2015. "Vox populi or vox masculini? Populism and Gender in Northern Europe and South America." *Patterns of Prejudice* 49 (1–2): 16–36. http://dx.doi.org/10.1080/0031322X.2015.1014197.

Mudde, Cas, and Cristóbal Rovira Kaltwasser. 2017. *Populism. A Very Short Introduction.* Oxford: Oxford University Press.

Norocel, Christian. 2013. "'Give Us Back Sweden!' A Feminist Reading of the (Re) interpretations of the Folkhem Conceptual Metaphor in Swedish Radical Right Populist Discourse." *Nordic Journal of Feminist and Gender Research* 21 (1): 4–20. https://doi.org/10.1080/08038740.2012.741622.

Norocel, Ov Cristian, Tuija Saresma, Tuuli Lähdesmäki, and Maria Ruotsalainen. 2020. "Discursive Constructions of White Nordic Masculinities in Right-Wing Populist Media." *Men and Masculinities* 23 (3–4): 425–446. https://doi.org/10.1 177/1097184X18780459.

Roose, Joshua M. 2019. "Non-Western New Populism: Religion, Masculinity and Violence in the East." In *Populism and the Crisis of Democracy. Volume 3: Migration, Gender and Religion*, edited by Gregor Fitzi, Juergen Mackert, and Bryan S. Turner, 111–129. London and New York: Routledge.

Rosdil, Donald L. 1991. "The Context of Radical Populism in US Cities: A Comparative Analysis." *Journal of Urban Affairs* 13 (1): 77–96.

Saresma, Tuija. 2018. "Gender Populism: Three Cases of Finns Party Actors' Traditionalist Anti-Feminism." In *Populism on the Loose*, edited by Urpo Kovala, Emilia Palonen, Maria Ruotsalainen, and Tuija Saresma, 177–200. Jyväskylä: Jyväskylän Yliopisto.

Schwichtenberg, Cathy. 1987. "Articulating the People's Politics: Manhood and Right-Wing Populism in –I The A-Team." *Communication* 9 (3–4): 379–398.

Scott, Eugene. 2018. "Joe Biden and the Case against 'Toxic Masculinity.'" *Washington Post*, March 21, 2018. https://www.washingtonpost.com/news/the-fix /wp/2018/03/21/bidens-hypothetical-threats-toward-trump-may-not-actually-help -decrease-sexual-assault/.

Shapiro, Ben. 2019. "Gillette Joins the Fight against 'Toxic Masculinity.'" *The National Review*, January 15, 2019. https://www.nationalreview.com/2019/01/ gillette-commercial-toxic-masculinity-debate/.

Shifman, Limor. 2013. "Memes in a Digital World: Reconciling with a Conceptual Troublemaker." *Journal of Computer-Mediated Communication* 18: 362–377.

Taggart, Paul A. 2000. *Populism*. Birmingham: Open University Press.

Vieten, Ulrike M. 2016. "Far Right Populism and Women: The Normalisation of Gendered Anti-Muslim Racism and Gendered Culturalism in the Netherlands." *Journal of Intercultural Studies* 37 (6): 621–636.

Winberg, Oscar. 2017. "Insult Politics: Donald Trump, Right-Wing Populism, and Incendiary Language." *European Journal of American Studies* 12 (2). https://doi .org/10.4000/ejas.12132.

Wodak, Ruth. 2015. *The Politics of Fear. What Right-wing Populist Discourses Mean*. London: Sage.

Part I

MASCULINE POPULISTS

Chapter 1

Iberian Swagger versus Feminist Masculinity

Populist Narratives of Masculinity in Contemporary Spain

Nicholas Manganas

Spain's transition to democracy in the mid-seventies ushered in a two-party system of government after thirty-six years of military dictatorship (1939–1975). Widely considered a model transition in studies of democratization, unofficial pacts of silence and forgetting decidedly left the traumatic politics of the past in the dustbins of history (Encarnación 2001; Graham 2004; Blakely 2005). The radical politics of the left and the worst excesses of the extreme right were delegitimized as Spanish political parties firmly situated themselves on the spectrum between the center-left and the center-right. In the 1980s, Spain emerged as a modern, forward-thinking nation-state as it joined the European Union and NATO. This post-dictatorship consensus, however, began to deteriorate with the onset of the Global Financial Crisis (GFC) also known as the Great Recession, in 2008. The Spanish economy was hit particularly hard and its two-party system of government frayed as new populist movements emerged to challenge the mainstream parties that were widely blamed for causing the crisis (Bosco and Verney 2012; Múnoz Molina 2013; Moreno-Caballud 2015).

On the left, a new political party Podemos (We Can) arose out of the 15-M anti-austerity movement in 2014. Known with the epithet *indignados* (indignant), Podemos has been accused of promoting a populism of the left that is anti-establishment and a threat to the unity of Spain (Vallín 2016; Díez 2019). Podemos's ponytailed leader Pablo Iglesias, a politics lecturer at Complutense University in Madrid, has called for a "feminist masculinity" that recognizes that the modern man must deconstruct himself in order to accommodate a just society for women (Alemán 2018). In November 2018, he caused a small

3

scandal when he stated that "feminist men screw better" (Alemán 2018). On the right, the political party Vox was established in 2013 but only achieved significant electoral success in 2018. Vox's anti-feminist discourse aided its electoral rise, winning an unprecedented fifty-two seats in the November 2019 general elections. Vox leader Santiago Abascal represents the *macho ibérico* (Iberian male) who struts his aggressive swagger as he argues against what he calls "feminazi" discourse that seeks to blame men for being men (Delgado 2018; Hedgecoe 2019). The electoral fortunes of both Podemos and Vox were the final blow to the political consensus attained with Spain's transition to democracy, ushering in a new era of Spanish politics.

Although there are countless iterations of masculinities in contemporary Spain, my focus in this chapter is on two variants: (1) the narrative of masculinity from the populist right that is closely tied to the traditional or hegemonic masculinity of the Franco era [1939–1975]; and (2) the counternarrative from the populist left that seeks to undermine normative definitions of masculinity. I argue that both Iglesias and Abascal's performance of masculinity repeat certain tropes to signal that they fit within "relatively tight bandwidths" of acceptable masculinities (Mundy and Denny 2019, 122) by, for example, emphasizing their heterosexuality and other traditional values of masculinity such as virility, strength, power, and toughness (Fouz-Hernández and Martínez-Expósito 2007, 83). But once their masculinity is firmly established as operating within an acceptable bandwidth, there is scope for them to differentiate their respective performances of masculinity to signal to the electorate their political dispositions. On the left, Iglesias juggles his performance of the mythic revolutionary hero with a call for a feminist masculinity. On the right, Abascal has returned an Iberian swagger to Spanish politics in his attempts to reorient Spain back toward traditional family values.

But as we shall see below, these narratives weave a complex web. At times, it is impossible to delineate where one narrative of masculinity begins and the other ends. And often, it is problematic to assume a neat division between left and right, as if one's political orientation was strictly aligned with one's performance of their gender. I argue, however, that each leader's performance of masculinity is tied to the construction of the political discourse they are selling to the electorate. Such constructions phantasmatically mirror the historical divisions of the two Spains as both versions of masculinity become a battleground between two different conceptualizations of Spain. The expression of populist masculinity, then, must be read as an underlying tool to lend credibility and legitimacy to each of the two Spains that are in an eternal, and irreconcilable, conflict with each other. Such a reading highlights that despite Abascal and Iglesias's performance of masculinity functioning at opposites ends of the bandwidth, they both follow the same political logic. That is, despite the complexity of their masculinities that forces them to negotiate and adapt to varying degrees of political exigencies, they each embody the burden of their respective political projects that intimately mirror the division of the two Spains. This case study underscores that although it is difficult, if not impossible, to define a specific populist form of masculinity (at least in contemporary Spain), the performances of populist masculinities are dictated by a discursive logic that reflects both the social and political space in which they circulate (Stavrakakis 2004, 256). Populist masculinities must, therefore, be understood in dialogue with the multiple histories of the nation-state, histories that are both complex and contested.

DISCOURSES OF POPULIST MASCULINITIES

Iglesias and Abascal's performances of masculinity could not, on the surface, be more different. They both firmly position themselves on opposites ends of the political spectrum and as such appeal to two very different electoral constituencies. My focus in this chapter is to situate their performances of masculinity along a historical continuum and unpack the political logic that underpins them. Aligned with Ernesto Laclau's discursive theory of populism (1980, 2005), I suggest that understanding populist masculinity as a discursive practice is a theoretically productive exercise as it takes into consideration a network of meanings that encompasses both linguistic and non-linguistic elements (Laclau and Mouffe 1985), as well as practices that are linked to the discursive logic that produces them (Stavrakakis 2004, 257). To paraphrase Laclau, to ask if there is such a thing as a populist form of masculinity is to start with the wrong question (2005, 11). Instead, we should be asking to what extent performances of masculinity by populist leaders (and their followers) have an affective dimension that is intimately tied to the political logic that seeks to reimagine the telling of the national story. Conceptualizing populist masculinity as a discursive practice underlines how the telling of national stories is reinscribed on the body, often contested, and frequently mirrors long-standing historical narratives.

It is only in recent years that scholarship has sought to explore the link between masculinity and the nation. Important scholarly work in the late twentieth century by theorists such as Judith Butler and R. W. Connell, deconstructed gender norms and highlighted the performative aspect of gender but fell short of explaining "*how* masculinity and nationalism work together" (Miller-Idriss 2017, 200). Still, the field of masculinity studies owes a great debt to both Butler and Connell. Butler's argument that gender is tenuous in space and time and exteriorized "through a stylized repetition of acts" (1990, 140) is an important insight into understanding populist masculinities. Connell, moreover, underlines that masculinity is more than just a personal identity, underlining the need to understand masculinity as an integral part of "organized social relations" (2005, 29). In my reading of how Spanish populist leaders of both the left and the right perform their masculinity (both embodied and discursive), I argue that contemporary manifestations of masculinity are not only historically conditioned, but also a facet of "large-scale social structures and processes" (2005, 39). I thus concur with Connell's assessment that we can only really understand masculinities in the plural (2005, 7).

Although difficult to define, Connell's loose definition of masculinity is instructive. She defines masculinity as "simultaneously a place in gender relations, the practices through which men and women engage that place in gender, and the effects of these practices in bodily experiences, personality and culture" (2005, 71). Hegemonic masculinity, according to Connell, is a masculinity that is both dominant and celebrated at any particular historical moment, and is always contestable (2005, 76–77). It is telling that she considers masculinity both a *place* and an *effect* and that these are inseparable. As I argue below, the manner in which Spain's two populist leaders perform their masculinity is starkly different yet each leader situates their performance within "relatively tight bandwidths" of masculinity (Mundy and Denny 2019, 122). As Mundy and Denny posit, although masculinities have become more flexible in recent decades, particularly due to the visibility of alternative masculinities in popular culture, "signifying manhood remains firmly rooted in relatively 'butch' grounds that connote a masculinity that's never confused with being feminine" (2019, 122). Thus, despite Abascal performing a version of hegemonic masculinity, and Iglesias's subversion of it, there is no blurring of their sexuality or any doubt that they are, indeed, "men." In that sense, their masculinity is enacted and emplaced within a normative spectrum of gender relations dictated by national and cultural traditions. Yet I am particularly interested in the *effect* of the practices of masculinity. I suggest that the performance of masculinity in populist politics can tell us much about what it means to be a man in contemporary Spain because as Johansson and Ottemo put it, "when historical conditions and relational patterns in society change, the hegemonic position can be challenged and questioned" (2015, 193). The effect is to also highlight the *limits* of such challenges to hegemonic masculinity. Despite the visibility of multiple ways of performing masculinity, I agree with Namaste who argues that hegemonic masculinity is the "form of manhood that [remains] most respected and valued" (2017, 248).

In the last decade or two, the contestation of hegemonic masculinity has led some scholars to argue that masculinity is in "crisis" (Robinson 2000; Clare 2000; Morgan 2006; Walsh 2010). This crisis has emerged hand in hand with the deepening of global integration that has effectively made many men (and women) "surplus citizens" (Kotouza 2019) in their own nation. Michael

Kimmel's *Angry White Men* (2017) documents a particularly American version of such a crisis suggesting that for many white, heterosexual, and typically working-class men, there is a sense that something fundamental and foundational has changed. For these men, the American dream has ended or become unattainable, as job losses and economic instability took away any last remnants of dignity, honor, and autonomy. They have lost their "sense of themselves as men," he argues, and they feel that loss as a humiliation (2017, 13). Like others, Kimmel did not see Trump's election coming, noting he underestimated the depth of disorientation and rage of those who he now refers to as "Trump's angry white men" (2017, ix). Kimmel's reading of contemporary masculinity highlights how intimately the performance of masculinity is tied to the nation. With the electoral success of other radical right populists from Brazil to India, there is understandable angst about what this might mean for both global and national politics and whether this turn toward populism is undermining the liberal-democratic consensus that was heralded with the end of the Cold War (Fukuyama 1992). It is troublesome, however, to apply the "angry white men" thesis to countries such as Brazil or India as each national context has its particularities. There is a risk, too, in overly relating the so-called crisis more to the *consequences* of men's feelings of loss and humiliation, such as voting for Trump, rather than of masculinity in and of itself. I thus agree with Mundy and Denny (2019, 9) who argue that masculinity is *always* in crisis: "By suggesting that men now find themselves in a state of crisis presupposes that at some point they were not" (2019, 10). In Spain, as I discuss below, the idea that masculinity as an identity construction is in crisis has a long historical trajectory.

If this chapter situates the performance of masculinities in the context of national identities, then it does so in conversation with other recent scholarship that seeks to address the question of "*how* masculinity and nationalism work together" (Miller-Idriss 2017, 200). Suvi Keskinen's analysis of radical right-wing texts in Finland, for example, demonstrates that the nation intersects with gender, race and class to produce and construct a number of antagonisms, such as that of the "concerned white men who struggle to save the white nation," which can be read as an attempt to "recentre white masculinity and the privileges of the position" (2013, 231). On this point, Miller-Idriss argues that "masculinity intersects with nationalistic ideals in ways that mutually reinforce masculinity and nationalism" (2017, 211). In her study of the iconography of far-right German youth, she suggests that this intersection between the nation and masculinity is particularly evident during times of crisis (2017, 211). Her analysis reveals that the nation has an affective and emotional appeal, demonstrating that both nationalism and masculinity "are jointly articulated and reinforced" (2017, 212). Catarina Kinnvall's study on populism and the masculinization of Indian politics further illustrates the nexus between masculinity and the nation. She explores the ways in which Hindu nationalism and gendered narratives of nationhood are reimagining the Indian state and its foreign policy (2019, 283). Her key point is that such a reimagining is always incomplete and thus has the potential to activate local and social resistances (2019, 284).

My analysis of the case study below demonstrates that in Spain, too, performances of populist masculinities intersect with the nation, and are mutually reinforced by the discursive logic of each leader's electoral strategy. If we agree with Mundy and Denny's assertion that "manhood has continually been thought to be in eminent danger, a state of emergency, a calamitous end" (2019, 10), then, at least in the Spanish context, masculinities cannot be separated from national narratives that are intimately tied to the telling of the national story. And this retelling has an emotional and affective appeal. But the ensuing case study also highlights some key differences between Spain and other nations that have seen a rise in populist parties in the past decade or so. In Spain, populist discourses are not as racialized nor as class based as in some other European countries. The fact that Spain is concurrently experiencing a populism of the right *and* the left, means that populist discourses tend to mirror domestic cleavages, rather than threats from outside. Populist discourses in Spain instead phantasmatically mirror older constituent divisions between the left and the right that can be traced back to the Spanish Civil War and beyond. In the next sections I trace some of those national divisions and suggest that they echo Connell's point that masculinity is a historically contingent performance (2005, 185).

Histories of masculinities in Spain

Spanish history, like all national histories, is oft-disputed, murky and complex. In agreement with Jacques Le Goff who argues that what is needed "is a constant rereading of the past in relation to the present" (1992, 18), I seek to bring to the foreground how the constitutive narrative of the two Spains (conservative and liberal Spains) continues to be manipulated by political elites to tell a "story" of the "nation" to the Spanish people (Manganas 2016, 232). The narrative of the two Spains has existed in Spanish political discourse and inflected debate about what Spain is since at least the early nineteenth century (Manganas 2016, 18). In his essay *Dia de difuntos de 1836* (*All Souls' Day 1836*), satirist José de Larra wrote "Aquí yace media España; murió de la otra media" (Here lies half of Spain. It died of the other half) (1836).[1] In 1909, less than a century later, the celebrated poet Antonio Machado coined the phrase *las dos Españas* (the two Spains) in a short untitled poem: "Españolito que vienes al mundo, te guarde Dios. Una de las dos Españas ha de helarte el corazón" (Little Spaniard just now coming into the world, may God keep you.

One of those two Spains will freeze your heart) (1983, 113). In this Manichean rendering of political ideology, Liberal Spain is accorded the values of the French Revolution and is anti-monarchical and pro-European. Conservative Spain is deemed traditionalist, centralist, pro-monarchical, anti-regionalist and parochial (Manganas 2016, 22). These two Spains clashed in the Spanish Civil War (1936–1939), leading to the establishment of the Franco dictatorship (1939–1975). That regime was characterized by a return to what were considered traditional Spanish values, overturning the modernizing policies of the liberal Second Republic (1931–1939). A return to traditional understandings of gender roles was one of the regime's key hallmarks, and despite some modernizing toward the latter half of its existence (particularly in the economic sphere), Spain experienced almost forty years of arrested development. Spain's transition to democracy was consensus-driven, underwritten by unofficial pacts to forget the traumas of the past. But by the early 2000s this consensus had begun to fall apart. First, with the recuperation of historical memory as the descendants of Republican families began demanding justice for family members who remained buried in unmarked mass graves around the country; and second, with the devastating effects of the Great Recession that led to successive Spanish governments implementing severe austerity politics. The emergence of populist parties from both the left and the right was the most obvious side effect of these developments.

The narrative division between the two Spains, however, has never been entirely reconciled. Balfour and Quiroga (2007, 21) have explored the idea of two Spains as a myth that was later propagated by the Franco dictatorship. Indeed, it is problematic to assume that each Spaniard as an individual can easily be situated within one of the two Spains. But discursively, the narrative division has informed much of contemporary Spanish politics, ranging from responses to both domestic and international terrorism, historical memory, austerity and gender politics (Manganas 2016). Thus, although I acknowledge the empirical limitations of the two Spains narrative, I maintain that it remains discursively potent because political and media discourses continue to engage with its historical legacy, whether mythic or not. In the early twenty-first century, the rise of populism(s) in many parts of the world bears witness to the global appeal of such Manichean fantasies; the United States' red states and blue states being one of the latest manifestations, with roots dating back to the American Civil War (1861–1865) and beyond.

If we accept Connell's premise that hegemonic masculinity is always historically contingent then it is possible to trace hegemonic masculinity throughout Spanish history and understand its import in developing the purported Spanish male character (2005, 77). Connell pinpoints the Spanish conquistadors as one of the first modern masculine cultural types (2005, 187) and much scholarship has explored masculinity, and its concomitant fear of feminization, from early Imperial Spain until the present day. Mariscal, for example, highlights that virility and manliness were highly valorized during the Spanish age of conquest, associating the masculine with strength and goodness while delimiting the feminine as weak (1991, 42). Donnell demonstrates that alongside this celebration of the masculine circulated cultural anxiety that Spain was at perpetual risk of being feminized (2003, 49). But this projection was existentially challenged by Spain's declining imperial power, symbolized by its defeat in the Spanish-American War (1898) when Spain lost its remaining four colonies. Known with the epithet "El desastre" (the disaster), the event led to a spiritual crisis that devolved, according to Donnell, into the "shame of emasculation," impacting on Spain's ability to project a masculine and virile image abroad (2003, 150–151).

In the twentieth century, such anachronistic permutations of masculinity were reconfigured, as new forms of masculinity emerged to challenge all iterations of hegemonic masculinity (Ryan and Corbalán 2017, 1). But the turbulent twentieth century was an age of extremes and the performance(s) of masculinities tended to yo-yo between a version of masculinity that harkened back to Spain's imperial glory, and another that sought to distance itself from its retrograde qualities. The twentieth century was characterized by what Colmeiro calls the "hetero-masculine national paradigm" (2017, 21). This model of masculinity was rooted in the ideology of national-Catholicism and within this paradigm, there was only one appropriate form of masculinity, abnegating homosexuality and all other forms of masculinity that did not fit within the confines of the national-Catholic ideal (Colmeiro 2017, 21). The Francoist formation of masculinity was embedded in the glorification of large families, but at the same time glorified the physicality and seductiveness of the *torero* (bullfighter) (Ryan 2017, 84–85). The hegemonic masculinity of Francoism closely resembled a militarized masculinity that sought to mold men into productive and disciplined members of a hierarchical state (DiGiovanni 2017, 64). Within this gender formation, discipline, violence and a commitment to nation and family were prized values, and there was a concerted effort to recuperate an imperial identity (DiGiovanni 2017, 64–66). The Franco regime thus painstakingly legitimated the "suffering self-sacrificing hero" (Colmeiro 2017, 22), whose masculinity was based on aggression and epitomized by the imperial myth of the Spanish Christian Warrior (DiGiovanni 2017, 67). The regime's enemies—leftists, communists, anarchists, homosexuals, non-Christians, and all supporters of the Republican side—were thus branded a threat to this masculine ideal.

The propagation of such "hegemonic masculinity" was state-driven, erasing alternative expressions of masculinity. Toward the end of the Franco regime, however, state censorship began to relax, and despite the regime's concerted efforts, Spanish sexual mores slowly evolved, aided by the advent of mass tourism in the country from the 1960s onward. By the early 1970s, the hegemonic masculinity of Francoist ideology began to be replaced with what Colmeiro calls "the sex-crazed, hysterical male, who is culturally repressed and complexed, obsessed with affirming his power and masculinity with foreign females" (2017, 28). Also known as the *macho ibérico*, this prototype of masculinity celebrated the short, fat, balding Iberian man who idealized money and business success (Colmeiro 2017, 28). The *macho ibérico*'s success in popular culture also demonstrated how fond the Spanish public had become of his bumbling, ridiculous, nature. Over the years, the *macho ibérico* prototype evolved into more muscular Adonis-like figures, such as Javier Bardem in Bigas Luna's film *Jamón Jamón* (1992). But as McKinnon argues, the most extreme forms of hypermasculinity betray an underlying anxiety (2003, 5) and the *macho ibérico* served to highlight how unstable Spanish forms of masculinity were during a time of political transition.

The end of the Franco regime in 1975 not only instituted a democratic parliamentary system but also allowed for Spanish prototypes of masculinity to evolve and align more closely with the rest of Western Europe. But as Namasate points out, these changes were slow because after nearly four decades of military dictatorship binary gender roles were "rigidly codified" and "deeply entrenched" (2017, 244). A loosening of gender norms was facilitated by a range of cultural and political shifts, including the widespread incorporation of women into the workforce, the decriminalization of homosexuality in 1979 and the end of mandatory military service in 2002 (DiGiovanni 2017, 76). By the 1980s, a new, more sophisticated, masculine prototype emerged. Referred to as the Spanish "new" man, this prototype was consolidated during the long period of Socialist rule (1982–1996), the first time the left had governed in Spain since the 1930s. Jordan and Morgan-Tamosunas brand the "new" Spanish man as "socially and emotionally reconstructed," displaying "gentleness, sensitivity [and] tolerance" (1998, 152). Taken alongside Spain's accession into the European Union in 1986, the hegemonic masculinity of the Franco era and the "sex-crazed hysterical male" increasingly became anachronisms. The films of Pedro Almodóvar further shook away the image of the retrograde Spaniard, as his films garnered international acclaim for their subversion of traditional gender roles.

Yet, there has been no easy, unproblematic evolution of masculine prototypes in contemporary Spain. Referring to masculinities in the plural implies that there are always multiple forms of masculinity in any given society. In 1996, after a series of corruption scandals, the Socialists were voted out of government and the leader of the center-right Popular Party, José María Aznar, returned a blustering version of masculine swagger back into mainstream political discourse in an attempt to recapture Spain's lost international glory and manly stature (see Spain's participation in the invasion of Iraq in

2003). In popular culture, too, the *macho ibérico* also made a comeback, particularly in the *Torrente* (1998–2014) film series, which Fouz-Hernández and Martínez-Expósito call an "ironic homage" to a dying breed of Spanish manhood (2007, 83). In their 2007 book *Live Flesh*, they argued that the *macho ibérico* is "a figure unable to survive in a newly globalized and at the same time de-centralized Spain" (27). The underlying message is that although the symbolic figure of the *macho ibérico* still circulated in Spanish culture, he was perceived rather ironically and survived merely for others to poke fun at him. However, despite the contestation of hegemonic masculinities and the popularization of certain prototypes of manliness such as the soft-mannered "new" man (Fouz-Hernández and Martínez-Expósito 2007, 83), the traditional *macho ibérico* was never completely extinguished. Scholars have perhaps underestimated the extant nostalgia in politics and popular culture (at least in certain sections of Spanish society) for at least some traits of the *macho ibérico* and many of the values of traditional Spanish masculinity that characterized the Franco era—strength, virility, muscularity, power and toughness (Fouz-Hernández and Martínez-Expósito 2007, 83).

For most of its democratic history, Spain has been immune to right-wing populism because of the legacy of Francoism and the widespread suspicion of extreme nationalism(s). It took the Great Recession to usher in a left populism, but the triple threat of economic crisis, the European refugee crisis and the referendum for Catalan independence, to finally open the doors for a populism of the right. Abascal's performance of hypermasculinity on the political stage has thus challenged Fouz-Hernández and Martínez-Expósito's contention that the *macho ibérico* is unable to survive in a globalized Spain. His performance of masculinity has also upended the unwritten consensus that the "new" Spanish man is the only legitimate version of masculinity in democratic politics. In my discussion below, I explore how both Abascal and Iglesias perform a version of the *macho ibérico* and "new" Spanish man prototypes and suggest that their performances coincide with their political positions, vis-à-vis the narrative division of the two Spains.

THE FEMINIST MASCULINITY OF THE POPULIST LEFT

Podemos emerged out of the 15-M movement that sprang up across Spain in 2011. Young *indignados* (indignant) voiced their frustration and malaise with a Spanish state that had failed to live up to its promise. With echoes of May 1968 in Paris, 15-M was inspired by both the Arab Spring and Occupy Wall Street. It spoke for the *ni-ni* (neither-nor) generation: young people who neither work nor study, are unable to live independently and whose best hopes are poor work contracts, low salaries and precarious working conditions (Adagio 2013, 147). By 2014, a small group of academics decided to institutionalize the movement by creating Podemos, though the party has always stressed that the 15-M movement and the political movement are not necessarily one and the same. Most of its support, according to Ramiro and Gómez (2017, 110–111), has come from educated parts of the electorate that are frustrated with their unfulfilled potential rather than the "losers of globalization" described in Kimmel's *Angry White Men* (2017). Its meteoric rise was a shock to the political system as support for the party peaked at around 20 percent of the electorate in 2015 (winning sixty-nine seats in the general elections). As Kennedy observes, the political backlash that Podemos has received has been brutal, called everything from "weirdos" to "catastrophic" for offering "Hugo Chávez-style utopias" (2014). The party clearly fits Mudde and Rovira Kaltwasser's definition of populism as it attacks elites (Podemos leaders call the Spanish elite *"la casta"* [the caste]); defends the "common people"; and calls for sovereignty to be returned back to ordinary Spaniards (2013, 151). But it is an inclusionary populism, framing its narrative of the "corrupt elite" against the "common people" from the left, ensuring its political message emphasizes socioeconomic equality, the inclusion of minorities, and a general cosmopolitan vision of the world (Mudde and Rovira Kaltwasser 2013; Kantola and Lombardo 2019, 112).

Its leader Pablo Iglesias is atypical in contemporary Spain. A lecturer in politics, he is named after the founder of the Spanish Socialist Party. With his sharp intellect and unkempt ponytail, his charisma lies more with his astute use of dialectics and the way he passionately communicates complex issues in ways that ordinary Spaniards can understand, rather than in his physical appearance (Rodríguez 2016; Caravantes 2019, 477). Iglesias, with his scholarly disposition and cowboy-like walk, is often caricatured in the media and is pejoratively called "el coletas" (the ponytailed guy) by his political opponents (Justo 2020; Garrido 2020; Cedeira 2020). Although he is not "typically" masculine and handsome, he often outperforms his political rivals during electoral debates (Gil 2019a; Rubio 2019). If anything, his refusal to do away with his scholarly image, such as by cutting his hair or wearing a tie, points to how far he wants to demonstrate that he and his party do not belong to the corrupt elite with their veneer of sophistication.

As Podemos emerged on a platform of anti-austerity, gender politics were not a particular priority for the party in its beginnings (Kantola and Lombardo 2019, 1117). But since then, it has made a concerted effort to stress its feminist credentials. In 2019 it renamed its coalition with Izquierda Unida (United Left), Unidas Podemos (Together we Can), using the plural feminine (Ramírez 2018). Podemos has also increased the number of women in the Spanish parliament and uses feminist language such as "bodily autonomy" in its political discourse. It has further brought visibility to feminism in political debates, deconstructed male privileges and spoken on the needs of marginalized women (Kantola and Lombardo 2019, 1115). There is thus ample evidence that Podemos fosters a space for feminist politics to be articulated both within the party itself and its messaging to the electorate (Kantola and Lombardo 2019, 1123). In an interview with author and psychoanalyst Jorge Alemán (2018), Iglesias was keen to stress his support for the feminist movement, claiming that in the current epoch it is occupying a historical role that was previously occupied by other social movements, leading the way in imagining new possibilities and community spaces.

Iglesias thus situates feminism in a historical context of revolutionary and emancipatory politics that aligns with his own scholarly framework that is anchored in Marxian and Gramscian theory, with echoes of both Laclau and Mouffe, two theorists lionized by many Podemos leaders (Tremlett 2015; Fernández 2018). Iglesias is skilled at adapting his language and the theoretical depth of his arguments according to his audience. In his interview with Alemán he was not hesitant to ruminate philosophically about how masculinity can comfortably cohabit with the sort of militant feminism that he admires. Besides his infamous quip that "los hombres feministas follan mejor" (feminist men screw better), Iglesias suggested that the key question in the current moment is how men can reclaim a type of feminine masculinity (Alemán 2018). This is a pertinent question in the context of how the feminist movement in Spain has mobilized in recent years, bringing with it a groundswell of popular support, particularly after the light sentencing of five young men in the *La Manada* rape case (2017), and the success of the women's strike on International Women's Day in 2017 (Molpeceres Arnáiz and Filardo-Llamas 2020). Both events mobilized women (and men) from both sides of politics, disconcerting the center-right which had initially ridiculed the strike and had not been particularly supportive of the #metoo movement. Alongside the successful long-running campaign to publicize gender violence and femicide (Spanish media reports regularly on the number of women killed each year much like other countries do the road death toll), the Spanish feminist movement has much to admire and continues the long historical trajectory of emancipatory politics initiated by the left during Spain's Second Republic (1931–1939).

Iglesias, in the tradition of the "new" Spanish man detailed above, thus seeks to accommodate what he calls the "machista" (misogynist) that lives inside all men with the political reality of a feminist movement that, in his view, is making progressive politics more interesting (Alemán 2018). For Iglesias, it is possible for men to maintain their masculinity while being a feminist, which is what the crude phrase "feminist men screw better" aims to make present (Alemán 2018). Although he acknowledges that this process is by no means easy, he suggests that all men have a responsibility to work toward a deconstruction of the male self (Alemán 2018). He thus takes the prototype of the "new" Spanish man one step further by suggesting that it is not enough for men to simply display "gentleness, sensitivity [and] tolerance (Jordan and Morgan-Tamosunas 1998, 152), but that men must continually refashion their masculinity in dialogue with the feminist movement in order to ensure social justice and the emancipatory potential of a leftist social project (Alemán 2018). However, Iglesias is not particularly insightful about how this reconciliation might be achieved, as he has only sparingly touched on these issues as his overwhelming focus remains on more concrete traditional left-wing policies. For example, one of the first acts that the Socialist/ Unidas Podemos coalition government enacted in early 2020 was an increase in the minimum wage to 1,000 euros a month (Cué 2020), a strong message to the electorate that Podemos's primary objective was to lift the standard of living of the Spanish working class. The fact that his position on a feminist masculinity remains limited to the quip that "feminist men screw better," opened him up to an array of criticism. Iglesias himself has been accused of displaying machismo which, according to Sánchez-Mellado, is a characteristic of both the political left and right (2018). In 2018 Iglesias publicly apologized to a female TV presenter for making sexist comments about her in a private WhatsApp chat a few years earlier (Sánchez-Mellado 2018). Despite the earnestness of his public apology, he was unable to avoid the perception that despite his open support for the Spanish feminist movement, both Iglesias and Podemos foster a masculine party culture (Caravantes 2019, 480). Iglesias's proclamation that "the politics of machos" has come to an end also sits in contrast to other features of masculinity that Iglesias displays. Iglesias, according to Kantola and Lombardo, is characterized by "an aggressive competitive discourse," "alpha-male behaviour," a "confrontational style," and performs the prototype of the "victorious revolutionary" (2019, 1113–1124). Caravantes argues that Iglesias displays a unique performance of charismatic masculine leadership, one more aligned with Bernie Sanders in the United States, that is less paternalistic, anti-intellectual and vulgar, and more educated and well-mannered (2018, 480). Even so, she perceives in his performance an overemphasis on winning, an adversarial style, and aggressive intellectualism (2018, 466–479).

Iglesias's complex performance of masculinity, however, is both historically contingent and compatible within a broader politics of the left in contemporary Spain. As the child of Socialist parents in the 1980s, Iglesias was socialized in the ethos of the Spanish "new" man with left-wing values and intellectual rationality (Ryan 2017, 80). His intellectual capacity allows him to argue in favor of a feminist masculinity, cognizant of the harm that patriarchy inflicts on many women in his country. His disavowal of a hypermasculine personification, however, is challenged at times, by his display of overt masculine traits, particularly in his projection of aggressive intellectualism (Caravantes 2018; Kantola and Lombardo 2019). Furthermore, despite not physically conforming to a traditional masculine image, his masculinity is performed within "relatively tight bandwidths" of acceptable masculinities (Mundy and Denny 2019, 122) that coincide with a long tradition of male leaders of the left. His soft revolutionary demeanor borrows from past leftist leaders such as Julio Anguita (former leader of the United Left) and Santiago Carrillo (former leader of the Spanish Communist Party), both writers and intellectuals whose politics emerged out of the legacy of the Second Republic. His performance of masculinity thus mirrors the historical divisions of the two Spains, particularly through the propagation of Podemos's romantic view of the spirit of the Second Republic that it wishes to recapture. Thus, when Iglesias displays an aggressive, confrontational, and even alpha-male, performance of masculinity, he is positioning himself to fight for and reclaim a Spain that was lost during that fateful civil war. In both Iglesias's and Podemos's discourse, the current democratic regime is cast as illegitimate, the democratic transition incomplete, as Spanish institutions are perceived to be dominated by the inheritors of Francoism. The elite "caste" are the beneficiaries of the half-hearted transition to democracy. Indeed, a typical Podemos event is smothered with the purple, yellow and red Republican flag, nary a contemporary Spanish flag in sight (Muro 2015; Velasco 2019).

But since joining a leftist coalition government with the centre-left Socialist Party and other smaller parties in 2020, Unidas Podemos has softened both its criticism of Spanish institutions such as the monarchy and its celebration of the former Second Republic and its symbols (Gil 2019b). The exigencies of forming part of a coalition government, such as the need for consensus and compromise with other parties, may very well erode its populist label as it is now deeply embedded in the institutional running of the country. Iglesias's performance of masculinity thus treads a fine line between the present demands of identity politics (deconstructing the male self); the burden of a historical leftist project that requires a revolutionary hero to reclaim it; and the constraints of governing for *all* Spaniards. Iglesias thus performs multiple masculinities that are always historically contingent and embedded within a historical continuum of acceptable leftist masculinities.

THE IBERIAN SWAGGER OF THE POPULIST RIGHT

The rise of Vox in Spanish politics was precipitous. As late as 2017, Spain was considered an "exception" in Europe for remaining "immune to the appeal of right-wing populism" (González-Enríquez 2017, 3). Spain's weak national identity and the legacy of the Franco regime were two key reasons, according to González-Enríquez, to explain why Spain was such an anomaly in European populist politics (alongside Portugal which shared a similar history of military dictatorship) (2017, 11–12). She adds: "It is difficult to imagine an extreme right-wing, xenophobic, anti-globalization, and/or anti-EU party gaining a foothold in Spain in the foreseeable future" (2017, 37). A year later, Vox won twelve seats in the Andalusian elections in 2018, forming part of a coalition government with center-right parties. In 2019 it consolidated those gains at the national elections winning 15.1 percent of the vote, making it Spain's third-largest political party. The populist right had finally gained traction in Spain.

But the emergence of Vox did not necessarily come out of the blue. The absence of populist right parties in Spanish politics simply meant that this constituency for a long time had been subsumed in the center-right Popular Party (Sancton 1996). Alonso and Rovira Kaltwasser pointed to the devastating impact of the Great Recession on Spanish society and suggested that there was an exceptional opportunity for a populist radical right party "to present itself as the real defender of the ideas and interests of the 'the people'" (2015, 39). After a series of corruption scandals and the mishandling of the economic crisis, a small number of individuals split from the Popular Party in 2013, establishing Vox with the aim of filling this void in Spanish politics. It borrowed heavily from other European far-right parties (anti-immigration and anti-Brussels) but also appealed to the traditional concerns of the Spanish right in its opposition to regional nationalisms in Catalonia and the Basque Country (Vox defends recentralizing the semi-federal system). As Alonso and Rovira Kaltwasser also stressed, Spanish politics is as much about nationalism, territorial integrity and traditional values as it is about the economy and socioeconomic equality (2015, 39). The pillars of Vox's electoral platform include fear of immigrants (they are taking *our* jobs), but particularly exploit the fear of national disintegration (the balkanization of Spain) (Arroyo 2019). But despite this opportune political context that was ripe for exploitation, the party achieved little electoral success in its early years until it was able to capitalize on voter discontent in the aftermath of Catalonia's 2017 ill-fated referendum, channeling it into an array of other issues, such as a strong discourse on law and order and attacks on gender violence laws (Pardo 2019). This platform was coupled with an attempt to recuperate a mythic past (i.e., the Reconquista when Christians liberated Spain from Muslims) and to reinstall pride in being Spanish (Arroyo 2019). Vox's voters, according to the newspaper *El País*, are politically disaffected, feel a sense of abandonment from the mainstream political system and are concerned about the crisis of Spanish identity (Abril 2020). Research by Spain's Centre for Sociological Research indicates that the typical Vox voter is male, young (between twenty-five and forty-four years old) and is more concerned about the economy, unemployment and health than immigration. However, 55.9 percent of voters acknowledged that the political crisis in Catalonia influenced their vote (Cortizo and Ordaz 2020).

Vox utilizes both the traditional and social media effectively to stoke the left/right divide in Spain by framing the tension between the two Spains as an existential crisis (Pardo 2020). For example, Vox fomented protests against the Socialist/Unidas Podemos coalition government's handling of the Covid-19 crisis (Campos 2020). Abascal recalled the divisions of the Spanish Civil War during a speech in the Congress of Deputies, suggesting that Iglesias had a pathological obsession with the 1930s and that the government had presided over ten times as many deaths as those killed in Paracuellos (the site of a series of massacres of civilians and soldiers by Republicans in 1936) (Guillén 2020). Such polarization is not necessarily new in contemporary Spanish politics, since both the center-left and center-right for years have been aligning their political messaging along such divisions (Manganas 2016). But Vox has certainly intensified this virulent discourse by echoing Trump in the United States, promising to "make Spain great again" (Pardo 2019).

Vox is Latin for "voice" and like most populist political parties, Vox claims to speak for the forgotten people that are in deep mourning for a Spain that they feel they have lost. Its discourse is thus permeated by a deep feeling of nostalgia for a past that has slipped out of their grasp. The range of concerns for Vox supporters are myriad, but they include the disappearance of the middle class, the sense that their towns and cities are no longer safe due to high levels of immigration, and high unemployment (Abril 2020). For such voters Vox is "a reaction to the state that Spain is in" and as such represents "hope" as it not only stands for the traditional values of God, family, and the homeland, but is perceived as caring more about the underprivileged than other political parties (Abril 2020). In the televised election debate, Abascal paraphrased one of the pioneers of Spanish fascism, Ramiro Ledesma Ramos: "For the most humble Spaniards, Spain is their only asset: only the rich can allow themselves the luxury of not having a homeland" (González 2019). This was a telling remark not only for its echoes of Spanish fascism, but because it pointed to how Abascal's idea of a Spanish "imagined community" (Anderson 1983) is intimately tied to the dignity ascribed to the nation. Such a rendering allows Abascal to display a protective masculinity in his defence of such an imagined community. The "patria" or the "nation" is thus set up as an ontological object of hope for a class of Spanish men who have lost their sense of their role and place in the world. In Abascal's worldview, there is no separating the emasculation of Spanish men and the emasculation of the nation; they are one and the same. His performance of hypermasculinity is thus a response to reclaim a Spain that might have won the battle of the civil war, but lost the long war against progressives (feminists, LGBT+ activists, regional nationalists etc.) that have slowly shaped Spain into a more diverse and inclusive society.

Abascal thus argues for a return to an imagined meritocratic society that includes eliminating all threats to a unified national identity and the need to tackle a "crisis in values" (Alabao 2018). Central to this aim is the exultation of the traditional family that, in Vox's view, preexists the state and is perceived as an institution to guarantee traditional gender roles. For instance, Vox has sought to implement a parental veto policy in regions where it forms part of a coalition government. This policy, also known as the "parental pin," allows parents to refuse permission to their children to be exposed to content in public schools that they deem subverts their ethical, social and sexual morals (Jones 2020). The workshops targeted by Vox include ones designed to counter gender violence and the bullying of the LGBT+ community (Gil Grande 2020). Consequently, many of Vox's policies are framed to preserve the traditional family, such as arguing for reducing divorce, sending gender violence cases to mediation, an increase in the birth rate as a means to halt non-European immigration, as well as being vehemently against abortion and same-sex marriage (Alabao 2018). These policies are underpinned by a virulent discourse of anti-feminism that consistently rails against "gender ideology" and "gender totalitarianism" from the progressive left (Azpiroz 2019). Overall, they perceive that the pendulum has swung too far in favor of women and that that this pendulum needs to swing back to the center in order to achieve true "equality" in Spanish society. Abascal targets politicians from the center-right for being weak and cowardly in their defence of territorial integrity and traditional values, and also attacks "progres" (progressives) whom he deems a privileged elite that is undermining "real" Spanish values. Abascal thus inverts Iglesias's call for a feminist masculinity by celebrating a hegemonic form of masculinity that contrasts starkly with the Spanish "new" man but is also closely aligned with older Spanish forms of masculinity that until now had almost been entirely delegitimized.

Abascal is physically muscular and attractive, has copious amounts of facial and body hair, and wears tight pants and shirts that cling to his body and gym-toned torso, all elements that are hallmarks of gay eroticism (González 2019). He, too, is often caricatured in the media: "es macho alfa ibérico con detalles patrióticos en la corbata" (He is an alpha *macho ibérico* with patriotric details on his tie) (Miranda 2019). His tone is often aggressive, and he represents the *macho ibérico* when he appears on a horse declaring the beginning of a reconquest, a war against Catalans, immigrants and feminists. But this is not a bumbling or ironic version of the *macho ibérico*, but rather, a romantic version of the *macho ibérico* appealing to dignity, honor and merit; a vision of men doing "cosas de hombres" (men's things) such as hunting and bullfighting (Delgado 2018). Abascal's performance of masculinity is so novel in Spanish politics that one female journalist commented that she sees Abascal twins everywhere: men on the streets imitate him; women are seduced by him (de La Lá 2019). But it also recalls the hegemonic masculinity propagated in the Franco era, rooted in the ideology of national-Catholicism, large traditional families, and a militarized masculinity that seeks to reinstall a pride in Spanish identity that is perceived to have been lost with Spain's transition to democracy. Abascal's performance of an alpha-male protector who is only violent to defend Spain against its enemies that wish to destroy it (Delgado 2018), thus echoes older constituent models of masculinity that can be traced to Spain's authoritarian past.

The most telling aspect of Abascal's rise and popularity is how easily he was able to activate a masculine prototype that was widely considered dormant. His emergence on the political stage reminds Spaniards that his Iberian swagger is intimately tied to the version of Spain he defends. But like Iglesias, his performance of masculinity is complex. He treads a fine line between his articulation of a paternal vision to save Spain from its enemies and his seeking to reclaim a "true" manliness where men do not need to apologize for being men. His confident swagger belies that he is aware of his charisma and physical appeal. But his unironic performance of hegemonic masculinity is characterized by his inconsistent discourse. While his virulent anti-feminist and anti-LGBT messaging helped in his electoral rise, he has recently attempted to reframe that narrative by claiming that Vox supports all Spaniards despite their color, sex and sexual orientation, suggesting, brazenly, that Socialist prime minister Pedro Sánchez abandon the left's historic hate against homosexuals (Arroyo 2020). Such mixed-messaging highlights that Abascal's performance is similarly historically contingent, vacillating between a longing for the past and the need to appeal to contemporary voters. Abascal has, therefore, returned an Iberian swagger back to the political stage and in the process challenged one of the foundational myths of Spain's transition to democracy: that the Spanish far right had firmly been delegitimized.

CONCLUSION

This comparative case study demonstrates that both Podemos and Vox have utilized the populist trope of the people versus an elite to foster a "moralistic imagination of politics" (Müller 2016, 26) and as such, both Iglesias and Abascal overcompensate by promoting a cultural and psycho-emotional aesthetic in the expression of their masculinity that is aimed to appeal to their base and sell themselves to the electorate (Valdivia 2019). Unlike Spain's center-left and center-right leaders who adopt a rather conservative approach to their display of masculinity, Iglesias and Abascal stretch the bandwidth of acceptable masculinities as much as they can in order to lend credibility and legitimacy to their defence of their politics and to their vision of Spain. On one end of the bandwidth, Iglesias positions himself at the center of a social narrative that idealizes him as the figure of the revolutionary hero who seeks to upend the current political system. On the other end, Abascal is an idealized patriarch, the protector who has emerged to defend and reclaim a political system that is at risk of disappearing.

The case study demonstrates that although Abascal and Iglesias's performances of masculinity could not, on the surface, be any more different, they both utilize the same political logic to affectively appeal to their electoral base, reflecting both the social and political space in which they circulate (Stavrakakis 2004, 256). Both performances thus sustain Connell's argument that masculinity is a historically contingent performance (2005, 185). Furthermore, the case study underlines the usefulness of conceptualizing populist masculinity as a discursive logic because it highlights that performances of populist masculinities are intimately tied to the telling of the national story. The discursive approach also underscores that each national context has its own national burdens. Spain's historical particularities have oriented political discourses toward internal, national divisions, and performances of masculinity correspondingly align with those national cleavages. This means that appeals to whiteness that might resonate in other parts of Europe are not readily activated in the Spanish context. But performances of populist masculinities in Spain do align with Miller-Idriss's contention that "masculinity intersects with nationalistic ideals in ways that mutually reinforce masculinity and nationalism" (2017, 211). The Spanish context demonstrates that such intersections are just as apparent on the left as they are on the right. Hence, the feminist masculinity of Iglesias and the Iberian swagger of Abascal, do not point to any specific form of masculinity. Rather, they reinforce that populist masculinities are better understood as a political logic that facilitates the selling of diverse political projects to the electorate, regardless of where they sit on the political spectrum.

There are two important insights we can glean from populist masculinities in Spain. First, populism should not be considered a new phenomenon but rather situated on a historical continuum. Although Podemos and Vox are relatively new parties, their political objectives and aesthetics draw heavily from the past and are in intimate dialogue with perceived historical losses and gains. The complexity of modern masculinities, however, means that both populist leaders must adapt their performance of masculinity to the current historical moment even if, at times, they risk becoming caricatures. It also points to the appeal that traditional hegemonic masculinity still has in contemporary society, concurring with Namaste's assessment that hegemonic masculinity is the "form of manhood that [remains] most respected and valued" (2017, 248). Second, and more importantly, it suggests that the populism should be considered a "political logic" instead of an ideology (Judis 2016, 14) because beyond promulgating an antagonism between the people and the elite, it is calculated to intimately echo long-standing historical narratives, whether from the left or the right. In Spain's case, the narrative of the two Spains has always circulated in political discourse, providing Podemos and Vox with a ready-made constituency to respond to its political messaging. The Spanish experience further demonstrates how easy it is for political parties to manipulate the affective bonds that a tortured national history still engenders in many of its citizens. It correspondingly shows that gender is not only inseparable from politics, but that populist performances of masculinity normalize a male ideal that is intimately tied to contested histories. The Spanish case underlines that populist movements have a tendency to align themselves with historical movements from either the radical left or right, avoiding the center altogether. Consequently, performances of populist masculinity tend to polarize, blurring the line between politicking and gender performance. Taking a historical perspective attests to how a perceived crisis in masculinity has a long genealogy. To paraphrase Le Goff, we must constantly reread masculinities of the past in relation to the masculinities of the present (1992, 18). This approach can tell us much about how performances of populist masculinities can be traced to earlier prototypes and historical events; emerging, circulating, and evolving into new forms that scholars must continue to question anew.

NOTE

1. All translations from Spanish to English are by the author except for the poem by Antonio Machado, translated by R. Bly (1983).

BIBLIOGRAPHY

Abril, Guillermo. 2020. "Why I Voted for Vox?" *El País*, February 22, 2020. https://english.elpais.com/eps/2020-02-21/why-i-voted-for-vox.html.

Adagio, Carmelo. 2013. "Youth Protests and the End of the Zapatero Government." In *Politics and Society in Contemporary Spain: From Zapatero to Rajoy*, edited by Bonnie N. Field, and Alfonso Botti, 143–160. New York: Palgrave Macmillan.

Alabao, Nuria. 2018. "La Guerra de Vox Contra el Feminismo." *Ctxt*, December 4, 2018. https://ctxt.es/es/20181129/Firmas/23216/Nuria-Alabao-machismo-en-vox-masculinizacionneofascismo-Santiago-Abascal.htm.

Alemán, Jorge. 2018. "Jorge Alemán 07—Conversación con Pablo Iglesias." *YouTube Video*, November 23, 2018. https://www.youtube.com/watch?v=b2w 5LXpHH4Q.

Alonso, Sonia, and Cristóbal Rovira Kaltwasser. 2015. "Spain: No Country for the Populist Radical Right?" *South European Society & Politics* 20 (1): 21–45.

Anderson, Benedict. 1983. *Imagined Communities*. London: Verso.

Arroyo, Luis. 2019. "Spain: The Far-Right Discourse during the Campaign." *The Progressive Post*, May 7, 2019. https://progressivepost.eu/debates/spain-the-far-right-discourse-during-the-campaign.

Arroyo, Luis. 2020. "Vox: Disección del Disparate sobre los Homosexuales." *infoLibre*, May 8, 2020. https://www.infolibre.es/noticias/opinion/columnas/2020/05/08/vox_diseccion_del_disparate_sobre_los_homosexuales_106578_1023.html.

Azpiroz, Ander. 2019. "¿Es Vox un Partido Machista?" *Diario Sur*, January 6, 2019. https://www.diariosur.es/nacional/partido-machista-20190106181653-ntrc .html.

Balfour, Sebastian, and Alejandro Quiroga. 2007. *The Reinvention of Spain: Nation and Identity since Democracy*. Oxford: Oxford University Press.

Blakeley, Georgina. 2005. "Digging Up Spain's: Past Consequences of Truth and Reconciliation." *Democratization* 12 (1): 44–59.

Bosco, Anna, and Susannah Verney. 2012. "Electoral Epidemic: The Political Cost of Economic Crisis in Southern Europe." *South European Society and Politics* 17 (2): 129–154.

Butler, Judith. 1990. *Gender Trouble: Feminism and the Subversion of Identity*. New York: Routledge.

Campos, Cristian. 2020. "Así Intenta Vox Convertir las Protestas del Barrio de Salamanca en su 15-M Contra el Gobierno." *El Español*, May 17, 2020. https://www.elespanol.com/espana/politica/20200517/intenta-vox-convertir-protestas-barrio-salamanca-gobierno/490202220_0.html.

Caravantes, Paloma. 2019. "New Versus Old Politics in Podemos: Feminization and Masculinized Party Discourse." *Men and Masculinities* 19 (3): 465–490.

Cedeira, Brais. 2020. "La Cifosis Dorsal de Pablo Iglesias: El Problema de Espalda que le Hace Andar Como un 'Cowboy.'" *El Español*, January 18, 2020. https://www.elespanol.com/reportajes/20200118/cifosis-dorsal-pablo-iglesias-problema-espalda-cowboy/460454967_0.html.

Clare, Anthony. 2000. *On Men: Masculinity in Crisis*. Sydney: Arrow Books.

Colmeiro, José. 2017. "Old Traditions and Revolutionary Tendencies: Performing Different Masculinities in Spanish Cinema." In *The Dynamics of Masculinity in Contemporary Spanish Culture*, edited by Lorraine Ryan and Ana Corbalán, 19–35. New York: Routledge.

Connell, R. W. 2005. *Masculinities*. 2nd Edition. Cambridge: Polity.

Cortizo, Gonzalo, and Ana Ordaz. 2020. "La Situación en Catalunya Condicionó el Voto de uno de Cada Cuatro Electores el 10N, Según el CIS." *El Diario*, January 16, 2020. https://www.eldiario.es/politica/situacion-Catalunya-condiciono-electores-CIS_0_985501738.html.

Cué, Carlos E. 2020. "El Día que Podemos Firmó la Paz con los Empresarios y Se Convirtió en un Partido de Gobierno." *El País*, January 29, 2020. https://elpais.com /politica/2020/01/29/actualidad/1580330582_196687.html.

De La Lá, Carla. 2019. "50 Sombras de Santiago Abascal." *La Razón*, January 16, 2019. https://www.larazon.es/familia/50-sombras-de-santiago-abascal-BC214585 48/.

De Larra, Mariano José. 1836. "El día de Difuntos de 1836. Fígaro en el Cementerio." *Biblioteca Virtual Miguel de Cervantes*, May 4, 2020. http://www.cervantesvirtu al.com/obra-visor/el-dia-de-difuntos-de-1836-figaro-en-el-cementerio--0/html/ff7 9053a-82b1-11df-acc7-002185ce6064_2.html#I_0_.

Delgado, Lionel S. 2018. "Enfadados con Todo: Vox y la Masculinidad." *El Salto*, December 9, 2018. https://www.elsaltodiario.com/vox/enfadados-con-todo-vox -masculinidad.

Díez, Rosa. 2019. "El Gobierno que Prepara Sánchez Romperá España." *Expansión*. https://www.expansion.com/economia/politica/2019/12/11/5df00ac2468aeb8 7388b46a1.html.

DiGiovanni, Lisa. 2017. "Militarized Masculinity: Boy's Socialization and the Post-War Graphic Novel of Carlos Giménez." In *The Dynamics of Masculinity in Contemporary Spanish Culture*, edited by Lorraine Ryan, and Ana Corbalán, 63–79. New York: Routledge.

Donnell, Sidney. *Feminizing the Enemy: Imperial Spain, Transvestite Drama, and the Crisis of Masculinity*. Lewisburg: Buckness University Press.

Encarnación, Omar G. 2001. "Spain after Franco: Lessons in Democratization." *World Policy Journal* 18 (4): 35–44.

Fouz-Hernández, Santiago, and Alfredo Martínez-Expósito. 2007. *Live Flesh: The Male Body in Contemporary Spanish Cinema*. London: I. B. Tauris.

Fernández, Fruela. 2018. "Podemos: Politics as a 'Task of Translation.'" *Translation Studies* 11 (1): 1–16.

Fukuyama, Francis. 1992. *The End of History and the Last Man*. New York: Free Press.

Garrido, José María. 2020. "La Señora del Barrio de Salamanca que Se Manifiesta contra 'el Coletas' Comunista de Podemos: "¡Vengo de la Iglesia!" *El Plural*, May 15, 2020. https://www.elplural.com/politica/espana/senora-barrio-salamanca-manifiesta-el-coletas-comunista-podemos-vengo-iglesia_239820102.

Gil, Iván. 2019a. "El Ganador de los Debates fue Iglesias, que Influyó en el Voto del 50% de Espectadores." *El Confidencial*, July 10, 2019. https://www.elconfidencial. com/espana/2019-07-10/el-ganador-de-los-debates-fue-pablo-iglesias-pero-no-influyo-en-el-sentido-del-voto_2116843/.

Gil, Iván. 2019b. "Podemos Aparca su Tendencia Republicana antes de Entrar en el Gobierno." *El Confidencial*, December 25, 2019. https://www.elconfidencial.com /espana/2019-12-25/podemos-iglesias-aparca-republica-gobierno-monarquia_238 8756/.

Gil Grande, Rocío. 2020. "'Pin Parental': ¿Qué Se Enseña en los Talleres que Vox Quiere Vetar?" *RTVE*, January 25, 2020. https://www.rtve.es/noticias/20200125/ pin-parental-se-ensena-talleres-vox-quiere-vetar/1996436.shtml.

González, David. 2019. "La Nueva Imagen Fornida de Santiago Abascal, el Líder de VOX Convertido en un 'Involuntario' Icono LGTB." *El Cierre Digital*, October 27, 2019. https://elcierredigital.com/ventana-indiscreta/312131704/santiago-abascal-vox-icono-LGTB.html.

González, Miguel. 2019. "Vox, Unchallenged at TV Debate, Enjoys Boost in the Polls." *El País (English Edition)*, November 6, 2019. https://english.elpais.com/elpais/2019/11/06/inenglish/1573029968_471791.html.

González-Enríquez, Carmen. 2017. "The Spanish Exception: Unemployment, Inequality and Immigration, but no Right-Wing Populist Parties." *Elcano Royal Institute*, Working Paper 3/2017. http://www.realinstitutoelcano.org/wps/wcm/connect/e9e0d7c1-7c71-4335-a2fb-15b219e62c5e/WP3-2017-GonzalezEnriquez-Spanish-Exception-unemployment-inequality-inmigration-no-right-wing-populist-parties.pdf ?MOD=AJPERES&CACHEID=e9e0d7c1-7c71-4335-a2fb-15b219e62c5e.

Graham, Helen. 2004. "The Spanish Civil War 1936–2003: The Return of Republican Memory." *Science and Society* 68 (3): 313–328.

Guillén, J. J. 2020. "Abascal Amaga con una Moción de Censura y Desafía al Gobierno Convocando Manifestaciones en Coche." *Heraldo*, May 6, 2020. https://www.heraldo.es/noticias/nacional/2020/05/06/abascal-amaga-con-una-mocion-de-censura-y-desafia-al-gobierno-convocando-manifestaciones-en-coche-1373354.html.

Hedgecoe, Guy. 2019. "Spain's Gender Gap." *Politico*, January 23, 2019. https://www.politico.eu/article/vox-feminism-spain-far-right-gender-gap/.

Johansson, Thomas, and Andreas Ottemo. 2015. "Ruptures in Hegemonic Masculinity: The Dialectic between Ideology and Utopia." *Journal of Gender Studies* 24 (2): 192–206.

Jones, Sam. 2020. "Row in Spain Over Far-Right Party's Parental Veto Policy for Classes." *Guardian*, January 21, 2020. https://www.theguardian.com/world/2020/jan/20/spains-government-vows-to-overturn-parental-pin-initiative.

Jordan, Barry, and Rikki Morgan-Tamosunas. 1998. *Contemporary Spanish Cinema*. Manchester: Manchester University Press.

Justo, David. 2020. "'La Gente es Muy Cabrona': Pablo Iglesias No Se Corta al Hablar de lo que le Han Hecho con esta Foto." *Cadena SER*, January 15, 2020. https://cadenaser.com/ser/2020/01/15/politica/1579068205_192366.html.

Judis, John, B. 2016. *The Populist Explosion: How the Great Recession Transformed American and European Politics*. New York: Columbia Global Reports.

Kantola, Johanna, and Emanuela Lombardo. 2019. "Populism and Feminist Politics: The Case of Finland and Spain." *European Journal of Political Research* 58: 1108–1128.

Kennedy, Paul. 2014. "The Breakthrough of Podemos in Spain Poses a Serious Challenge for the Country's Two-Party System." *LSE EUROPP Blog*, March 16, 2020. https://blogs.lse.ac.uk/europpblog/2014/06/09/the-breakthrough-of-podemos-in-spain-poses-a-serious-challenge-for-the-countrys-two-party-system/.

Keskinen, Suvi. 2013. "Antifeminism and White Identity Politics: Political Antagonisms in Radical Right-Wing Populist and Anti-Immigration Rhetoric in Finland." *Nordic Journal of Migration Research* 3 (4): 225–232.

Kimmel, Michael. 2017. *Angry White Men: American Masculinity at the End of an Era*. New York: Nation Books.

Kinnvall, Catarina. 2019. "Populism, Ontological Insecurity and Hindutva: Modi and the Masculinization of Indian Politics." *Cambridge Review of International Affairs* 32 (3): 283–302.

Kotouza, Dimitra. 2019. *Surplus Citizens: Struggle and Nationalism in the Greek Crisis*. London: Pluto Press.

Laclau, Ernesto. 1980. "Towards a Theory of Populism." *Screen Education* 34: 87–93.

Laclau, Ernesto. 2005. "Populism: What's in a Name?" In *Populism and the Mirror of Democracy*, edited by Francisco Panizza, 32–49. London: Verso.

Laclau, Ernesto, and Chantal Mouffe. 1985. *Hegemony and Socialist Strategy*. London: Verso.

Le Goff, Jacques. 1992. *History and Memory*. Translated by S. Renall, and E. Claman. New York: Columbia University Press.

Luna, Bigas, dir. 1992. *Jamón Jamón*. Madrid: Lolafilms.

Machado, Antonio. 1983. *Times Alone: Selected Poems of Antonio Machado*. Translated by R. Bly. Middletown, CT: Wesleyan University Press.

MacKinnon, Kenneth. 2003. *Representing Men: Maleness and Masculinity in the Media*. London: Arnold.

Manganas, Nicholas. 2016. *Las dos Españas: Terror and Crisis in Contemporary Spain*. Eastbourne: Sussex Academic Press.

Mariscal, George. 1991. *Contradictory Subjects: Quevedo, Cervantes, and Seventeenth Century Spanish Culture*. Ithaca: Cornell University Press.

Miller-Idriss, Cynthia. 2017. "Soldier, Sailor, Rebel, Rule-Breaker: Masculinity and the Body in the German Far Right." *Gender and Education* 29 (2): 199–215.

Miranda, Beatriz. 2019. "El Voto y la Imagen. El Vox de Santiago Abascal: Estilo Anodino, 'Preti' y con Símbolos Patrióticos." *El Mundo*, November 6, 2020. https ://www.elmundo.es/album/loc/famosos/2019/11/06/5dc1834721efa0d9308b4658 _1.html.

Molpeceres Arnáiz, Sara, and Laura Filardo-Llamas. 2020. "Llamamientos Feministas en Twitter: Ideología, Identidad Colectiva y Reenmarcado de Símbolos en la Huelga del 8-M y la Manifestación Contra la Sentencia de 'La Manada.'" *Dígitos. Revista de Comunicación Digital* 6: 55–78.

Moreno-Caballud, Luis. 2015. *Cultures of Anyone: Studies on Cultural Democratization in the Spanish Neoliberal Crisis*. Translated by Linda Grabner. Liverpool: Liverpool University Press.

Morgan, David. 2006. "The Crisis in Masculinity." In *Handbook of Gender and Women's Studies*, edited by Kathy Davis, Mary Evans and Judith Lorber, 109–124. London: Sage Publications.

Mudde, Cas, and Cristóbal Rovira Kaltwasser. 2013. "Exclusionary vs. Inclusionary Populism: Comparing Contemporary Europe and Latin America." *Government and Opposition* 48 (2): 147–174.

Müller, Jan-Werner. 2016. *What is Populism?* Philadelphia: University of Pennsylvania Press.

Mundy, Robert, and Harry Denny. 2019. *Gender, Sexuality, and the Cultural Politics of Men's Identity: Literacies of Masculinity.* London: Routledge.

Múñoz Molina, Antonio. 2013. *Todo Lo Que Era Sólido.* Barcelona: Seix Barral.

Muro, Miriam. 2015. "La 'Transversalidad' de Podemos Naufraga en un Mar de Banderas Republicanas." *Libertad Digital,* January 31, 2015. https://www.libertad digital.com/espana/2015-01-31/cientos-de-banderas-republicanas-y-lemas-contra -el-pp-en-la-marcha-de-podemos-1276539540/.

Namaste, Nina B. 2017. "Identifying the Male: Language, Humour, and Gender Performance in Companyia T De Teatre's *Homes!*" In *The Dynamics of Masculinity in Contemporary Spanish Culture,* edited by Lorraine Ryan and Ana Corbalán, 244–260. New York: Routledge.

Pardo, Javier. 2020. "Periodistas y Medios de Comunicación, en el Punto de Mira de Vox." *El Plural,* April 15, 2020. https://www.elplural.com/politica/espana/ periodistas-medios-comunicacion-punto-mira-vox_237829102.

Pardo, Pablo. 2019. "Make Spain Great Again." *Foreign Policy,* April 27, 2019. https ://foreignpolicy.com/2019/04/27/vox-spain-elections-trump-bannon/.

Ramírez, María. 2018. "Can #MeToo Fix Spain's Language Problem?" *The Atlantic,* July 27, 2018. https://www.theatlantic.com/entertainment/archive/2018/07/can -metoo-fix-spains-language-problem/566003/.

Ramiro, Luis, and Raúl Gómez. 2017. "Radical-Left Populism during the Great Recession: Podemos and its Competition with the Established Radical Left." *Political Studies* 65 (15): 108–126.

Robinson, Sally. 2000. *Marked Men: Masculinity in Crisis.* New York: Columbia University Press.

Rodríguez, Emmanuel. 2016. *La Política en el Ocaso de la Clase Media. El Ciclo 15M-Podemos.* Madrid: Traficantes de Sueños.

Rubio, Ricardo. 2019. "Pablo Iglesias, Ganador del Debate de Atresmedia Según la Encuesta de Europa Press en Twitter." *Europa Press,* April 24, 2019. https://www. europapress.es/nacional/noticia-pablo-iglesias-ganador-debate-atresmedia-encuesta-europa-press-twitter-20190424150626.html.

Ryan, Lorraine. 2017. "Memory and Masculinity in Almudena Grandes's *El Corazón Helado.*" In *The Dynamics of Masculinity in Contemporary Spanish Culture,* edited by Lorraine Ryan, and Ana Corbalán, 80–98. New York: Routledge.

Ryan, Lorraine, and Ana Corbalán. 2017. "Introduction: The Reconfiguration of Masculinity in Spain." In *The Dynamics of Masculinity in Contemporary Spanish Culture,* edited by Lorraine Ryan, and Ana Corbalán, 1–18. New York: Routledge.

Sánchez-Mellado, Luz. 2018. "Perdónanos, Mariló." *El País,* December 14, 2020. https://elpais.com/elpais/2018/12/13/gente/1544720379_470343.html.

Sancton, T. 1996. "War of the Spanish Succession." *TIME International* 147 (10): 12–16.

Stavrakakis, Yannis. 2004. "Antinomies of Formalism: Laclau's Theory of Populism and the Lessons from Religious Populism in Greece." *Journal of Political Ideologies* 9 (3): 253–267.

Tremlett, Giles. 2015. "The Podemos Revolution: How a Small Group of Radical Academics Changed European Politics." *Guardian,* March 31, 2015.

https://www.theguardian.com/world/2015/mar/31/podemos-revolution-radical-academics-changed-european-politics.

Valdivia, Pablo. 2019. "Narrating Crisis and Populism in Southern Europe: Regimes of Metaphor." *Journal of European Studies* 49 (3–4): 282–301.

Vallín, Pedro. 2016. "Podemos Sí es Populista." *La Vanguardia*, November 20, 2016. https://www.lavanguardia.com/politica/20161120/411995710184/podemos-populismo-pablo-iglesias.html.

Velasco, Lourdes. 2019. "Iglesias, Garzón y la Bandera Tricolor." *Cope*, April 14, 2019. https://www.cope.es/actualidad/espana/noticias/iglesias-garzon-bandera-tricolor-20190414_394913.

Walsh, Fintan. 2010. *Male Trouble: Masculinity and the Performance of Crisis*. New York: Palgrave Macmillan.

Chapter 2

Signifying Illiberalism

Gender and Sport in Viktor Orbán's Facebook Photos

Katinka Linnamäki

In 2010, when the Hungarian right-wing populist government, consisting of Fidesz and KDNP, began its second term with a two-thirds parliamentary majority, an "illiberal turn" took place in Hungary (Laczó 2018). The populist Fidesz not only survived the transition from opposition to a governing force, but the two-thirds majority enabled it to amplify the populist logic and stabilize its hegemonic position in the Hungarian political scene.[1] This chapter argues that the illiberal turn, dismaying "liberal" gender equality, also affected the Hungarian gender order.

Recent research thematizes the connection between populism, liberalism and gender by connecting populism to the global crisis of the neoliberal hegemony and seeing it as anti-hegemonic mobilization against the racial, religious and sexual threat that global neoliberalism poses on local hegemonic (white, heterosexual, ethno-national, Christian) masculinities (Barát 2017). Populist rearticulations of hegemonic masculinities happen through appropriations of spaces and activities that historically excluded women (Bonde 2009). Prime examples of such spaces and activities are sport- and especially football-related ones in Hungary, the politicization of which has been a major endeavor of Fidesz. Through financial support, new tax laws, extensive stadiums, and through politicizing new and existing football clubs, the party reclaims traditional masculinities that combine national pride and heroism, like the figure of the famous 1956 match hero Ferenc Puskás (Molnár 2007; Szerovay and Itkonen 2018). The politization of football also shapes the masculinity of the party's long-term leader, Hungarian PM Viktor Orbán, known as a football player and sports fan (Goldblatt and Nolan 2018).

This chapter analyses how the illiberal political shift is articulated through the signifier "sport" in Viktor Orbán's visual representation. It considers Orbán as a gendered performative signifier of both illiberal populism (Laclau 2018) and of hegemonic masculinity in Hungary (Connell and Messerschmidt 2005). According to the relational understandings of politics (Laclau 2018) and gender (Connell 2009), binary relations construct social actors, for example, "us" and "them"; men and women. These exclusions can be signaled in space, for instance, with national borders or gendered toilets. In this sense, space and spatial signifiers like distance can successfully constitute certain relations between in- and out-groups, as well as between masculinities and femininities in a certain society. The chapter aims to entangle these relations through a multimodal approach, combining critical feminist (Goffman 1988) and qualitative content analysis with compositional interpretations (Rose 2001) of the visual material on Orbán's Facebook page. At the beginning, I give a short overview of recent literature on populism and gender and the populist leader, and conceptualize the representation of Orbán as a gendered performative signifier. Next, I briefly discuss populism in the Hungarian political context and deliver the analysis of the visual material of Orbán's Facebook page. At the end, I sum up the results and answer the question of how Orbán's Facebook representation of sports signifies illiberalism and the illiberal turn.

POPULISM, MASCULINITY, AND THE LEADER AS GENDERED PERFORMATIVE SIGNIFIER

For populist scholars, charismatic leaders are typical parts of populist movements (Taggart 2004; Mudde and Kaltwasser 2014; Wodak 2015; Laclau 2018). The ideational approach (Mudde 2017; Mudde and Kalwasser 2018; Hawkins 2019) defines populism as a set of ideas based on the moral superiority of "the people" over "the elite," representing the general will of "the people" (Mudde 2017). As opposed to modern ideologies, the group of "the people" is not defined through sociocultural or socioeconomic categories but constructed on a moral basis that the populist leader defines (Mudde 2017, 9). This leaves the leader in a problematic omnipotent position beyond "the people" versus "the elite" dichotomy. Gender-related literature that draws on this approach mostly focuses on the external appearances of gender in right-wing populist politics—for example, policies (Mudde and Kaltwasser 2015) or political representation (Abi-Hassan 2018)—while gender concepts in populist discourses are under-researched.

The post-foundational approach defines populism as a "logic of articulation" that does not represent but constitutes social agents (Laclau 2018;

Mouffe 2018). Thus, populist politics cannot be defined by its content (in terms of who or what it represents), but as a "particular logic of articulation of those contents—whatever those contents are" (Laclau 2014, 153). In the populist logic, distinct political demands—different in target and nature—are grouped together, forming an "equivalential chain" (Laclau 2014, 156). Hegemony—that is, the totality of these heterogeneous political demands—is constituted by discursive means, such as by signifiers, that fulfill two roles: first, they are an integral part of the equivalent chain of the unfulfilled demands; second, they are signifying the whole chain of equivalence (Laclau 2018). Performativity is understood here as the constitutive action of articulation of "the people" and their antagonistic frontier (Palonen 2019). I argue that the anti-essentialist approach best serves the intention to combine populism with critical gender research, as both dismiss the concept of pre-discursive identities and agree that identities are constituted through exclusions (Butler 1990, 1993; Connell 2009; Laclau 2018).

Building on non-essentialist gender theory, R. W. Connell (2005) introduces the concept of hegemonic masculinity; a performed masculinity that signifies and connects legitimized masculinities in a society, and that, similarly to a signifier in the Laclauian sense, also constitutes its antagonistic outside: femininity and illegit, marginalized masculinities. Gender is defined as a "structure of social relations that centers on the reproductive arena, and the set of practices that bring reproductive distinctions between bodies into social processes" (Connell 2009, 10). Bodies are not just expressing social norms, but as "both objects . . . and agents in social practice," bodies also performatively shape social norms (Connell and Messerschmidt 2005, 851).

Recent research often conceptualizes populism as a reaction to the threat to hegemonic (white, heterosexual, ethno-national, Christian) masculinity (Barát 2017; Keskinen 2013). As ethno-nationality is often constituted through analogy to the heterosexual nuclear family (Norocel 2010), its threat is often signified by "gender ideology," an umbrella term signifying the harm that gender equality allegedly poses on hegemonic masculinity (Kuhar and Paternotte 2017, 255). Thus, gender becomes a "symbolic glue" expressing a combination of a wide range of right-wing populist mobilizing logics: nationalist (Korolczuk and Graff 2018, 799; cf. Aharoni and Féron 2020), religious (Gunnarsson Payne 2019; Moghadam and Kaftan 2019), anti-colonialist (Korolczuk and Graff 2018), or neoliberal (De Lange and Mügge 2015). Accordingly, gender is not just a discursive topic but a constitutive element in the populist logic. I consider "gender order"—that is, wider gendered patterns in a society (Connell 2009, 73)—to be just like nationalism, a constitutive element in the articulation of "the people," "a practical resource that can be exploited in constructing political identities and defining lines of political opposition and conflict" (Brubaker 2020, 44; cf. Keskinen 2013). I also emphasize that right-wing populist parties often foster traditional family constellations with traditional gender order (Norocel 2010, 2011); nationalism (Sanger 2019); and reclaim spaces and activities "where men can meet without women," such as sports (Bonde 2009, 1541). I consider the populist appropriations of traditional masculine positions as articulations of populist hegemonic masculinities, which are often represented, for instance, by populist leaders.

Emilia Palonen (2009, 2018) points out that a strong long-term leader assures a party's hegemony and its lack of inner contestation the best. Benjamin Moffitt (2016) claims that political leaders signify the equivalential chain not only with their names—like Orbanism (cf. Koenen 2015)—but also through their embodied performances, thus expanding the Laclauian concept of performativity to the "constitutive effect of political action on political identity" (40). Similarly, Francisco Panizza (2005) highlights that a populist leader signifies the hegemonic unity through not just their words but also their "body and personal life" (Panizza 2005, 20). As an example, research on South America has shown how leaders signify the populist regime through their media representation (Salojärvi 2019). This understanding of embodied performativity resonates with the concept of hegemonic masculinity, which performatively "embodie[s] the currently most honored way of being a man" (Connell and Messerschmidt 2005, 832). Importantly, feminist criticism also points out that political signifiers, such as the leader, are often imperceptibly gendered, leading to gendering of both the hegemonic and anti-hegemonic movements, interfering with the gender order of a society (Motta 2013).

All of the above, the entangling populism, nationalism and masculinity, can be well recognized in the Hungarian context. I conceptualize the representation of Viktor Orbán as a gendered performative signifier of the party Fidesz and since 2010 of the illiberal democracy in the country and in an international context (Koenen 2015), as well as a representation of the illiberal hegemonic masculinity in the country. This chapter combines the understudied affective performative dimensions of signifiers with their feminist critic. It focuses on how the leader as a gendered performative signifier constitutes and connects both the populist logic as well as the gender order.

POPULISM IN HUNGARY

In post-communist Hungary, the elite and anti-elite positions were not bound to certain parties, but interchanged between the two biggest camps, the right and the left. Both camps utilized populist rhetoric and framed their opponent as "the elite." Their political identities based upon the rejection of the other rather than on their actual policies, which Palonen calls a system of "competing populisms or bipolar hegemony" (2009, 318). The starting point of the era of competing populisms dates back to 1994, when, after the dissolution of the liberal camp, Fidesz and the Hungarian Socialist Party (MSZP) signified right versus left became the two exclusive political poles in Hungary (Fowler 2004; Palonen 2009).[2] Changing in power and in opposition they were interchangeably accused of elitism or claimed to represent "the people." "The people" were signified by "nation," which became one of the most important signifiers in the logic of polarization. It was used for signifying either the right-wing understanding of the ethnic Hungarian population, also beyond state borders, or the left-wing understanding of the nation-state of Hungary. Accordingly, "nation" was politicized to constitute competing hegemonic identities and politics of the past (Palonen 2009, 2018).

The Hungarian illusion about democracy and faith in the polarized party system shattered in 2006, when a tape recording, in which former PM Ferenc Gyurcsány (MSZP) admitted that the party lied about the economic state of the country to win the elections, leaked out, shortly after the Socialist-Liberal coalition took office (Becker 2010). As Palonen (2012) puts it: "Gyurcsány had shaken the country . . . by going against the traditional tactic of calling the opposite camp liars" (944). In this "crisis of representation"—the populist moment in a Mouffean sense—the newly founded far-right party Jobbik and the center-right Fidesz accelerated riots on the streets of Budapest, and a new type of illiberal populism started to replace the old system of competing populisms (Palonen 2018, 4).

Accordingly, illiberalism means a "symbolic-constitutive rejection of the liberal left as illegitimate to rule or participate in (defining 'real') democracy" (Palonen 2018, 9) in Hungary. In order to legitimize illiberalism and to avoid arising counter-populist anti-elitist movements within the country, illiberal populism needs to shift the line of antagonism beyond the country borders and expropriate both the anti-elitist and the elitist positions and signifiers in Hungary. Even though Orbán as Hungarian PM necessarily performs elitism, he also needs to signify anti-elitism himself. He also needs to reject liberalism and signify illiberalism in terms of gender (Grzebalska, Kováts, and Pető 2017). This chapter aims to explain the reconciliation of the elitist and anti-elitist positions in the social media representation of Orbán and its connectedness to the Hungarian, illiberal gender order.

MATERIAL AND METHOD

I have chosen Orbán's Facebook images for the analysis, because, according to recent research, Facebook is the most relevant social media in Hungary (Lévai 2018).[3] Although Orbán is also represented in official party pictures and memes, his self-articulation on Facebook enables him to present himself in a seemingly more personal context than in official images directly picturing him in his party affiliation and political position. This not only offers him the opportunity to distance his representation from his elite status as Hungarian PM, but also leads to a wide spectrum of representations, whose interplay I intend to analyze. Besides, the Facebook material enables a synchronic study from 2008 to 2018. Even though Orbán has had his own personal Facebook page since only 2011, Fidesz's Facebook page contains pictures of him from 2007 onward.

First, I limited the material to only timeline photos, capturing Orbán's "visually holistic profile" (Techopedia 2012), which added up to 373 images. Then I analyzed the pictures regarding their content and limited the material only to those where Orbán is pictured with somebody else. Finally, I conducted a brief content analysis (Rose 2001, 38–39) and categorized the pictures into content categories based on their similar features in terms of actors and activity. I limited the material to only those categories that appear both before and after 2010: Orbán as part of the party Fidesz; Orbán with his family members; and Orbán during his free time activities, interacting with people. This added up to 193 images in total: 75 before 2010 and 118 after 2010. For the detailed qualitative analysis, I applied a multimodal approach (Hand 2017, 219), including the title, place and date of the images into the analysis. I applied a combination of the visual methods of qualitative content analysis (Rose 2001, 54–69), compositional interpretation (Rose 2001, 40–45; 69–77) and feminist visual analysis (Goffman 1988). Before 2010, Orbán is represented either as part of the party Fidesz or during his activities outside party-related occasions, mostly related to other public events. In both categories he is represented as a young, approachable man, often as a young father who brings his children to party events. After 2011, family occasions are strictly divided from party events. Orbán is mostly pictured in his own home among his adult female family members and occupies the position of an older man who is the target of their affection. In addition, his party leader imagery has changed from his earlier approachable representation. As Hungarian PM, he is often pictured either alone or accompanied by other famous politicians, religious leaders or national and international celebrities (musicians, actors, athletes); or during his national and international visits, often during traveling. He is pictured as a strong leader, separated from other party members, who are often younger than him. Finally, after 2010, a new category appears in the material, picturing Orbán during sports-related events and activities: thirty-three images among the timeline pictures and ten among the mobile uploads. These images overlap with the other categories: his representation as Hungarian PM and as a family-oriented father, as well as a private person in his free time or during his travels, representatively combining

Orbán's various roles around the signifier of "sport." In the following, I draw on two examples from both categories before 2010 and examples representing him during sports activities after 2010, representing each subcategory listed above.

ON THE WAY TO ILLIBERALISM

The shift toward illiberal democracy and illiberal populism had already started in 2006, after the infamous "lie-speech" of the Socialist PM Gyurcsány. Fidesz, starting out as a left-liberal youth party in the eighties, shifted toward the right in 1992 after the political failure of the right-wing government at that time. Between 1998 and 2002 it transitioned to a pro-European, progressive-nationalist, civic party and became a statist-conservative force from 2006 on (Palonen 2009, 329). In opposition between 2002 and 2010, Fidesz aimed to represent anti-elitism and to articulate "the people." The party leader Orbán stopped showing up in the Hungarian Parliament, arguing for a more indirect connection to the people, and changed his formal managerial look to a more casual "countryside" one (Palonen 2009, 324; 2012, 948; 2018, 7). The first picture I analyze (*Image 1*) is from Fidesz's twenty-second birthday party in March 2010 (Fidesz 2010). We see all the prominent Fidesz politicians gathering outside the party's office, and Orbán is pictured in an intimate moment with his wife.

The figures are all pictured engaging with others—with their wife, child, or fellow party members—and no one is taking up a distinguished central position, which will change after the elections. Orbán and the other male figures are pictured in relaxed, semi-formal outfits, in jeans with t-shirts or suit jackets, performing the masculinity of a younger generation. This visual connection to the party's liberal and young party identity from the early 1990s—even if the party members are middle-aged adults in the image—and the representation of youth through the twenty-two-year-old party, creates a continuum in the party's identity, mitigating and legitimizing its chameleon-like transformations in the last decades. Some of the party members—all male figures in the picture—wear long hair and mustaches and are in positions that could be seen as feminine (by twisting their bodies, leaning sideways, crossing their legs or arms and touching their faces). Orbán is performing the role of a gentle partner, pressing his forehead against his wife's forehead, holding her hands, while looking up into her eyes. With another figure holding a child, I conclude that these male figures are performing a masculinity which is compatible with the party's image at the time, characterized by "a more progressive western-oriented twist of conservatism" (Palonen 2009, 324).[4] Accordingly, the masculinity performed in this image is a soft family-centered one, and femininities and female figures are not excluded from the party event either. Before 2010, in general, a small number of women appeared in official events of Fidesz, sometimes even on the prestigious position on stage (but never during a speech).

During his unofficial activities, Orbán has a chance to meet with people as a private person, to represent himself as "one of the people." In *Image 2* (Fidesz 2008) Orbán is captured during the 1st of May celebrations in 2008, traditionally a socialist celebration of work, hence associated with the socialist MSZP. However, the location, Tabán, where the picture was taken, is in Budapest's elitist 1st district, which has had a right-wing mayor since 1990. Through the place, Orbán already attempts to combine elitist and anti-elitist signifiers.

In *Image 2* (Fidesz 2008), similarly to *Image 1* (Fidesz 2010), Orbán is performing a young, approachable masculinity. He is sitting on a bench during the 1st of May celebration, wearing a checked shirt without a tie, surrounded by plastic beer cups. He is accompanied by two male and two female figures sitting around the table with him, whereas a group of photographers are standing behind them. As for gender relations, women are not excluded from this representation: the closest figures to the camera are female ones, even though we see them mostly from behind. Further, the female figure on the left is the most active besides Orbán—she is grabbing a beer cup—while the other one is facing Orbán and mirroring his position. All figures around the table express a similar distance between each other, and gender does not play a significant role in the spatial arrangement (like on *Image 1*, Fidesz 2010).

However, the group of photographers changes the symmetry between the four main figures. With them around the table, Orbán becomes the center of the group and the center of attention: all the camera objectives are pointing directly at him. The focal point of the image is at his eye level, which further suggests that he is the central figure of the composition. His highlighted status is also signaled by, first, that he is the most active figure in the group (he is gesticulating with his hands); second, that whereas all other figures are looking at him, he is avoiding eye contact and, as his chin is slightly raised, stares above the heads of the people he is engaging with. His position, indicating that he tries to turn away from the cameras, however, suggests that he finds the media attention uncomfortable. I consider this picture a prototype of the evolving illiberal masculinity and logic, in which Orbán combines the populist low culture with the elitist, high position in his representation, in an attempt to exclude the oppositional party from the signification of any of them and disrupt the long-lived "competing populisms" in the country (Palonen 2009, 318).

ILLIBERAL POPULISM

After 2010, images picturing Orbán during his free time activities increase in number, especially during his football game visits. The increasing number of Orbán's participation in sports and football events signals the era of illiberal populism. Because the signifiers "sport" and "football" combine popular (low culture) elements with nationalism, through incorporating them in his representation as PM, which highlights his elite status, Orbán achieves what he already tried to represent before: a disrupted polarization, and the exclusion of the left-wing opposition from the signification through the seizure of both the elitist and the populist position in the country.

Sports, especially football, has a long history of symbolizing certain national identities in Hungary: for example, Hungary's cultural superiority in contrast to Austria during the dualist era; its belonging to Western Europe in opposition to its neighboring countries during the interwar era; or the superiority of socialism above capitalism during the totalitarian socialist era (Győri Szabó 2019, 131). Since 2010 sport has again gained huge significance in Hungarian politics and has risen to be a strategic area among domestic matters (Szerovay and Itkonen 2018). Successful national sports can grant a country and its elites prestige and economic, diplomatic and sometimes technological advantages. National sports have an important affective, performative attribute as well: they signify societal solidarity between the fans, regardless of their background, and neutralize the societal, cultural and political differences among them (Péter 2010). National sport is also a gendered signifier and has a strong affective influence on masculinities. The target audience of these sport events are the male population, whereas women are often portrayed in a sexualized, inferior position (Péter 2013). Moreover, athletes often shape hegemonic masculinity in a society, like football icon Ferenc Puskás, signifying communism by being the "the humble son of the proletariat" (Molnár 2007, 306). Through expropriating his legacy, Fidesz can also successfully reconcile the elitist (governmental) and anti-elitist (unity of the fans and reference to the working class) standpoints; and signify the gender order in Hungary though the signifiers "sport" and "football."

Football and athletics as a visual trope in general appear with different meanings in the material. It represents Orbán's identity as an athlete (*Image 3*, Orbán 2017); it introduces the home/not home distinction (*Image 3*, Orbán 2017; *Image 4*, Orbán 2014; *Image 5*, Orbán 2016), thus blurring the line between "nation" and "demography"; and, finally, it provides a platform where Orbán can personally meet and perform "the people" of the illiberal populist logic (*Image 5*, Orbán 2016; *Image 6*, Orbán 2015).

In *Image 3* (Orbán 2017) Orbán is pictured on a plane, on his way to the European Parliament. He is standing, holding a pen and paper. In the background, but framed opposite Orbán, we see a printed image of a male football player attached to the wall of the airplane as part of an advertisement. Orbán's compositional position and body pose echoes the male football player's in the image. However, while the football player is portrayed in a physical pose, sweating in sports gear, Orbán is pictured standing straight and relaxed in a formal and clean outfit. While the athlete is portrayed giving out a shout, Orbán is pictured using a pen and paper as tools of communication. Moreover, the football player in the background is a person of color, Romelu Lukaku. As a Belgian football player, he is representing Brussels not just in a symbolic but also in a concrete geographical sense. Thus, the signifier "football" introduces the home/not home distinction, which easily translates to the national inside/outside dichotomy (De Cleen and Stavrakakis 2017; Brubaker 2020).

The similarities between the figures' positions Orbán as a strategic, disciplined, persistent athlete. However, compared to the physical athlete, Orbán is pictured as a (white) thinker and a speaker (politician). Orbán does not only perform the strategic thinker and competitive figure of a football player. His formal outfit, the pen and paper, and his actual place in business class on an airplane refer to the figure of a businessman, which is one of the most powerful symbols of masculinity in global society (Connell and Wood 2005). Thus, the image successfully portrays Orbán's masculinity as a combination of both elitist (businessman) and anti-elitist (football player) signifiers.

After 2010, female figures are eliminated from the representation of Fidesz in the material. However, there is a new category of women represented: female figures with outstanding human accomplishments—in most cases, female elite athletes. They are portrayed with a private and personal connection to Orbán, usually with no other party member (for instance, the sports minister) being present. These female figures are portrayed in close physical distance to Orbán and they are often touched by him, either through a hug or a handshake, or occasionally through a kiss on the cheek, like in *Image 4*.

Image 4 ("*Bravo, Niki!*" Orbán 2014) portrays Orbán and the female figure he is facing, similarly to *Image 3* (Orbán 2017), positioned on a horizontal line. However, there is much less distance between the figures than before: they share the central position of the picture. Orbán is leaning close to the female athlete with the intention of kissing her on the cheek. The difference in the distance and the gesture (confrontation/kiss), compared to the previous image (*Image 3*, Orbán 2017) eliminates the home/not home opposition, and refers to a closeness that is only possible in the home country. Moreover, the figures are performing a gendered action: the female athlete is being kissed as a sign of respect and congratulations by the male PM. This gesture shifts the equal status of the male and the female figures into a hierarchized one, which is also signaled—besides Orbán's controlling gesture of approval—by the angle of the camera, focusing on Orbán's face, and the lowered focal point, highlighting their difference in height.

"Sport," however, is not used just to signify the home/not home dichotomy (*Image 3*, Orbán 2017), but also the "nation." In *Image 5* (Orbán 2016), Orbán is pictured at a football match, surrounded by other football fans: two male and two female figures. A young male child is sitting in front of Orbán, and Orbán holds him with both hands. Similarly to *Image 4* (Orbán 2014), "home" is signified by the physical closeness between the figures, intensified by the colors of the national flag of Hungary, which have been almost fully monopolized by Fidesz since 2002 (Palonen 2009, 324). Evoking the national colors in connection to the signifiers "sport" and "football" enables Orbán to create a continuity within the history of the party, and to shift the line of antagonism from a domestic matter to the country borders.

The three male figures in the front of the image, including Orbán, are building a circle with Orbán holding the child in the center. The two female figures of the image remain outside of this circle, partly covered by the men. The male figure standing right next to Orbán connects them to Orbán by one of his shoulders pointing at Orbán and the other pointing at the female figure behind him. However, the spatial composition of the image has another layer: even though Orbán is part of the circle of the three male figures, people are also gathering behind and around him, changing his side position into a central one, suggested by the position of camera pointing directly at him (like in *Image 2*, Fidesz 2008). Consequently, the horizontal line as the main compositional feature of the previous images is transformed into the shape of a (half-)circle, and Orbán occupies the center position in it. He is pictured in a higher, more highlighted position than the rest of the group, made up of everyday Hungarian political supporters. His high-status position is visible in his outfit, straight body posture, direct gaze into the camera, relaxed facial features, and by the fact that his eye level is higher than that of the others. It is also indicated by his separation from the crowd by a row of seats.

Image 6 ("*We cheered for Katinka Hosszú, Boglárka Kapás and László Cseh*," Orbán 2015) is an example of how the highlighted position of Orbán translates into a high position outside the country borders. We see Orbán standing on the tribune of a swimming hall in Kazan, with his wife and one of his daughters, looking down to the competitors with a warm smile on his face. He is occupying a physically higher position than the sitting female figures and represents a different, more relaxed type of elite masculinity than the other male figures in the background, who are wearing formal suits. By contrast, Orbán has a warm facial expression and wears a relaxed outfit. Moreover, his closeness to the athletes is highlighted as he is leaning over the facade, as if he would rather be right among the figures below than on the tribune among "the elite."

THE HUNGARIAN ILLIBERAL LOGIC
AND GENDER ORDER

Orbán uses the signifiers "sport" and "football" in several ways to visually and affectively constitute the illiberal populist logic. First, Orbán's own identity as an athlete represents him as a football enthusiast private person on the one hand (Goldblatt and Nolan 2018) (*Image 5*, Orbán 2016), and as a disciplined, hard-working politician who believes in fair play on the other (*Image 3*, Orbán 2017). Second, visiting football matches connects Orbán to "the people"; however, his formal clothing on the tribune reflects his elite status—the politician who supports sports with state funds—that he tries to cover with nationalistic accessories and by the fact that he seems to enjoy his free time just like every other Hungarian in the country (*Image 5*, Orbán 2016; *Image 6*, Orbán 2015). Third, the signifier "football" gives a new spatial dimension to the top-down relation between "the people" and "the elite," as it brings the antagonistic frontier, opponents in a football game, down to an equal horizontal ground, instead of the vertical top-down one (*Image 3*, Orbán 2017). Finally, it transforms this horizontal level into a home/not home differentiation. This successfully eliminates the polarization within the country, because by extending of the line of antagonism to the country border it successfully replaces the antagonistic ethno-nationalistic versus republic-based understanding of the nation, the main signifier of the competing Fidesz and MSZP hegemonies.

The signifier "home" combines the nationalistic logic with the populist one and does not signify subjects with Hungarian nationality, but "the people" of the Hungarian populist logic. Orbán is constituted in relation to figures in non-leading positions, where he is occupying a central position, paired with a high-position body language and pose. Orbán's high position is not identical with the controlling elite, but with the "core" (the innermost point) of the Hungarian nation. First, this inside-outside—as opposed to a top-down—articulation of a leader portrays him as one among "the people." Second, the inside-outside dichotomy strengthens the nationalistic logic, and "the people" are defined through a centrum-periphery differentiation (De Cleen and Stavrakakis 2017; Brubaker 2020). Thus, Orbán positions himself at the core of the Hungarian nation, and this morally highly evaluated position both connects him with and differentiates him from the rest of "the elite" (*Image 6*, Orbán 2015) as well as from the rest of "the people" (*Image 4*, Orbán 2014).

"Home" also refers to an emotionally charged space, evoking a sense of belonging, which is signaled through closeness and family members (*Image 4*, Orbán 2014; *Image 5*, Orbán 2016; *Image 6*, Orbán 2015). Consequently, the gender aspects within "home" are gaining significance. Female figures are usually pictured in the background, either standing slightly behind Orbán or as part of a group surrounding him (*Image 5*, Orbán 2016; *Image 6*, Orbán 2015). They are repeatedly portrayed in the position of witnessing or photographing (often with a smile) a moment when Orbán is connecting to, standing close to, or even being touched by another male figure. It highlights the distance between the hegemonic masculine and the everyday feminine positions in the Hungarian gender order. This is contrasted by the physical male touch, which marks the main frontier between masculinities and femininities of the current Hungarian gender order, portrayed as directly connected to male and female figures (*Image 5*, Orbán 2016). The male touch on Orbán highlights his hegemonic status, as male figures reach out for him; however, the fact that he never returns these touches (nor the looks of these male figures) and remains overall passive during these interactions highlights his difference from other masculinities in the Hungarian gender order. Despite these separating elements, most of the time he is portrayed in the middle of pictures, as a central figure (*Image 5*, Orbán 2016), which creates the desired combination of difference (elitism) and belonging (anti-elitism) in his position. This highlighted position is also evidenced by the lack of pictures in the material of Orbán posing with male athletes. By posing only with female athletes, Orbán reserves the hegemonic masculine position for himself.

The schematic picture (figure 2.1) sums up the structure of the Hungarian gender order. It is constituted along the overdetermined home/not home and centrum/periphery differentiations. Orbán occupies the hegemonic masculine position of top and center. The next circle, closest to him, is the circle of the Hungarian masculinities whose immediate connection is often indicated by a male touch in the material, while femininities—portrayed as female figures—are positioned on the periphery. We can conclude that this gender order clearly divides masculinities and femininities and attributes carefully separated and hierarchized gender roles to male and female actors. Accordingly, Fidesz propagates traditional gender roles with its politics (Szikra 2013, 11), a shift that started in 2010.[5] Before that, it positioned itself as a progressive party, performing a soft masculinity and to some extent gender equality (*Image 1*, Fidesz 2010; *Image 2*, Fidesz 2008). Gender equality is often used as a signifier of liberalism in right-wing political discourse (Grzebalska, Kováts, and Pető 2017). Thus, the shift toward a "non-liberal" gender order based on traditional gender roles is in line with the illiberal turn in Hungary. As gender equality also signifies elitism (Grzebalska, Kováts, and Pető 2017), its dismissal is another way for Orbán to lessen his elitist position.

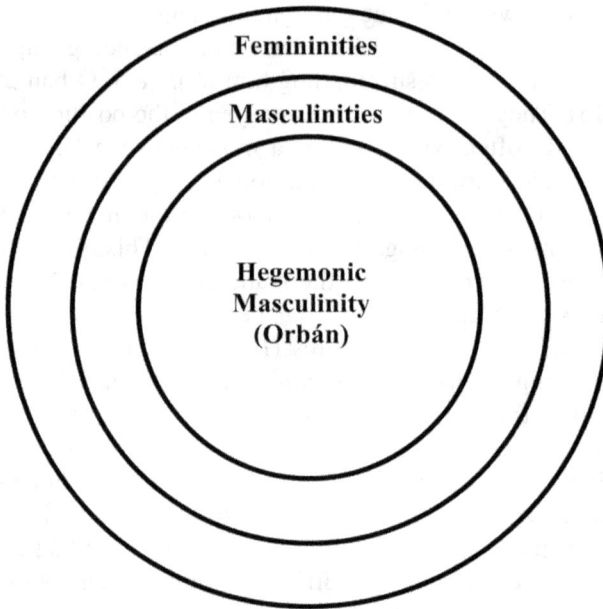

Figure 2.1 The Hungarian gender order

CONCLUSION

In this chapter I conceptualized Viktor Orbán as a gendered performative signifier of the Hungarian illiberal populism, and showed how the illiberal turn resulted in a new illiberal masculinity and gender order in Hungary. Since 2010, through the signifiers "sports" and "football," Orbán represents himself both as an elite athlete as well as a sports fan. Through this representation he successfully signifies both "the people" and "the elite" positions at the same time and maintains the disrupted polarization within the Hungarian political scene. As Hungarian sociologist Erzsébet Barát argues, to mask their vulnerability, populist leaders, who are one of "us," need to represent themselves simultaneously as "one of us" and "above us" (2017, 538). In line with this, I add that this representation of Orbán also serves to reserve the post-polarized status of Hungarian politics and the illiberal logic. Importantly, with the help of "sport," he is introducing the home/not home antagonism. First, it successfully combines the populist top-down and the nationalist inside/outside dimensions, and constitutes an illiberal spatial logic based on the blurred lines between the two understanding of Hungary: state and ethno-nation (De Cleen and Stavrakakis 2017; Brubaker 2020). The leader position of Orbán in Hungary is articulated through his "core" position in the country: he is the center ("elite") and also the "most home," the most "us" ("the people").

The signifier "home" combines the nationalistic logic with the populist one. It does not signify subjects with Hungarian nationality but "the people" of the Hungarian illiberal populist logic. Second, "home" is a gendered signifier because it represents a specific gender order inside "home." As "the people" of the illiberal democracy are constructed through a gendered signifier, it articulates a new illiberal gender order among them as well. The Hungarian gender order is constructed along a central/periphery dimension. The central position is occupied by the hegemonic masculine position, whereas femininities are cast to the periphery, which is the order reflected in Fidesz's politics as well (Szikra 2013).

NOTES

1. As a result, Fidesz won both parliamentary elections with a two-thirds majority in the years 2014 and 2018.
2. The system of competing populisms intensified after the overwhelmingly negative campaigning during the 1998 and 2002 elections (Palonen 2009).
3. Even though Orbán has also had an Instagram page since 2014, Facebook has better coverage of the last 10 years and his Facebook page has more than 666,000 followers, while his Instagram page has fewer than 49,000 (Orbán 2020).
4. Their other aim was to differentiate themselves as progressive party from the old regime and first and foremost from their main opponent, the Hungarian Socialist Party (MSZMP), which is often labelled as the successor party and connected to the old communist regime, at least in the rhetoric of Fidesz (MTI 2011).
5. The focus on traditional gender roles in the government's family politics is also clearly visible in the new Hungarian constitution (cf. Országgyűlési Hivatal, Law CCXI/2011 on the defense of families).

BIBLIOGRAPHY

Abi-Hassan, Sahar. 2018. "Populism and Gender." In *The Oxford Handbook of Populism*, edited by Cristóbal Rovira Kaltwasser, Paul Taggart, Paulina Ochoa Espejo, and Pierre Ostiguy, 426–444. Oxford: Oxford University Press.
Aharoni, Sarai B., and Élise Féron. 2020. "National Populism and Gendered Vigilantism: The Case of the Soldiers of Odin in Finland." *Cooperation and Conflict* 5 (2): 86–106.
Barát, Erzsébet. 2017. "Populist Discourses in the Hungarian Public Sphere from Right to Left (And Beyond)?" *Journal of Language and Politic* 16 (4): 535–550.
Becker, Jens. 2010. "The Rise of Right-Wing Populism in Hungary." *SEER: Journal for Labour and Social Affairs in Eastern Europe* 13 (1): 9–40.
Bonde, Hans. 2009. "The Great Male Cycle: Sport, Politics and European Masculinity Today." *The International Journal of the History of Sport* 26 (10): 1540–1554.

Brubaker, Rogers. 2020. "Populism and Nationalism." *Nations and Nationalism* 26 (5): 44–66.

Butler, Judith. 1990. *Gender Trouble. Feminism and the Subversion of Identity.* New York and London: Routledge.

Butler, Judith. 1993. *Bodies That Matter: On the Discursive Limits of Sex.* New York and London: Routledge.

Connell, R. W. 2005. *Masculinities.* 2nd Edition. Cambridge: Polity Press.

Connell, Raewyn. 2009. *Gender. In World Perspective.* 2nd Edition. Cambridge: Polity Press.

Connell, Robert W., and James W. Messerschmidt. 2005. "Hegemonic Masculinity: Rethinking the Concept." *Gender and Society* 19 (6): 829–859.

Connell, Robert W., and Julian Wood. 2005. "Globalization and Business Masculinities." *Men and Masculinities* 7 (4): 347–364.

De Cleen, Benjamin, and Yannis Stavrakakis. 2017. "Distinctions and Articulations: A Discourse Theoretical Framework for the Study of Populism and Nationalism." *Javnost—The Public* 24 (4): 301–319.

De Lange, Sarah L., and Liza M. Mügge. 2015. "Gender and Right-Wing Populism in the Low Countries: Ideological Variations across Parties and Time." *Patterns of Prejudice* 49 (1–2): 61–80.

Fidesz (@FideszHU). 2008. "No Title Added." *Facebook Photo*, May 2, 2008. https://www.facebook.com/FideszHU/photos/a.16215044306/16215299306/?type=3&theater.

Fidesz (@FideszHU). 2010. "No Title Added." *Facebook Photo*, March 29, 2010. https://www.facebook.com/FideszHU/photos/a.419584059306/419588319306/?type=3&theater.

Fowler, Brigid. 2004. "Concentrated Orange: Fidesz and the Remaking of the Hungarian Centre-Right, 1994–2002." *Journal of Communist Studies and Transition Politics* 20 (3): 80–114.

Goffman, Erving. 1988. *Gender Advertisement.* New York: Harper & Row Publishers.

Goldblatt, David, and Daniel Nolan. 2018. "Viktor Orbán's Reckless Football Obsession." *The Guardian*, January 11, 2018. https://www.theguardian.com/news/2018/jan/11/viktor-orban-hungary-prime-minister-reckless-football-obsession.

Grzebalska, Weronika, Eszter Kováts, and Andrea Pető. 2017. "Gender as Symbolic Glue: How 'Gender' Became an Umbrella Term for the Rejection of the (Neo)liberal Order." *Political Critique*, January 13, 2017. http://politicalcritique.org/long-read/2017/gender-as-symbolic-glue-how-gender-became-an-umbrella-term-for-the-rejection-of-the-neoliberal-order/.

Gunnarsson Payne, Jenny. 2019. "Challenging 'Gender Ideology': (Anti-) Gender Politics in Europe's Populist Moment." *The New Pretender*, February 10, 2019. http://new-pretender.com/2019/02/10/challenging-gender-ideology-anti-gender-politics-in-europes-populist-moment-jenny-gunnarsson-payne/.

Győri Szabó, Róbert. 2019. "Football and Politics in Twentieth Century Hungary." *The International Journal of the History of Sport* 36 (2–3): 131–148.

Hand, Martin. 2017. "Visuality in Social Media: Researching Images, Circulations and Practices." In *The SAGE Handbook of Social Media Research Methods*, edited by Luke Sloan, and Anabel Quan-Haase, 215–232. New York: SAGE Publications.

Hawkins, Kirk A. 2019. "The Ideational Approach." In *Routledge Handbook of Global Populism*, edited by Carlos de la Torre, 57–73. London: Routledge.

Keskinen, Suvi. 2013. "Antifeminism and White Identity Politics. Political Antagonisms in Radical Right-Wing Populist and Anti-Immigration Rhetoric in Finland." *Nordic Journal of Migration Research* 3 (4): 225–232.

Koenen, Krisztina. 2015. "Orbánismus in Ungarn: Ursprünge und Elemente der "Illiberalen Demokratie" [Orbanism in Hungary Origins and Elements of 'Illiberal Democracy']." *Osteuropa* 65 (11–12): 33–44.

Korolczuk, Elżbieta, and Agnieszka Graff. 2018. "Gender as 'Ebola from Brussels': The Anticolonial Frame and the Rise of Illiberal Populism." *Signs: Journal of Women in Culture and Society* 43 (4): 797–821.

Kuhar, Roman, and David Paternotte, eds. 2017. Anti-gender Campaigns in Europe: Mobilizing against Equality. Lanham, Maryland: Rowman & Littlefield.

Laclau, Ernesto. 2014. "Populism. What's in a Name?" In *Ernesto Laclau: Post-Marxism, Populism and Critique*, edited by David Howarth, 152–164. London: Routledge.

Laclau, Ernesto. 2018. *On Populist Reason*. London: Verso.

Laczó, Ferenc. 2018. "Populism in Power in Hungary. Consolidation and Ongoing Radicalization." *Eurozine*, March 27, 2018. https://www.eurozine.com/populism-power-hungary/.

Lévai, Richárd. 2018. "Közösségi média adatok 2018 [Social Media Data 2018]." *Közösségi Kalandozások*, February 6, 2018. https://kozossegikalandozasok.hu/2018/02/06/kozossegi-media-adatok-2018/.

Moffitt, Benjamin. 2016. "Understanding Contemporary Populism: Populism as a Political Style." In *The Global Rise of Populism: Performance, Political Style, and Representation*, edited by Benjamin Moffitt, 28–50. Stanford: Stanford University Press.

Moghadam, Valentine M., and Gizem Kaftan. 2019. "Right-Wing Populisms North and South: Varieties and Gender Dynamics." *Women's Studies International Forum* 75 (7–8): 102244.

Molnár, Győző. 2007. "Hungarian Football: A Socio-Historical Overview." *Sport in History* 27 (2): 293–317.

Motta, Sara C. 2013. "'We Are the Ones We Have Been Waiting For': The Feminization of Resistance in Venezuela." *Latin American Perspectives* 40 (4): 35–54.

Mouffe, Chantal. 2018. *For a Left Populism*. London: Verso.

Mudde, Cas. 2017. "Populism: An Ideational Approach." In *The Oxford Handbook of Populism*, edited by Cristóbal Rovira Kaltwasser Paul Taggart, Paulina Ochoa Espejo, and Pierre Ostiguy, 27–48. Oxford: Oxford University Press.

Mudde, Cas, and Cristóbal Rovira Kaltwasser. 2014. "Populism and Political Leadership." In *The Oxford Handbook of Political Leadership*, edited by R. A. W. Rhodes and Paul't Hart, 376–388. Oxford: Oxford University Press.

Mudde, Cas and Cristóbal Rovira Kaltwasser. 2015. "Vox Populi or Vox Masculini? Populism and Gender in Northern Europe and South America." *Patterns of Prejudice* 49 (1–2): 16–36.

Mudde, Cas, and Cristóbal Rovira Kaltwasser. 2018. "Studying Populism in Comparative Perspective: Reflections on the Contemporary and Future Research Agenda." *Comparative Political Studies* 51 (13): 1667–1693.

MTI. 2011. "Benyújtották a törvényjavaslatot, amely kimondaná, hogy az MSZP osztozik az MSZMP felelősségében [A Bill was Filed Stating that the MSZP Shares the Responsibility of the MSZMP]." *HVG*, November 20, 2011. https://hvg.hu/itthon/20111120_mszp_osztozik_mszmp_felelosseg.

Norocel, Ov Cristian. 2010. "Constructing Radical Right Populist Resistance: Metaphors of Heterosexist Masculinities and the Family Question in Sweden." *NORMA: Nordic Journal for Masculinity Studies* 5 (2): 169–183.

Norocel, Ov Cristian. 2011. "Heteronormative Constructions of Romanianness: A Genealogy of Gendered Metaphors in Romanian Radical-Right Populism 2000–2009." *Debatte: Journal of Contemporary Central and Eastern Europe* 19 (1–2): 453–470.

Orbán, Viktor (@orbanviktor). 2014. "Bravo, Niki!" *Facebook Photo*, September 6, 2014. https://www.facebook.com/orbanviktor/photos/a.311926051092/10152675387896093/?type=3&theater.

Orbán, Viktor (@orbanviktor). 2015. "Hosszú Katinkáért, Kapás Boglárkáért és Cseh Lászlóért szorítottunk [We cheered for Katinka Hosszú, Boglárka Kapás and László Cseh]." *Facebook Photo*, August 8, 2015. https://www.facebook.com/orbanviktor/photos/a.10151703698051093/10153483765826093/?type=3&theater.

Orbán, Viktor (@orbanviktor). 2016. "Most kell szerénynek lenni [This is the Time to be Humble!]." *Facebook Photo*, June 18, 2016. https://www.facebook.com/orbanviktor/photos/a.311926051092/10154173566871093/?type=3&theater.

Orbán, Viktor (@orbanviktor). 2017. "Brüsszel felé. Harcra föl! // On the way to Brussels. Time to fight!," *Facebook Photo*, March 5, 2017. https://www.facebook.com/orbanviktor/photos/a.311926051092/10154943221816093/?type=3&theater.

Orbán, Viktor (@orbanviktor). 2020. *Instagram*. https://www.instagram.com/orbanviktor/.

Országgyűlési Hivatal. 2011. "2011. évi CCXI. törvény a családok védelméről. [Law CCXI / 2011 on the defense of families]." *Budapest*, December 2, 2011. https://www.parlament.hu/irom39/05128/05128.pdf.

Palonen, Emilia. 2009. "Political Polarisation and Populism in Contemporary Hungary." *Parliamentary Affairs* 62 (2): 318–334.

Palonen, Emilia. 2012. "Transition to Crisis in Hungary: Whistle-Blowing on the Naked Emperor." *Politics & Policy* 40 (5): 930–957.

Palonen, Emilia. 2018. "Performing the Nation: The Janus-faced Populist Foundations of Illiberalism in Hungary." *Journal of Contemporary European Studies* 26 (3): 308–321.

Palonen, Emilia. 2019. "Rhetorical-Performative Analysis of the Urban Symbolic Landscape: Populism in Action." In *Discourse, Culture and Organization: Postdisciplinary Studies in Discourse*, edited by Tomas Marttila, 179–198. London: Palgrave Macmillan.

Panizza, Francisco. 2005. "Introduction: Populism and the mirror of democracy." In *Populism and the Mirror of Democracy*, edited by Francisco Panizza, 1–32. London: Verso.

Péter, László. 2010. "Szabadidő—VB, a macsó férfiak, a háziasszonyok és a társada-lom működésének háromszögében [Leisure—World Cup in the Triangle of Macho Men, Housewives and Society]." *Péter László okoskodó naplója*, June 15, 2010. http://peterlaci.blogspot.com/2010/06/szabadido-vb-macso-ferfiak.html?m=1.

Péter, László. 2013. "Fociológia—Focilabda a hölgyek feneke? Futball és masz-kulinitás [Fociology—Soccer Ball is the Bottom of the Ladies? Football and Masculinity]." *Péter László okoskodó naplója*, June 20, 2013. http://peterlaci. blogspot.com/2013/06/fociologia-futball-es-maszkulinitas.html?m=1.

Rose, Gillian. 2001. *Visual Methodologies: An Introduction to the Interpretation of Visual Materials*. London: Sage.

Salojärvi, Virpi. 2019. "Populism in Journalistic Photographs: Political Leaders in Venezuelan Newspaper Images." *Iberoamericana—Nordic Journal of Latin American and Caribbean Studies* 48 (1): 28–39.

Sanger, Nadia. 2019. "A Matter of Race and Class: Notes on Populist Feminism in Theorising from the South." *Agenda* 33 (3): 70–73.

Stavrakakis, Yannis. 2018. "Paradoxes of Polarization: Democracy's Inherent Division and the (Anti-) Populist Challenge." *American Behavioral Scientist* 62 (1): 43–58.

Szikra, Dorottya. 2013. *Megszorító intézkedések és ezek hatása a nemek társadalmi egyenlőségére Magyarországon—Műhelytanulmány [Restrictive Measures and their Impact on Gender Equality in Hungary—Workshop Paper]*. Budapest: Friedrich Ebert Stiftung. http://library.fes.de/pdf-files/bueros/budapest/10836.pdf.

Szerovay, Mihály, and Hannu Itkonen. 2018. "Global and Local Interactions in Football: The Changing Field of Professional Football Stadiums in Finland and Hungary in the 2000s." *Sport in Society* 21 (12): 1897–1916.

Taggart, Paul. 2004. "Populism and Representative Politics in Contemporary Europe." *Journal of Political Ideologies* 9 (3): 269–288.

Techopedia. 2012. "Facebook Timeline." https://www.techopedia.com/definition/28 406/facebook-timeline.

Wodak, Ruth. 2015. *The Politics of Fear: What Right-Wing Populist Discourses Mean*. London: Sage.

Chapter 3

Strong Borders and Masculine Orders

The Role of Crisis Frameworks and the US-Mexico Border in the Context of Trump's Populist Masculinity

Joshua D. Martin

The election of Donald J. Trump as the forty-fifth president of the United States has engendered significant shifts in US politics and culture and has forced scholars to examine the complex mechanisms that helped pave the way for his ascent. A real-estate entrepreneur, political novice, and former reality TV celebrity, Trump emerged onto the national US political stage and was met with both skepticism and scorn given his political inexperience and long history of questionable behaviors. Despite Trump's defiance toward political convention, his populist appeal shouldn't necessarily be understood as a wholesale anomaly, especially when we consider his masculine brand in conjunction with his favorite political commodity: the US-Mexico border.

From the inception of his campaign, the border emerged as a source of perennial fascination for Trump. Indeed, throughout his campaign, Trump's discourse regarding the border garnered him significant media attention and impressive political capital. His campaign promise to construct a nearly 2,000 mile wall along the United States' southern border became a hallmark of his political brand, operating both as a symbol for his "America First" orientation and the leadership qualities that Trump, as he himself asserted, was uniquely qualified to enact. Scholars across disciplines have examined Trump's appeal from several critical approaches, arguing, for example, that Trump exploited middle-class disenchantment following neoliberal economic reforms (Fuchs 2018, 263), that he capitalized on social media infrastructure to create ideological echo chambers and distrust toward existing power structures (Cummings 2019, 64), and that he employed a rhetoric of xenophobic racialization that reduced immigrants to pernicious Others

(Robertson 2018, 74–76). Despite these important contributions, existing scholarship has not adequately examined how Trump's language about the border complements the populist masculinity that bolstered his political persona. After all, questions of masculinity are ultimately questions of power, and in order to better understand political culture and conflict, "it becomes necessary to study the powerful (men)" who wield influence and profoundly shape social life (Messerschmidt 1999, 2). What role, then, did Trump's border discourse play in the context of his masculine brand, and what discursive mechanisms specifically contributed to this appeal?

THEORETICAL ORIENTATION AND ARGUMENT

Through an interdisciplinary lens combining critical discourse analysis alongside masculinity studies, I analyze in this chapter three case studies in Trump's political discourse regarding the US-Mexico border: a rally he held in the border state of Arizona (August 2016), his final debate performance with former secretary of state and democratic presidential rival Hillary Clinton (October 2016), and select Twitter messages from his 2016 presidential campaign and tenure. Accordingly, I argue that Trump discursively created social and economic threats through a crisis framework, staging would-be calamities and emergencies that subsequently necessitated brazen actions from a stalwart and novel leader. As critical discourse scholars Isabela and Norman Fairclough contend, "Crises have a rationalizing function, the function of restoring rationality where it has been undermined" (2012, 2), thus allowing political actors to craft narratives that demand a call to action against the backdrop of social, economic, and political reforms. Masculine personas often prove critical to this operation, too, since "images of productive masculinity," as political theory scholar James Martin notes, "supply authoritative metaphors with which audiences can easily identify" (2014, 154). In Trump's discursive framework, the US-Mexico border functioned as a staging ground for this political operation, reflecting said crises and reinforcing qualities and actions that found their logical conclusion in Trump's populist masculine brand. Positing status quo political actors as effete and incompetent alongside Mexican immigrants whom he configured as invasive and criminal, Trump foregrounded a dyadic specter of feminizing liabilities that necessitated decisive masculine actions and qualities that he, by his own admission, was uniquely qualified to employ.

Just as all masculinities emerge from unique discourses, historical phenomena, and cultural frameworks, they likewise condition a consciousness of self and other, of nation and neighbor, through hierarchies of exclusion, hegemony, and belonging (Connell 2005, 71–72; Connell 1998, 5; Kimmel 1996,

44). In the examples studied here, Trump discursively leveraged animus against immigrants and seasoned politicians while glorifying a nativism that demanded a populist strongman presence in the face of impending havoc. Within this crisis framework, Trump positioned his political brand as an overdue necessity for both a return to order and, more broadly, the preservation of the republic at large. Whereas many US presidential candidates have historically championed a "strength through diversity" trope, Trump regressed into an ephemeral "greatness," a necessarily vague concept that complemented the emotional gravitas of his populist disdain toward the political status quo and Latino non-nationals. Since populisms flourish in response to real or perceived crises, the US-Mexico border proved essential to Trump's masculine front, as it created a symbolic terrain of threats and debilities that invited appeals to aggressive actions and novel leadership.[1] In the end, Trump's border language foregrounded an aspirational horizon of toughness and novelty that, in turn, ensured a continuity for a populist strongman presence that has altered US political culture. This chapter concludes by examining Trump's 2019 national emergency declaration as a perpetuation of his crisis framework and the populist masculinity that it necessitates.

THE US-MEXICO BORDER IN POLITICAL SPEECH AND THE NATIONAL IMAGINARY

The geopolitical border between the United States and Mexico has continued to attract attention in the national imaginary following both the militarization of the region and the expanded integration of both countries' economies in and beyond the 1980s. Since then, the border has often been unfairly represented as a bedrock of crime, danger, and disease (Chávez 2012, 49), and it has afforded many, especially politicians, a symbolic landscape to craft visions of both national identity and national security (Diener and Hagen 2010, 193; Ackleson 2005, 168). In political speech, the border trope is particularly effective at encoding hierarchies of belonging and moral rectitude, and it is often used to either harness nationalist sympathies or rally commonality, depending on the framing of the interlocutor (DeChaine 2012, 2–3). No matter the motive, crisis frameworks often complement language about the border given the latter's inextricable ties to "sovereignty, implications of legal status, civil, social and political rights, obligations, and access to public resources" (Vertovec 2004, 984). Crisis frameworks, in turn, demand strong and immediate emotional investments from audiences while directing them toward specific lines of action (Fairclough and Fairclough 2012, 3–5), and as such, they provide political actors an expedient discursive tool to advance specific interests (Klein 2007, 6–7). Border-related phenomena shortly preceding Trump's campaign brought to the fore questions of national security and rightful belonging, thus setting the stage for the emotional urgency Trump infused in his mischaracterizations concerning both border-crossers and the region at large.

Throughout 2014 and 2015, political instability in Central America instigated mass migration to the United States' southern border, culminating in what was widely regarded as a crisis as tens of thousands of migrants (primarily youth) sought asylum at the southern border (Park 2014). Right-wing commentators in particular often disparaged the cautious and cerebral response of Trump's predecessor, Barack Obama, as insufficient to mitigate threats that loomed at or outside the country's borders. What's more, throughout the 2016 election cycle, questions of immigration polled high in lists of voters' top concerns, and widespread anxiety and exasperation with political convention ultimately worked to Trump's advantage given his enduring preoccupation with restoring safety and ensuring prosperity in light of weak (i.e., "feminine") border policies. What discursive tactics, then, did Trump employ, and how did they supplement his populist masculinity?

STAGING TRUMP'S CRISIS FRAMEWORK:
MORALS, METAPHORS, AND MASCULINITY

Trump's fascination with constructing a physical barrier along the border, of course, cannot be separated from his unfavorable representations of Latin American, and especially Mexican, immigrants. During his campaign launch within the Trump Tower in Manhattan, for example, he represented the latter as largely malevolent, terming them criminals and rapists who endangered the body politic (Burns 2015). His animus became markedly more salient in the ensuing months as his popularity grew. After securing the Republican nomination for president, for example, Trump spoke at a campaign rally in Phoenix, Arizona, on August 31, 2016, where he represented Mexican immigrants in equally grim terms, casting them as malicious characters allied with crime and destruction, and employing a crisis framework that would prove critical for endowing such representations with power and longevity.

Lambasting undocumented immigrants, Trump bemoaned "crime all over the place" and delineated a causal relationship between "millions more illegal immigrants" and "thousands of more violent, horrible crimes" (Trump 2016). He criticized existing trade deals and current immigration laws, too, portraying them as incongruent with citizens' labor needs and law-and-order civility, respectively. Trump also invited to speak on his behalf the family members of several US citizens killed by undocumented immigrants. Gruesome details emerged, and the speakers invariably identified Trump as "the only man who is going to save our country," and as the man "who's going to change this country for the better" (Trump 2016). One speaker later asserted that had Trump been president in years past, "the border would have been secure and our children would not be dead today" (Trump 2016). Politics and political speech inevitably connect with questions of morality (Lakoff 2009, 43; Lawler and Schaefer 1990, ix), but they also rely deeply on metaphors that often intersect with gender and space.

In this crisis framework, the border emerged as a powerful staging ground whereby Trump allied his candidacy with law-and-order civility and common-sense (however, ill-defined) socioeconomic reform. Accordingly, Trump's framing of threats created what critical discourse scholar Otto Santa Ana would likely identify as "a cognitive ordering of events and a moral ordering of responsibilities" (2013, 217), thus compelling audience members to opt for his candidacy—the only efficacious and morally sound alternative to status quo politics. Importantly, Trump's hierarchy of winners and losers located US nationals as undeserving victims in positions of feminine vulnerability, inviting rescue from a salvific masculine figure. The gendered dimensions of Trump's crisis framework thus became increasingly conspicuous, and for good reason.

Just as metaphor helps shape our consciousness (Lakoff and Johnson 1980, 3), gendered imagery likewise plays an important role, especially in regards to how we interpret social phenomena. After all, "gender roles provide ready-made platforms to craft agency in ways that affirm structures, conventions, and expectations" (Martin 2014, 153). Indeed, many of Trump's comments here relied on a gender dichotomy: feminizing weakness and incompetence vs. masculine strength and efficacy. For example, after referring to Hillary Clinton's and Barack Obama's legacies as riddled with "weak, weak policies. Weak and foolish policies," Trump later promised "strong mandatory minimum sentences" as punishment for undocumented immigrants who reenter the US without documents (Trump 2016). Typecasting Latin Americans in negative frameworks has long allowed US politicians to boost their political ambitions, even as far back as the nineteenth century (Greenberg 2005, 15–18; Gómez 2007, 27). Trump, however, created crises in ways that augmented his abrasive masculine front. In his crisis framework, for example, both his audience and the nation at large suffered the brunt of feminizing liabilities: undocumented immigrants, whom he configured as penetrative forces, and incompetent politicians, whom he represented as powerful and exploitative elites. Accordingly, Trump's aggressive masculine persona promised stability and safety, evoking gendered and spatial imagery for which the US-Mexico border was especially well suited.

Unsurprisingly, then, Trump's narrative arc encompassed his political rivals as well, locating them alongside maligned immigrants given their alleged shared disregard for civic duty and law and order. "President Obama and Hillary Clinton," Trump asserted, "support the release of dangerous, dangerous, dangerous criminals from detention," later adding that Clinton aspired to promote "low-skilled immigration," which would inevitably create a "Trojan horse" of potential assailants (Trump 2016). Trump extended his suspicion to Syrian refugees too, lamenting the supposed incompetence of politicians who push "open borders and let everybody come in and destroy our country" (Trump 2016). If immigrants and political refugees were anathema to US safety and way of life, then career politicians, in Trump's crisis framework, were accessories to this faceless and impending threat.

While Trump's crisis framework relied heavily on impending threats to public safety, it also exacerbated an underlying monetary concern, too. Specifically, it evoked a larger threat to the nation's economic sustainability, thus inviting the need for a strongman protector figure who boasted business success. Consider Trump's false claim from the same rally that "these illegal [immigrant] workers draw much more out from the system than they can ever possibly pay back," thereby hurting "vulnerable American workers" who likewise suffered the ill effects of free-trade deals (Trump 2016).[2] The crisis, again, relied on notions of gender and space: both the penetrated nation and disenfranchised US workers stood as violated and "feminine" figures, and the border functioned as the site where Trump's aggressive masculine actions could remedy said problems. By staging such crises accordingly, Trump positioned himself as a guardian who spoke for "the silent majority" (as his campaign termed them)—that is, the everyday US citizens left behind or shafted by forces far beyond their control. A billionaire who had spent much of his life navigating the terrain of American capitalism and espousing the self-made man ethos,[3] Trump brandished a masculine resolve that evoked stability and reassurance in light of this two-fold specter of feminizing liabilities.

THE NEED FOR NOVELTY:
CASTING THE BORDER WALL AS A PANACEA

Trump's crisis framework continued to yield impassioned responses from loyalists and detractors alike throughout his campaign. The third (and last) presidential debate of the 2016 presidential election cycle occurred on October 19. In his comments, Trump directly blamed both Clinton and Obama for several geopolitical problems and then immediately transitioned to undocumented immigration, thus raising the twofold specter of antagonists invoked in his rally comments. With the election less than a month away, the stakes could not have been higher, especially when considering the October 8 publication by the *Washington Post* of a 2005 audio clip where Trump openly bragged about sexually assaulting women.[4] Rather than recoil from his masculinized tactics, Trump openly embraced them, using gendered language and spatial metaphors to once again juxtapose his own strength alongside feminizing liabilities, and ultimately framing his border positions as a necessary regulation of violence. Consider briefly his reference to grieving mothers who had lost children to undocumented immigrants:

> We need strong borders. In the audience we have four mothers of—I mean, these are unbelievable people that I've gotten to know over a period of years whose children have been killed, brutally killed, by people that came into the country illegally. You have thousands of mothers and fathers and relatives all over the country. (Politico Staff 2016)

The focus on anguished mothers and murdered citizens positioned Trump as a no-nonsense architect of safety and security. That he antagonized both Obama and Clinton (figures he had decried as incompetent on border policy) alongside non-nationals (penetrative and feminizing agents) only sharpened the gendered and spatial contours of his crisis framework, thus inviting masculine action. Similar to the framing used in his rally, Trump located impending crises from the perspective of public safety, claiming, "We have to keep the drugs out of our country. Right now, we're getting the drugs, they're getting the cash. We need strong borders" (Politico Staff 2016). Then, he transitioned the crisis terms to economic terrain, tying conventional trade agreements to the specter of economic fragility and casting Clinton's policies as anachronistic and injurious: "You would have a disaster on trade and you will have a disaster with your open borders" (Politico Staff 2016). In Trump's crisis framework, the dyadic specter of effete political actors and criminal immigrants created a series of feminizing debilities that harmed the greater public.

Presenting these threats against the backdrop of the border created a springboard for a larger rumination on the sovereignty and survival of the republic, a discursive strategy that established Trump's populist brand as an avenue toward tangible solutions and that configured "[m]anliness as a heroic pragmatism," to borrow scholar Suzanne Clark's phrasing (2000, 19). As such, Trump's framework created an effective impetus (an imagined crisis that was both immediate and existential) that resonated powerfully when considered alongside a hierarchy of winners (status quo politicians and non-nationals) and losers (law-abiding citizens). Indeed, Trump's reliance on language that evoked danger and vulnerability created the impression that only a strong, law-and-order leader could remedy and secure a fractured nation. Juxtaposed alongside his rival Hillary Clinton, a well-established political figure whom Trump caricatured as a globalist and rule-stepping elite, Trump capitalized on his aggression, professed strength, and stated fearlessness to compel voters to prioritize his novel candidacy.

Politicians have long staged conventional masculine qualities to acquire political capital (Dittmar 2018, 48), and presidential politics in the United States, as masculinities scholar Jackson Katz contends, "has long been the site of an ongoing cultural struggle over the meanings of American manhood" (2016, 1). In recent years, too, some have also used the border to "exploit fears with spatial metaphors" (Staudt 2009, 13), cultivating a tough façade to showcase their fearless patriotism. But Trump harnessed a crisis framework with an emotional urgency unlike his predecessors. In political speech, such moves are particularly advantageous. In his assessment of political discourse by Republican politicians, cognitive linguist George Lakoff contends that many typically espouse a "strict father morality," thus establishing their candidacies as especially attractive for voters whose political worldview prioritizes hierarchy, causal thinking, and patriarchal conventions (2009, 76–78). When Trump denigrated immigrants and established politicians through his crisis framing, he antagonized them as feminizing burdens, representing both as moral and economic drains forestalling substantive progress. The emotional gravity of such caricatures was structurally conducive to Trump's populist masculinity, since his façade of strength and safety promised to mitigate looming crises. As Trump claimed early in the debate, for example, "We have no country if we have no border. . . . We need the wall" (Politico Staff 2016).[5] A powerful synthesis of spatial and gendered imagery, of geopolitics and national identity, the US-Mexico border continued operating as an effective staging ground for Trump's crisis framing and paternal bravado.

TWEETING TOUGHNESS IN A CLIMATE OF CHAOS: THE BORDER AND CRISIS FRAMEWORKS FROM @REALDONALDTRUMP

Since the early days of his campaign, Trump accrued impressive political capital via Twitter, as he maximized the emotional appeal of his messages by creating an alarmist echo chamber that exploited Twitter's decentralized infrastructure (Turner 2018, 148). The brevity of Twitter's message capacity also aided Trump in that he flipped narratives hostile to his candidacy, converting apparent negatives into enduring positives (Cummings 2019, 64). Known for hyperbole and an idiosyncratic preference for dubious, if not unequivocally false, assertions,[6] Trump used border language in his tweets that bolstered the hierarchy of winners (undocumented immigrants and status quo politicians) and losers (the body politic) that he employed in the preceding examples.

Twitter afforded Trump several advantages that augmented his populist appeal, especially in regards to his border discourse and masculine persona. For example, Trump brandished his unapologetic populism to legitimize "public displays of disaffection," using a hybrid media environment to attract attention and authorize widespread disenchantment with the political status quo in ways unseen in previous presidential elections (Wahl-Jorgensen 2018, 80–82). What's more, the symbolic dimensions of the border only amplified the masculinist dimensions of his appeal. Consider the following examples, as they foregrounded the same twofold specter of antagonists while honing gendered and spatial imagery to aggrandize pseudo crises:

El Chapo and the Mexican drug cartels use the border unimpeded like it was a vacuum cleaner, sucking drugs and death right into the U.S. (@realdonaldtrump, July 13, 2015).

I am watching the Democrat Party led (because they want Open Borders and existing weak laws) assault on our country by Guatemala, Honduras and El Salvador, whose leaders are doing little to stop this large flow or people, INCLUDING MANY CRIMINALS, from entering Mexico to U.S. (@realdonaldtrump, October 18, 2018)

Without a Wall there cannot be safety and security at the Border or for the U.S.A. BUILD THE WALL AND CRIME WILL FALL! (@realdonaldtrump, January 24, 2019)

People have been saying for years that we should talk to Mexico. The problem is that Mexico is an "abuser" of the United States, taking but never giving. It has been this way for decades. (@realdonaldtrump, June 2, 2019)

Consistently, as other messages in his Twitter feed make evident, he tweeted toughness in a climate of chaos, and in so doing, Trump mapped weaknesses, aggressors, and debilities that demanded urgent action.

Importantly, Trump's language established the United States in a position of susceptibility that, when considered alongside his proposed border wall, summoned powerful gendered and spatial imagery conducive to his abrasive masculine guise. In this framework of persistent and looming crises, Trump's Twitter feed reinforced the perception of an interminable assault on civil society, which also lacked effective leadership. Represented as such, the body politic emerged as an endangered and assaulted (i.e., "feminine") figure, whose long-term safety demanded a strongman figure consonant with Trump's populist masculinity and its associated qualities: aggression, novelty, undaunted candor, and unconventional policy brawn. Here, though, data paled to demagoguery. As with his past mischaracterizations, the threats that Trump outlined were invariably overstated, misrepresented, or nonexistent, as attested by data and research.[7] Arguably, though, the effects of these representations mattered more than their factual accuracy, at least in the realm of political expediency. After all, as political science scholar Stephen J. Farnsworth notes, much in-depth reporting by established US newspapers received far less attention during the 2016 election cycle than Trump's salacious tweets (2018, 133). The crisis framework proved crucial for such an operation, and the border an integral tool that both reflected said crises and reinforced Trump's abrasive masculine qualities.

BEYOND POPULIST BRAVADO: CONTEXTUALIZING THE EFFICACY OF BORDER BARRIERS

The logistics of Trump's proposed border wall have varied significantly since his campaign launch in 2015.[8] Since then, numerous researchers, government officials, and security experts have asserted that the project would accomplish little in terms of minimizing undocumented immigration or the transfer of illicit drugs, and history likewise does not support Trump's characterizations of a border wall as an effective panacea.[9] As of May 2020, Trump has neither extensively addressed the root causes promoting US-bound undocumented immigration, nor has he proposed legislative reforms to improve the asymmetrical ties between the US and Mexico that have normalized such labor and migratory flows. In terms of acquiring political capital, though, such nuances need not matter when a crisis framework already yields impressive results. Since his election, rather than implement sound policy as part of his presidential persona, Trump has continued to bolster a populism that configures his aggressive masculine front as a necessary and long overdue response, as these case studies have demonstrated. Moreover, the masculinized nature of Trump's commitment to constructing a border wall hasn't been lost on some of his political detractors.

Following a contentious meeting with Trump in early December 2018, House Speaker Nancy Pelosi expressed her frustration regarding Trump's unwavering conviction to build his long-promised border wall with Mexico, as its hefty price tag impeded negotiations to finalize the federal government's budget. "It's like a manhood thing for him. As if manhood could ever be associated with him. This wall thing," she lamented (Siegel 2018). She later clarified that she "was trying to be the mom" (Siegel 2018) in her attempt to create order and avoid a shutdown of the federal government, thereby challenging a gender dynamic (masculine strength and resoluteness vs. feminine weakness and incompetence) that Trump had long harnessed as a political tool. Neither such criticism nor political roadblocks deterred Trump from positioning the border at the forefront of the national imaginary. Again, the powerful symbolic dimensions of the crisis framework merit consideration. As Naomi Klein notes, "Without a story, without our moorings, a great many people become vulnerable to authority figures" who exploit phenomena that they frame as shocking (2017, 7).

After nearly four years of discursively using the border as a catalyst for impending and imaginative mayhem, Trump codified his crisis framework by declaring a national emergency in regards to the southern border on February 15, 2019. The executive maneuver allowed Trump to augment his power by reallocating nearly $8 billion in military funds to partially fund his wall, depriving the US military of promised finances and sharply contradicting his campaign assurance that Mexico would fund the project (Baker 2019). In his televised address to the nation on January 8, 2019, Trump recycled several of the discursive tools that he had incorporated in his rallies, debates, and social media activity. Consider the following remarks:

> [Undocumented immigration] strains public resources and drives down jobs and wages. . . . Our southern border is a pipeline for vast quantities of illegal drugs including meth, heroin, cocaine, and fentanyl. . . . Some have suggested a barrier is immoral. . . . The only thing that is immoral is the politicians to do nothing and continue to allow more innocent people to be so horribly victimized. (*New York Times* 2019a)

In Trump's schema of threats and liabilities, immigrants emerged as unequiv-ocal culprits, status quo politicians their unassuming enablers, US citizens the exploited victims, and his wall a solution that was both logical and moral. The resulting hierarchy of victors and victims invited conventional mascu-line qualities that Trump translated into national virtues: strength, autonomy, combativeness, decisiveness, and order.[10]

Though the border afforded Trump a powerful tool to stage specters and flout his populist brand, his preference for hyperbole and the illusory has long informed his public businessman persona. In his coauthored memoir *Trump: The Art of the Deal*, Trump asserts, "The final key to the way I promote is bravado. I play to people's fantasies. People may not always think big themselves, but they can still get very excited by those who do" (1987, 58). Through his crisis framework, Trump created a fantasy of anticipative great-ness by promising to "make America great again." And though his hyperbolic representations of the border and border-crossers lacked merit, he nonethe-less presented them as common-sense truths, thus bringing to mind Trump's preference for what he terms "truthful hyperbole"—that is, "an innocent form of exaggeration—and a very effective form of promotion (1987, 58). Just as populism relies on emotional urgency, so too did Trump exacerbate his audience's emotional trepidations: a hunger for economic stability, a respect for law and order, and a political orientation unambiguously opposed to convention. Combined with a populist masculine brand, the crisis framework was crucial for this operation, and the border trope was, and remains, one of its most powerful accessories.

CONCLUSION

As this chapter has demonstrated across three particular case studies, Trump implemented a crisis framework in his discourse regarding the US-Mexico border, where the latter functioned as a staging ground for aggressive actions and masculine bravado that configured him as a masculine protector figure capable of ensuring safety and security. Accordingly, Trump staged a twofold specter of feminizing debilities that he exacerbated through gendered and spatial imagery. Undocumented immigrants emerged as invasive agents of crime and destruction, and status quo politicians stood as incompetent actors who prevented tangible and common-sense progress. In this framework, then, the body politic appeared as a vulnerable and exploited collective in a hierarchy of winners and losers. In the end, the border both reflected said crises and reinforced the alleged urgency for a novel leader capable of exacting fearless and aggressive leadership. Trump's border wall thus appeared as an attractive solution to reinstate stability and order in the face of ominous calamity.

While US presidents across the political spectrum have invoked unflattering representations of the border to advance career ambitions, Trump was unique by summoning the region in such hyperbolic terms as a dystopian realm of danger, drugs, and doom. While Trump's exaggerated language and antagonistic characterizations might prove questionable or abhorrent during other historical epochs, in this crisis framing, he elevated them as overdue virtues, emblematic of a fighting spirit necessary for redirecting the political, social, and economic trajectories of the nation back toward the horizon of "greatness" and away from feminizing liabilities. Accordingly, Trump configured his aggressive actions at the border as both essential and moral, as they aimed to forestall imminent havoc and preserve the republic at large, in spite of data contesting both his representations of immigrants and the efficacy of border barriers. Accordingly, his antagonistic caricatures of Latin American immigrants and hardline border proposals helped authorize a dichotomous and insular political orientation that configured his populist masculinity as a tool to achieve safety and strength. While the landscape of US presidential politics is sure to evolve, the border is likely to remain a powerful tool in political discourse. Accordingly, scholars should continue to examine the masculine dimensions of Trump's populist appeal while likewise considering the discursive mechanisms that endow such representations with authority and durability in the first place. By doing so, we draw closer to a more informed understanding of a political persona that continues to alter US politics and culture.

NOTES

1. Consult de la Torre (2015, 1–3) and Hawkins and Littvay (2019, 1–2) for more information regarding how externalizing Others (including immigrants and political elites) in binary opposition to a homogenized "we the people" lends emotional urgency to populisms.

2. Research does not support Trump's claims that immigrants are a drain on the economy, such as with tax evasion (Chomsky 2007, 40). In fact, research has shown that undocumented immigrants actually complement, rather than threaten, the work of skilled US laborers (Davidson 2013).

3. The ideology of the "self-made man" has strongly informed the evolution of US masculinities. As Kimmel observes, while self-made man identity was once measured "by accumulated wealth and status [and] by geographic and social mobility" (1996, 16), the negative socioeconomic effects created by neoliberal reforms of the 1980s have configured entitlement and victimization as its new hallmarks, thus weaponizing a resentment that Trump exploited (2017, 15–21).

4. Off camera during an episode filming of the program *Access Hollywood*, Trump claimed to host Billy Bush, "I'm automatically attracted to beautiful [women]—I just start kissing them. It's like a magnet. Just kiss. I don't even wait. And when you're a star, they let you do it. You can do anything. Grab 'em by the pussy. You can do anything" (Fahrenthold 2016).

5. Trump echoed similar comments made in 1984 by then President Ronald Reagan, who asserted in a news conference, "But the simple truth is that we've lost control of our own borders, and no nation can do that and survive" (Reagan 1984). Since then, discourse tying border security to the survival of the nation has been a powerful rhetorical tool in presidential election cycles.

6. *The Washington Post* documented 16,241 "false of misleading claims" by the 1,095th day of Trump's presidency (2020).

7. Research does not support Trump's repeated claims that immigrants (undocumented or otherwise) are more likely to commit crimes in the United States (Flagg 2019).

8. Trump claimed early in his campaign that he would construct a nearly 2,000 mile barrier made of concrete and that Mexico would pay for its construction. He later modified on several occasions his original plan regarding length, materials, and financing construction costs.

9. Investigative reporting confirms that most illicit drugs entering the United States pass through legal ports of entry, as opposed to open and unfenced terrain (Ferman 2019; Ward and Singhvi 2019). What's more, Trump's proposed wall would

likely do little, if anything, to curb undocumented immigration given the dynamic and complicated nature of both immigration and labor demands (Nixon 2018).

10. The *New York Times*' fact-check analysis of Trump's national address highlighted numerous assertions that were misleading or blatantly false, including his characterizations of crime and drug trafficking (*New York Times* 2019b).

BIBLIOGRAPHY

Ackleson, Jason. 2005. "Constructing Security on the U.S.-Mexico Border." *Political Geography* 24 (2): 165–184. https://doi.org/10.1016/j.polgeo.2004.09.017.

Baker, Peter. 2019. "Trump Declares a National Emergency, and Provokes a Constitutional Clash." *New York Times*, February 15, 2019. https://www.nytimes.com/2019/02/15/us/politics/national-emergency-trump.html.

Burns, Alexander. 2015. "Donald Trump, Pushing Someone Rich, Offers Himself." *New York Times*, June 16, 2015. https://www.nytimes.com/2015/06/17/us/politics/donald-trump-runs-for-president-this-time-for-real-he-says.html?hp.

Chávez, Karma R. 2012. "Border Interventions: The Need to Shift from a Rhetoric of Security to a Rhetoric of Militarization." In *Border Rhetorics: Citizenship and Identity on the US-Mexico Frontier*, edited by D. Robert DeChaine, 48–62. Tuscaloosa: University of Alabama Press.

Chomsky, Aviva. 2007. *"They Take Our Jobs!": And 20 Other Myths About Immigration*. Boston: Beacon Press.

Clark, Suzanne. 2000. *Cold Warriors: Manliness on Trial in the Rhetoric of the West*. Carbondale: Southern Illinois University Press.

Connell, R. W. 2005. *Masculinities*. 2nd Edition. Berkeley and Los Angeles: University of California Press.

Connell, R. W. 1998. "Masculinities and Globalization." *Men and Masculinities* 1 (1): 3–23. https://doi.org/10.1177%2F1097184X98001001001.

Cummings, Lance. 2019. "The Dark Alchemy of Donald Trump: Re-inventing Presidential Rhetorics through Christian and 'New Age' Discourses." In *President Donald Trump and His Political Discourse*, edited by Michele Lockhart, 52–70. New York: Routledge.

Davidson, Adam. 2013. "Do Illegal Immigrants Actually Hurt the U.S. Economy?" *New York Times*, February 12, 2013. https://www.nytimes.com/2013/02/17/magazine/do-illegal-immigrants-actually-hurt-the-us-economy.html.

De la Torre, Carlos. 2015. "Introduction: Power to the People? Populism, Insurrections, Democratization." In *The Promise and Perils of Populism: Global Perspectives*, edited by Carlos de la Torre, 1–28. Lexington: University Press of Kentucky.

DeChaine, D. Robert. 2012. "Introduction: For Rhetorical Border Studies." In *Border Rhetorics: Citizenship and Identity on the US-Mexico Frontier*, edited by D. Robert DeChaine, 1–15. Tuscaloosa: University of Alabama Press.

Diener, Alexander C., and Joshua Hagen. 2010. "Conclusion: Borders in a Changing Global Context." In *Borderlines and Borderlands: Political Oddities at the Edge of the Nation-State*, edited by Alexander C. Diener, and Joshua Hagen, 189–194. Lanham: Rowman & Littlefield.

Dittmar, Kelly. 2018. "Disrupting Masculine Dominance? Women as Presidential and Vice-Presidential Contenders." In *Gender and Elections: Shaping the Future of American Politics*, edited by Susan J. Carroll, and Richard L. Fox, 48–77. 4th Edition. New York: Cambridge University Press.

Fahrenthold, David A. 2016. "Trump Recorded Having Extremely Lewd Conversation about Women in 2005." *Washington Post*, October 8, 2016. https://www. washingtonpost.com/politics/trump-recorded-having-extremely-lewd-conversation-about-women-in-2005/2016/10/07/3b9ce776-8cb4-11e6-bf8a-3d26847eeed4_story. html.

Fairclough, Isabela, and Norman Fairclough. 2012. *Political Discourse Analysis: A Method for Advanced Students*. New York: Routledge.

Farnsworth, Stephen J. 2018. *Presidential Communication and Character: White House News Management from Clinton and Cable to Twitter and Trump*. New York: Routledge.

Ferman, Mitchell. 2019. "Trump Laid Out Evidence That a Wall Is Needed. We Took a Hard Look." *New York Times*, January 25, 2019. https://www.nytimes.com/2019 /01/25/us/border-wall-mexico-usa-contraband.html.

Flagg, Anna. 2019. "Is There a Connection Between Undocumented Immigrants and Crime?" *New York Times*, May 13, 2019. https://www.nytimes.com/2019/05/13/ upshot/illegal-immigration-crime-rates-research.html.

Fuchs, Christian. 2018. *Digital Demagogue: Authoritarian Capitalism in the Age of Trump and Twitter*. London: Pluto Press.

Gómez, Laura E. 2007. *Manifest Destinies: The Making of the Mexican American Race*. New York: New York University Press.

Greenberg, Amy S. 2005. *Manifest Manhood and the Antebellum American Empire*. New York: Cambridge University Press.

Hawkins, Kirk, and Levente Littvay. 2019. *Contemporary US Populism in Comparative Perspective*. Cambridge: Cambridge University Press.

Katz, Jackson. 2016. *Man Enough? Donald Trump, Hillary Clinton, and the Politics of Presidential Masculinity*. Northampton: Interlink Books.

Kimmel, Michael. 2017. *Angry White Men: American Masculinity at the End of an Era*. New York: Nation Books.

Kimmel, Michael. 1996. *Manhood in America: A History*. New York: Free Press.

Klein, Naomi. 2017. *No Is Not Enough: Resisting Trump's Shock Politics and Winning the World We Need*. Chicago: Haymarket Books.

Klein, Naomi. 2007. *The Shock Doctrine: The Rise of Disaster Capitalism*. New York: Metropolitan Books.

Lawler, Peter Augustine, and Robert Martin Schaefer. 1990. "Introduction." In *American Political Rhetoric: Essential Speeches and Writings*, edited by Peter Augustine Lawler and Robert Martin Shaefer, ix–x. 2nd Edition. Savage: Rowman & Littlefield.

Lakoff, George. 2009. *The Political Mind: A Cognitive Scientist's Guide to Your Brain and Its Politics*. New York: Penguin Books.

Lakoff, George, and Mark Johnson. 1980. *Metaphors We Live By*. Chicago: University of Chicago Press.

Martin, James. 2014. *Politics and Rhetoric: A Critical Introduction*. New York: Routledge.

Messerschmidt, James W. 1999. *Nine Lives: Adolescent Masculinities, the Body, and Violence*. Boulder: West View Press.

New York Times. 2019a. "Full Transcripts: Trump's Speech on Immigration and the Democratic Response." January 8, 2019. https://www.nytimes.com/2019/01/08/us /politics/trump-speech-transcript.html.

New York Times. 2019b. "Trump's Speech to the Nation: Fact Checks and Background." January 9, 2019. https://www.nytimes.com/2019/01/08/us/politics/ trump-speech.html.

Nixon, Ron. 2018. "To Pay for Wall, Trump Would Cut Proven Border Security Measures." *New York Times*, January 8, 2018. https://www.nytimes.com/2018/01 /08/us/politics/trump-border-wall-funding-surveillance.html.

Park, Haeyoun. 2014. "Children at the Border." *New York Times*, October 21, 2014. https://www.nytimes.com/interactive/2014/07/15/us/questions-about-the-border -kids.html.

Politico Staff. 2016. "Full Transcript: Third 2016 Presidential Debate." *Politico*, October 20, 2016. https://www.politico.com/story/2016/10/full-transcript-third -2016-presidential-debate-230063.

Reagan, Ronald. 1984. "The President's News Conference." *Ronald Reagan Presidential Library and Museum*, June 14, 1984. https://www.reaganlibrary.gov/ research/speeches/61484d.

Robertson, O. Nicholas. 2018. "The Myth of Immigrant Criminality: Early Twentieth-Century Sociological Theory and Trump's Campaign." In *Nasty Women and Bad Hombres: Gender and Race in the 2016 US Presidential Election*, edited by Christine A. Kray, Tamar W. Carroll, and Hinda Mandell, 74–87. Rochester: University of Rochester Press.

Santa Ana, Otto. 2013. *Juan in a Hundred: The Representation of Latinos on Network News*. Austin: University of Texas Press.

Siegel, Benjamin. 2018. "'It's Like a Manhood Thing for Him': Pelosi on Trump and Border Wall." *ABC News*, December 11, 2018. https://abcnews.go.com/Politics/ manhood-thing-pelosi-trump-border-wall/story?id=59758174.

Staudt, Kathleen. 2009. "Violence at the Border: Broadening the Discourse to Include Feminism, Human Security, and Deeper Democracy." In *Human Rights Along the U.S.-Mexico Border: Gendered Violence and Insecurity*, edited by Kathleen Staudt, Tony Payan, and Z. Anthony Kruszewski, 1–28. Tucson: University of Arizona Press.

Trump, Donald. 2016. "Transcript of Donald Trump's Immigration Speech." *New York Times*, September 1, 2016. https://www.nytimes.com/2016/09/02/us/politics/ transcript-trump-immigration-speech.html.

Trump, Donald J., with Tony Schwartz. 1987. *Trump: The Art of the Deal*. New York: Ballantine Books.

Turner, Fred. 2018. "Trump on Twitter: How a Medium Designed for Democracy Became an Authoritarian's Mouthpiece." In *Trump and the Media,* edited by Pablo J. Boczkowski, and Zizi Papacharissi, 143–149. Cambridge: The MIT Press.

Vertovec, Steven. 2004. "Migrant Transnationalism and Modes of Transformation." *International Migration Review* 38 (3): 970–1001. https://doi.org/10.1111/j.1747 -7379.2004.tb00226.x.

Wahl-Jorgensen, Karin. 2018. "Public Displays of Disaffection: The Emotional Politics of Donald Trump." In *Trump and the Media*, edited by Pablo J. Boczkowski, and Zizi Papacharissi, 79–86. Cambridge: The MIT Press.

Ward, Joe and Anjali Singhvi. 2019. "Trump Claims There Is a Crisis at the Border. What's the Reality?" *New York Times*, January 11, 2019. https://www.nytimes.com /interactive/2019/01/11/us/politics/trump-border-crisis-reality.html.

Washington Post. 2020. "President Trump Made 16,241 False or Misleading Claims in His first Three Years." January 20, 2020. https://www.washingtonpost.com/ politics/2020/01/20/president-trump-made-16241-false-or-misleading-claims-his- first-three-years/.

Chapter 4

The Masculinist Restoration Project in the Rhetoric of Anti-Gender Movements

The Case of Turkey

Didem Unal

In the current Turkish context marked by a dramatic shift toward authoritarianism, the anti-feminist and anti-gender political agenda has been intrinsic to the foundation of a new political regime under the Justice and Development Party (AKP) [JDP] rule. Especially in the post-2011 period, as the AKP consolidated its power through new electoral victories and turned away from the ideal of "liberal Muslim democracy" that characterized its early years in power (Coşar and Özman 2004), its gender policy vision became increasingly dominated by a familialist and pronatalist policy vision and increased the grip of hegemonic gender roles on women's and LGBT people's lives (Acar and Altunok 2013; Güneş-Ayata and Doğangün 2017; Kandiyoti 2016). The religio-conservative backlash in the gender regime, reinforced through various ideological elements such as nationalism, familialism, pronatalism, anti-gender ideology, anti-feminism and pro-Islamism, has propagated for a naturalist gender order and proposed regulation of abortion and reproductive rights as a cure to the alleged demoralization of society (Cindoglu and Unal 2017; Korkman 2015). The mode of politics feeding into this backlash revolves around a highly masculinist leadership style that perpetuates populist antagonisms between the so-called national will and secular elite and derives its power from aggressiveness, vulgarity, ruthlessness and machismo (Eksi and Wood 2019; Ozbay and Soybakis 2020). In recent years, this hypermasculine political power has increasingly fostered a masculinist identity politics based on the construction of an endangered masculinity and mobilization against the concept of gender (Çağatay 2019; Özkazanç 2019). This affective entanglement of the authoritarian right-wing populist regime with masculinist identity politics leads to a new anti-democratic public space where anti-feminist and anti-gender claims and demands are becoming more coherent and visible in the public debate. It is worth noting that the terms "anti-feminist" and "anti-gender" here connote both rhetorical styles and policy perspectives that draw on antagonistic vilification and exclude pluralism and deliberative processes while arguing for traditional gender hegemony (Kováts 2017). While the former constructs a homogenous enemy out of feminists and feminisms, the latter vilifies theoretical work, empirical research and activist voices that draw on the concept of gender, gender equality and its policy tools (Kováts 2017). As such, they operate hand in hand in disseminating "gender populism," that is, the political appropriation of a simplifying understanding of gender as a "natural," dichotomous order (Saresma 2018).

Against this background, this chapter investigates the "masculinist restoration project" in the discursive repertoires deployed by various actors in Turkey with the aim of reinforcing anti-feminist, masculinist and anti-gender political positions. It situates the political agenda, the organizational strategies, and the rhetorical styles of the rising anti-gender movement vis-à-vis the AKP regime and pro-government women's organizations such as KADEM (Women and Democracy Association) that promote it (Doyle 2018; Koyuncu and Özman 2019). Kandiyoti (2013) defines the "masculinist restoration project" in Turkey as a patriarchal project of restoring "patriarchy as usual" at the current political moment when notions of female subordination can no longer be hegemonic because of women's demands for equality, their activism, and the demise of the idea of male-breadwinner. This attempt at restoring masculinist privileges employs the rhetoric of "the crisis of masculinity," that is, the thesis that invokes the idea of loss of hegemonic masculine values in a gender order that is allegedly coopted by feminist acquisitions and leads to insecurities in men's psyche and societal roles (Mellström 2018). The masculinist restoration project as a form of comprehensive restructuring of discourse, policy and gender vocabulary is not unique to Turkey; it is increasingly gaining ground across the world through mobilization of political agendas that sanction male domination in public and private spheres (Gotell and Dutton 2016; Marwick and Caplan 2018; Nicolas and Agius 2017). It is a particular form of counter-movement that opposes feminism and its advocates, promotes the "rights of men" in a society perceived to be dominated by women and mobilizes primarily to serve to the interests of fathers and spouses with regard to issues such as divorce laws, alimony, child custody, and violence (Blais and Dupuis-Déri 2012). Its anti-gender agenda is based on a mobilization against what they call "genderism," that is, gender mainstreaming, gender equality policies and recognition of sexual diversity (Kuhar and Paternotte 2017). In Turkey, masculinist actors utilize a form of polarizing propaganda that promises to ensure cultural authenticity and societal moral integrity around the hegemonic gender order not tainted by "western feminism." They vernacularize the transnational flows of the global anti-gender rhetoric through anti-Western and pro-Islamist framings that constantly appeal to nationalist sentiments operationalized by masculinist politics. In recent years, this masculinist demagoguery has become more visible and ideologically coherent in its resistance against feminist acquisitions and reinvigorated masculinist demands in conjunction with the proliferation of discourse on family and masculinist pride under AKP rule.

This chapter exposes how the masculinist restoration project in Turkey unfolds in public debate as anti-gender actors (1) propagate against "gender ideology" and call for reviving "cultural authenticity" through the Islamic tradition, anti-Westernism and nationalism, (2) marginalize feminism as an anti-family and anti-Islam standpoint and accuse it for deprivileging men as a social group, and (3) proliferate the discourse of endangerment of men's rights and ask for abandonment of recent feminist acquisitions in the legal sphere. Two main public debates, namely the debate on the *Council of Europe Convention on preventing and combating violence against women and domestic violence* (the Istanbul Convention) and women's right to alimony in cases of divorce are given special attention to map out the discursive boundaries of anti-gender positions. The analysis makes use of recent scholarly studies on rhetorical strategies and collective action frames used in populist and anti-gender mobilizations (Aslanidis 2018; Corredor 2019; Foroughi et al. 2019; Harsin 2018). It mainly focuses on the time frame between 2019 and 2020 during which anti-gender discourses significantly proliferated and gained efficacy in the formulation of a political agenda. The data consists of major anti-gender groups' and public figures' interviews, press statements, columns and social media texts in the specified time period. Press statements both in pro-government and oppositional news sources were used to identify the main topics, demands and concerns in the anti-gender agenda, while social media data, which mainly includes anti-gender actors' postings on Twitter, was gathered to detect the discursive and politically strategic tools and the interpretive schema used to reinforce the efficacy of masculinist demands.

Within this frame, the chapter argues that the anti-gender political climate that has been mediated until now through the discourse of an Islamically accentuated "complementarity of genders" framework is further fueled by novel actors in the current era who are motivated to respond to the alleged crisis of masculinity by restoring masculinist values in the legal sphere. This new stream of backsliding not only rejects the feminist ideal of gender equality but also challenges the AKP's "gender justice" vision formulated with reference to Islam and rhetorically works to deprive it from moderately accommodating a conservative pro-woman discourse enacted through docile, pro-AKP women's organizations. It assumes an affective tone, utilizing the sentiments of hate, rage and resentment, vernacularizes transnational anti-gender frames through an anti-Western logic based on Islam and leads to a ruthless performance of hypermasculine discourse in Turkey.

THE GLOBAL UPSURGE OF
ANTI-GENDER MOVEMENTS

Anti-gender actors in the current era utilize the concept of "gender ideology" to connote the opposition to a broad spectrum of recent sociopolitical reforms, namely sexual and reproductive rights, same-sex marriage, new reproductive technologies, gender mainstreaming, and protection against gender violence (Graff and Korolzcuk 2018; Kováts 2017). The simultaneity of anti-gender movements and traveling practices point out that they share certain striking commonalities across different geographies especially with regard to their antagonistic rhetoric and their opposition to LGBTQ issues, gender mainstreaming and gender theory (Kuhar and Paternotte 2017; Graff et. al 2019; Verloo and Paternotte 2018).

Anti-gender movements can emerge along and from within right-wing populist politics and share its conservative totalizing civilizational project that envisages idealized femininities and masculinities based on the hegemonic gender order (Saresma 2018). They aim to radicalize the right-wing populist rule to the extent that they urge right-wing populist actors to annul existing legal frameworks that adopt gender ideology and/or attempt to prevent them from ratifying such legal arrangements. The recent public debates about the Istanbul Convention in Hungary, Bulgaria, Slovakia, Poland and Turkey are emblematic of this (Darakchi 2019; Özkazanç 2019). Anti-gender critics of the Convention in these contexts regard the Convention as a "Trojan horse" or "Ebola from Brussels" that would proliferate "gender ideology" and introduce a "third sex" and same-sex marriage (Graff and Korolzcuk 2018).

These groups make use of right-wing rhetorical style that draws upon simplifications, imaginary antagonisms and promotion of manipulative sources of information. Known as the products of the "post-truth" era (Foroughi et al. 2019), these rhetorical styles discredit objective facts in knowledge production and appeal to fabricated knowledge in shaping the public opinion. In this symbolic order, gender becomes an "empty signifier" that is ascribed with a stereotyped political image of the opponents, that is, local and transnational feminist and LGBTQ actors and provides leeway for political opportunism (Mayer and Sauer 2017). In what follows, the discussion introduces the political agenda, the organizational strategies and rhetorical styles of the recently proliferating anti-gender actors in Turkey and discusses the implications of their masculinist restoration project for the gender regime.

AKP, ANTI-GENDER POLITICS, AND GENDER COMPLEMENTARITY

Scholars use different typologies to explain the authoritarian shift in AKP rule in the post-2011 period such as "competitive authoritarianism" (Esen and Gumuscu 2016), "electoral authoritarianism" (Kaya 2015) or "authoritarian neoliberalism" (Tansel 2018). Following Norris and Inglehart (2019), this chapter utilizes the term "authoritarian populism" as an analytical lens to point out that authoritarian and populist characteristics blend together in the party's discourse and policy. Discourse and policy on gender and sexuality functions as a "political glue" or "symbolic glue" in AKP rule, bringing together various ideological elements such as nationalism, conservatism, pro-Islamism, neoliberalism and antifeminism in the same pot (Cindoglu and Unal 2017; Kandiyoti 2016; Kováts and Põim 2015). In this narrative ecology, idealized features of masculinity and femininity provide a hegemonic rationale for social relations at all levels of social organization (Acar and Altunok 2013; Güneş-Ayata and Doğangün 2017; Korkman 2015; Unal and Cindoglu 2013). Moreover, heteronormative nuclear family is set up as a means of protection against loss of values, moral decay, erosion of cultural authenticity (Akkan 2018; Candas and Silier 2014; Coşar and Yegenoglu 2011).

This hegemonic gender order is further reinforced through a communication style and performative rhetoric that relies on polarization and stereotypes, thereby perpetuating antagonisms and grievances on the political spectrum (Eksi and Wood 2019). Its tone is affective, engaging in an elaborate emotional work through targeting feminists as adversaries, enemies, scapegoats: "Feminists . . . don't accept the concept of motherhood" (*Guardian* 2014), women and men cannot be equal (*Guardian* 2014), birth control is treason to nation (*BBC* 2016), abortion is murder (*BBC* 2012), "childless women are 'deficient'" (*Guardian* 2016). The AKP's neo-conservative populist project implicated in these statements is amplified by strong references to the Sunni Islamic tradition (Mutluer 2019). These religious references serve as catalysts to invoke majority anxieties about societal moral decay in the face of global feminist and LGBTQ agenda, increasing divorce rates and the decline of family (Özkazanç 2019; Yarar 2020). They also serve as remedies on the technical policy level through redefining key concepts, tools and mechanisms of gender equality politics (Koyuncu and Özman 2019).

The Islamic idea of *fıtrat* (disposition), which refers to human beings' biological and divinely ordained nature according to the Islamic thought, provides a useful ground for conservative gender populist arguments to replace the feminist idea of gender equality with the principle of the "complementarity of genders." As a result, a new terminology emerges out of this religio-populist anti-gender stance fused with the Islamic worldview. In this new symbolic order, Islam is presented as a just religion that is attentive to human beings' "true" selves and is thus superior to the liberal equality politics of "gender ideology" (Eslen-Ziya 2020; Koyuncu and Özman 2019). Familial unity, familial care and motherhood are praised through Islamic references (Adak 2020; Kocamaner 2019). Moreover, this religio-conservative equity vision is further blended with a religio-nationalist discourse that displays pronatalist tones and regards children as incarnations of Turkish nation's future (Korkman 2015). It is this reshuffling of the gender regime through pronatalism, familialism, gender complementarity and gender justice perspectives that has paved the way to the rising efficacy of anti-gender actors' masculinist restoration project in Turkey.

ANTI-GENDER ACTORS IN TURKEY
AND THEIR DEMANDS

When compared to the examples in Europe, the rising public visibility of the anti-gender movement as a countermovement to the feminist and LGBTQ activists is a relatively recent phenomenon in Turkey. It has mainly gained momentum through new discursive opportunity structures arising from the recent reshuffling of the gender regime. Özkazanç (2019) identifies the 2019 Feminist Night Walk as an important political moment where the anti-gender movement came to the surface. Contesting feminist activists' call for mobilization on the International Women's Day, an anti-gender group called *Turkish Family Assembly* released a statement on Twitter, asking imams to recite their demands in mosques on the 8th of March (*GazeteDuvar* 2019). Condemning gender ideology as a terrorist project, anti-gender actors demanded the annulment of the Istanbul Convention and the Law No. 6284 that aims to combat domestic violence and violence against women, opposed women's rights to alimony, and asked for new legal arrangements with regard to alimony rights and child custody in favor of men (*Bianet* 2018). They also raised other demands regarding the lifting of the ban on under-age marriages and the reenactment of the "head of the family" status in the Civil Code, which was annulled with the reform of the Civil Code in 2001. As these demands have found resonance in AKP officials' discourses, *Turkish Family Assembly* has emerged as a significant actor setting the anti-gender agenda and mobilizing a public debate around it. Main social actors involved in this campaign also include radical Islamist columnists writing in pro-government media and Islamist NGOs fiercely criticizing the Istanbul Convention (*MepaNews* 2020). There are also some public figures, such as Sema Maraşlı, who have recently emerged as vocal female actors in the emerging men's movement and aim to gain power positions in the media through self-positioning at the forefront of anti-gender activism (Maraşlı 2018).

Although organized around a very loose structure, the current anti-gender mobilization in Turkey displays the agility and the capacity to influence the public debate through various networks in media channels. As recent polls suggest (*Diken* 2020), it does not represent "demands from below" but rather fabricates a masculinist agenda to ensure the restoration of masculine privileges. The pro-government media resonates and legitimizes anti-gender actors' claims and demands by giving voice to the "alternative facts" that they proclaim against "gender ideology" in target policy areas, namely, divorce laws, alimony, child custody, and violence (D'Ancona 2017). In a similar vein, the AKP government aligns with the anti-gender movement, stating that the public reaction against the Istanbul Convention and women's right to alimony in case of divorce shall be soon addressed on policy level (*T24* 2019a). President Erdogan recently declared that the Istanbul Convention is not binding, and the government will review the Convention in line with sociocultural sensitivities (*Ahvalnews* 2020). One can safely argue that the AKP's accommodation of anti-gender masculinist claims in its policy vision amplifies the movement's efficacy in public debate and generates a discursive space where new masculinist demands can be articulated. The discussion below maps out the discursive boundaries within which the recent debates on the Istanbul Convention and women's rights to alimony have unfolded in anti-gender actors' accounts.

THE DEBATE ON THE ISTANBUL CONVENTION

The Istanbul Convention, which was opened for signature in May 2011, is a comprehensive international agreement on violence against women and domestic violence with a monitoring mechanism that requires states to fully address male violence as a form of gender-based violence, to take measures to prevent it and to prosecute the perpetrators. As of March 2020, thirty-four countries had ratified the Convention, while twelve signatures were not followed by ratifications (*Council of Europe*, 2020). Turkey signed the Convention in November 2011 with the support of all political parties in the parliament and ratified it in March 2012. The convention came into force in August 2014, making Turkey liable to prevent any form of male violence based on gender, sexual orientation and gender identity.

Moreover, Law No. 6284 was accepted on March 8, 2012, providing legal basis for protective and preventive measures against male violence such as ensuring victims have access to shelter, legal and psychological support and implementing barring/eviction orders requiring the perpetrator to stay away from the victim (Ayhan 2017). The law stipulates that these measures must be implemented regardless of the victim's marital status. Feminist organizations regard it as a significant step in preventing violence against women and use it as a pressure mechanism to urge the state to fully implement the existing legal framework to eliminate femicides (Yinanç 2017).

According to *We Will Stop the Femicides Platform*'s reports, 1,323 women were killed in Turkey in the last three years by their husbands, boyfriends or male kin (*Kadın Cinayetlerini Durduracağız* 2020). Despite these alarming statistics, the implementation of the law on preventing male violence is quite problematic and at risk. The Islamically accentuated conservative gender regime designed to protect family unity fails to acknowledge the systemic and institutional underpinnings of male violence and prefers to address it on moralistic grounds by pathologizing perpetrators and treating violence cases as individual incidents (Akyuz and Sayan-Cengiz 2016). On the other hand, the recent proliferation of anti-gender propaganda poses another major threat to a sustainable feminist struggle against male violence.

Opposition against the Istanbul Convention operates as a major frame in anti-gender mobilization in Turkey. Its repertoires of contention mainly consist of online activism with hashtags such as "Stop the Istanbul Convention," "Istanbul Convention kills," and "Family above everything" (Kaplan 2020a). Anti-gender actors operationalize these hashtags as collective action frames that enable them to develop a shared understanding about the alleged problem of "gender ideology" and a "schemata of interpretation" to take collective action (Benford and Snow 2000). These frames, that is, "schemata of interpretation" used in mobilization and collective action, provide activists discursive-cognitive patterns to diffuse grievances toward contentious action, and to crystallize their collective identity for a broad audience (Aslanidis 2018; Snow et al. 2014). They operate both on diagnostic and prognostic grounds in that the diagnostic phase identifies the social problem and the grievances associated with it, while the prognostic phase suggests solutions and strategies (Aslanidis 2018). Accordingly, anti-gender actors blame the Istanbul Convention for propagating gender ideology and dismantling the family unity. While this diagnostic framing attributes blame to feminists for the alleged moral decay in society, prognostic framing proposes the annulment of the Convention to overcome the dissolution of family unity: "The idea of genderless people cultivated by the feminist-LGBT movement blows up the foundations of the family institution" (Kaplan 2020b); "This Convention legitimizes adultery and destroys our family structure. Abolish it right away!" (*Diyanet-sen*, 2020).

Anti-gender actors also utilize opposition to the Istanbul Convention as a major frame to set a clear line separating the AKP's anti-feminism from its seemingly pro-woman discourse propagated by pro-government women's organizations (GONGOs) such as KADEM (Women and Democracy Association). Recently, KADEM has been the target of a series of anti-gender attacks in media because of its support for the Istanbul Convention. Several columnists in the pro-government media have attacked KADEM, arguing that it is co-opted by feminist lobbies and does not serve national interests (*Independent Türkçe* 2019). As a result, KADEM suddenly emerged as an anti-family actor in the public debate and found itself caught up in a crossfire. While feminist groups criticize it for not being feminist, anti-gender actors target its policy agenda for being feminist.

The argument about KADEM's alleged feminism is indeed very ironic because as a "government-controlled shadow civil society actor" (Doyle 2018), KADEM regards feminism as a Western ideology that supposedly defines genders in a constant clash and clearly positions itself as an anti-feminist organization (Koyuncu and Özman 2019). Echoing the AKP's gender complementarity perspective, KADEM suggests that the Islamic concept of justice is superior to the gender equality framework. Similar to conservative women's organizations on the right-wing of the political spectrum across the globe (Bachetta and Power 2013), it appropriates feminist rhetorical frames, aligns them with the conservative agenda and formulates a seemingly woman-friendly policy framework that would be in tandem with the AKP's gender complementarity model. As a result, it offers the impression that it can compensate for the AKP's overtly misogynist official discourse. The rising anti-gender movement aims to rhetorically transform this seemingly woman-friendly policy vision in the AKP's gender politics into an overtly masculinist policy vision in the legal and sociopolitical realms.

This masculinist restoration project built on a vision of "uncompromised" pro-familialism and male hegemony operationalizes an aggressive affective discourse on male victimization that revalorizes masculine privileges. It regards the Istanbul Convention as a key site where the alleged male victimization crystallizes. Anti-gender actors frequently frame barring decisions made in accordance with the Istanbul Convention and the Law No. 6284 as symbolic cases that expose the alleged loss of male privileges. The president of the *National Family Platform*, Adil Çevik states:

Men are thrown out of their homes without any evidence. You are supposed to pay 700 liras even in cases where you throw out a pet but there is no penalty for throwing out the father. Once thrown out of his home, the father's honor in the neighborhood is irreversibly shattered. (*Sivilsayfalar* 2018, translation mine)

Moreover, this discourse on male victimization operates through language that shrinks the discursive space where violence against women can be addressed as gender-based violence with systemic, institutional underpinnings. As such, it rhetorically situates itself in public debate both vis-a-vis the feminist movement and KADEM's seemingly woman-friendly policy vision.

THE ALIMONY DEBATE

In conjunction with their framing of the Istanbul Convention as a threat to family unity, anti-gender groups frame women's right to alimony as a trigger to divorce and demand a new legal framework regarding alimony rights. According to the current legislation, a spouse who risks poverty after divorce and who is not the faulty party, can demand alimony for an unlimited time. Echoing anti-gender actors' demands, President Erdogan recently announced that there will be amendments in the existing legislation, ensuring that alimonies be awarded in accordance with the marriage duration (*Milliyet* 2019). The fact that anti-gender actors' political agenda successfully resonates in the AKP's policy vision suggests a complex political alliance where AKP officials translate anti-gender demands into a moderate political standpoint with the populist claim that they reflect "social realities." On the other hand, while the AKP's approach to alimony rights is mainly dominated by familialist reflexes geared toward protecting family unity, anti-gender actors mostly mobilize around the discourse of male victimhood. The rhetoric of "evil women who inherently tend to misuse alimony rights" enables anti-gender actors to perpetuate the discourse of male victimhood. On her Twitter account, Sema Maraşlı, a well-known actor in anti-gender circles, states: "Women demand everything that they can associate with the concept of rights. They call it alimony rights to steal money from ex-husband's pocket. They commit adultery and demand the right to abortion" (Maraşlı 2020a, translation mine).

This rhetoric of "evil women" and male victimization provides anti-gender actors leeway to criticize the AKP for undermining its familialist vision through disprivileging men, feminist groups for being anti-family and anti-man, and GONGO's, such as KADEM, for utilizing its clientelist ties to the AKP to serve feminist goals (*Yeniakit* 2019a). This multiple critique and the discourse of male victimhood is further amplified through demands to change the existing legislation regarding under-age marriage. In this regard, different narrative parts of the anti-gender rhetoric, that is, women's right to alimony and under-age marriage are framed together to code male vulnerability as a tragic loss. Anti-gender actors frequently remind the public that men involved in marriages involving minors are not necessarily rapists or sexual aggressors and are mostly subject to unjust imprisonment (Sönmez 2019).

This symbolic order manufacturing victimhood through interlocking narratives amplifies anti-gender demagoguery's resistance to democratic deliberation and operates through a static, fixed understanding of a nation defined as a homogenous entity that is marked by so-called "culturally authentic" social realities, such as early marriage. It centers on a political vision that promises to "bring order into chaos" by defining chaos as the erosion of male privileges and inhibits society's capacity to organize a progressive public debate about the heterogeneity of the nation (Johnson 2017).

CONTEXTUAL SPECIFICITIES

Although the anti-gender movement in Turkey borrows largely from the global upsurge of anti-gender movements in its vilification of gender ideology and its deployment of the rhetoric of "the crisis of masculinity," contextual specificities provide a fertile ground for its consolidation. It blends anti-Western sentiments fused with pro-Islamist and nationalist reflexes that are mostly deployed to criticize the foundational role of Western norms and ideas in the history of modern Turkey (Atasoy 2009; Kadıoğlu 2010). In a press statement, the head of the Turkish Family Assembly makes an analogy between the rhetoric of "gavur" and the Istanbul Convention: "At that time, [late Ottoman/early 20th century] it was improper to call *gavur* as *gavur*. In a similar vein, in the current era you cannot call pervert laws such as CEDAW, the Istanbul Convention or the Law No. 6284 pervert" (*Habervakti* 2020, translation mine).

The Turkish word "gavur" literally refers to unbelievers and infidels (Iğsız 2008). The rhetoric of "gavur" in the context of Turkish modernization is generally used to justify exclusionary discourse and discrimination against religious minorities and implies the attempts to define the nation over ethnic and religious purity and "non-Western cultural authenticity" (Iğsız 2008). The reference to the word "gavur" in the statement above is no coincidence. It serves the reinforcement of anti-gender political claims through anti-Western and pro-Islamist reflexes that call the feminist "lobby" *gavur*, alien or the opposite of "yerli ve milli" [homegrown and national] (Mutluer 2019). Accordingly, the Istanbul Convention and its gender ideology is historically defined over the East/West divide and interpreted as the continuation of top-down modernization experience in Turkey that is framed as an elite project carried out at the expense of so-called national values, traditions and norms (Kadıoğlu 2010). This anti-Western rhetoric suggests that the Istanbul Convention epitomizes the cultural hegemony of Western norms and ideas that allegedly contradict Islamic traditions and norms: "Precautions against violence against women should be implemented in line with our societal concerns and family structures; they should not be forced by feminist ideologies or the European Union" (*Diyanet-sen* 2020). In line with these anti-Western and pro-Islamist reflexes, anti-gender actors frame both the Istanbul Convention and the "feminist and LGBTQ lobby" as the "Trojan horse" of Western powers employed to disempower the nation, dismantle the family institution and to generate a moral decay (*Star* 2020).

Moreover, nationalist and pronatalist ideological elements easily integrate into this anti-Western rhetoric with a recourse to the paranoia created around the wellbeing of children. Casting family as an institution of safety and outcasting any conception of it as a problematic category, anti-gender actors liberate family from violence, fear and anxiety and idealize it as an entity untouched by power asymmetries. In line with this conception, anti-gender actors suggest that the demise of the family institution will deprive children of moral education and economic, social and psychological security (Eraslan 2019). This rhetoric of "children in danger" echoes the nationalist concerns of the AKP's pronatalist and familialist policy perspective that idealizes family as a micro-geography of the AKP's conservative social engineering and projects the nation's future upon the ideal of raising pious children and youth (Lüküslü 2016; Mutluer 2019). It also blends with the anti-gender myth that represents the gender terminology of the Istanbul Convention as a tool of "feminist lobbies" to create "genderless children" and/or to encourage transgender identities in children. An Islamic scholar and academic from anti-gender circles states: "A twelve-year-old girl will be abducted from her family by force and her sex change operation will be paid by the Social Security Institution" (*T24* 2020).

ESSENTIALIST FRAMING

Anti-genderism in the global context deploys an essentialist framing method to present feminism as a monolithic category without internal diversity and targets it as a major "enemy," thereby evoking moral panic about the decay of "core" societal values (Paternotte and Kuhar 2018; Kováts 2017). In the Turkish context, anti-gender actors vernacularize this rhetoric through anti-Western and pro-Islamist framings where recent feminist acquisitions such as the Istanbul Convention are accused of bearing the hallmarks of the "mentality of the Crusades" and being antithetical to so-called socio-cultural and religious realities (*Yeniakit* 2019b). This narrative also frames feminism as a threat to the ontological security of the Turkish state, depicting feminists as terrorists. Sema Maraşlı states: "Terrorists on the mountains and feminists in the city simultaneously attack our beautiful country. Feminists are even more dangerous than terrorists" (*T24* 2019b, translation mine).

This framing of feminism as an attack on the ontological security of the state stems from an understanding of a masculinist state that favors male privileges. The masculinist state grants paternalistic protection to women on the condition that they are docile and submissive (Young 2003). In this equation, paternal authority invests the survival of the nation in the protection of women and envisions a hierarchical interplay between femininities and masculinities where subordination of women to men is ensured and submissiveness and docility are demanded from women in return for protection from internal and external security threats. This patriarchal bargain corresponds to affirmation of docile femininities and marginalization of "subversive" identities. Anti-gender actors utilize this masculinist protection model to code feminism as more dangerous than terrorism. Moreover, this masculinist protection model implies close collaboration with the nationalist political imaginary in Turkey that rests on the idea of national purity and paternalistic protection of women as the carriers of the cultural authenticity and of the difference between the material and the spiritual (Altan-Olcay 2009).

Anti-gender actors' essentialist framing of feminism as a "major enemy" suggests a countermovement dynamic that situates anti-genderism in an antagonistic relationship with feminism and defines its raison d'être over the goal to invert feminist claims about gender and sexuality (Corredor 2019). They aim to establish political alliances and gather support to maintain this counter mobilization, suggesting that a considerable segment of society feels threatened by the feminist movement's achievements and the integration of the feminist terminology into the public debate. This claim about the hegemonic sociopolitical force of the feminist movement serves to cover up the shrinking of space for feminist activism and policy in the recent era. Especially in the post-2011 period, the public space where gender discourse and policy can be formulated through the prism of gender equality has considerably diminished and feminist activism has been marginalized under the pervasive grip of the authoritarian political regime (Aksoy 2018; Doyle 2018; Unal 2019). Feminist NGOs have been increasingly outcast from decision-making processes and replaced with GONGOs that affirm the government's anti-gender, anti-feminist perspective (Koyuncu and Özman 2019). Casting the "gender ideology" as a hegemonic or master narrative in society despite this dramatic crackdown on feminist policy and activism, the anti-gender imaginary engages in a quest for a narrative monoculture, that is, a narrative ecology dominated by a single dominant narrative where other narratives are silenced and/or eliminated (Foroughi et al. 2019). In this narrative monoculture, feminists and other actors accused of serving "gender ideology" cease to be interlocutors but rather become enemies to be demonized.

POST-TRUTH EPISTEMOLOGY

The post-truth epistemology of the current populist era implies that the boundaries between truth and lies have become blurred (D'Ancona 2017; Foroughi et al. 2019). Anti-gender and masculinist communication make considerable use of this epistemology that undermines principles of diversity, tolerance, reason, and truth-seeking. Such communication combines post-truth epistemology with a populist rhetoric that creates adversaries and claims legitimacy through scapegoating feminists and gender ideology.

Anti-gender post-truth epistemology operationalizes different communication styles such fake news production or "rumor bombing," which refers to statements whose veracity is in question (Harsin 2018). These post-truth statements are far from being "innocent rumors" but are powerful rhetorical instruments making use of archetypes, plot lines, characters, images, icons, symbols and other narrative elements to vilify "gender ideology" and to incite the discourse of male victimhood. Stories about husbands, boyfriends, male teachers, prayer leaders at mosques and school shuttle drivers who are claimed to be victims of false accusation in male violence cases become epitomes of discrimination against men in anti-gender post-truth statements. These men are usually depicted as innocent, lower-class family men who work hard to provide for their families:

A 64-year-old honorable family man who works hard as a shuttle driver was falsely accused of assaulting three girls in the shuttle without anyone noticing and sentenced to 15 years. It is evident that this is a lie. His only wrongdoing is not going back to pick up the girls who were late for the shuttle. (Maraşlı 2020b, translation mine)

Female guardians conspire against the male teacher who refused to respond to their demands and accuse him of assaulting their daughters. After the teacher was sentenced to 33 years, they repent and confess their false accusation. What if they didn't? (Maraşlı 2020c, translation mine)

The court cases at stake and the names involved are always held anonymous and the same narrative elements recur in most of the stories: Innocent honorable men who are victims of sexual slander, evil women who conspire against men and a failing justice system. This demonization, scapegoating and claims to male victimhood operate to produce different kinds of adversarial relationships between religious people and seculars who are held responsible for sexual slander, honorable men and evil feminists, and also between "true" Muslims and Islamic feminists who argue for women's right to alimony. These highly affective narrative forms claim truthfulness by using social media as echo chambers where anti-gender truth claims can be established regardless of their factuality. They appropriate social media to invent, spread and perpetuate false stories driven by their political agendas, dislocate the notion of truth and further exacerbate the discourse of male victimhood (Harsin 2018; Marwick and Caplan 2018).

Unsurprisingly, this discourse of victimhood is in tune with the AKP's employment of resentment and vilification of opponents as affective pillars of its authoritarian populist rule (Yılmaz 2017). Resentful subject formation of Turkish Islamist identity that casts pious Muslims as victims of ultra-secular policies of the modernization process is elevated to a new level during the AKP period where populist antagonisms transgress the "secular versus pious" dichotomy and operationalize an "us versus them" mentality to vilify the opponents of the political regime (Tokdoğan 2020). The AKP's assertions of victimhood suggest an antagonistic struggle that intensifies the reactionary mode in the hegemonic social imagination and exclude conditions of democratic pluralism and deliberation. Anti-gender post truth narratives that proliferate the discourse of male victimhood take root in this symbolic ecology fueling feelings of resentment, agony, hate and rage.

CONCLUSION

The recently upsurging anti-gender movement in Turkey has emerged in a symbolic ecology perpetuated by anti-gender, anti-feminist, and masculinist traits of the current authoritarian populist regime. This chapter has demonstrated that the masculinist anxieties of the anti-gender mobilization operate in close connection with the constitutive elements of AKP rule, such as pro-Islamism, familialism, pronatalism, neoconservatism, nationalism, and anti-feminism. AKP officials and the pro-government media frequently resonate with anti-gender demands in target policy areas, namely, divorce laws, alimony, child custody and violence against women and generate discursive opportunity structures that amplify the anti-gender movement's efficacy in public debate.

This chapter has also demonstrated that the anti-gender mobilization is not a simple spillover or a continuation of the AKP's anti-feminist politics. Although it largely borrows from the AKP's religiously accentuated reshuffling of the gender regime, it comprises new ideological components and rhetorical styles, such as hijacking the feminist egalitarian discourse to defend men's and fathers' rights, and operationalizing the discourse of male victimhood and the rhetoric of the crisis of masculinity. These discursive techniques are utilized to push the AKP to annul the existing legal mechanisms ensuring gender equality and to reinvent and re-engineer the sociocultural and legal fabric through an aggressive affective discourse on male victimization.

The anti-gender reaction to the Istanbul Convention and women's alimony rights figures as the main site where the movement's actors develop repertoires of contention and collective action frames to develop a shared understanding about the alleged problem of "gender ideology." This symbolic framing process is fueled by a pro-Islamist, nationalist and anti-Western outlook and by a male victimization discourse that works to purify the AKP's policy vision from a seemingly pro-woman discourse. In this sense, it coopts the AKP's anti-feminist, yet seemingly woman-friendly stance represented by GONGOs such as KADEM and works to radicalize it in the legal sphere.

This narrative ecology deploys certain discursive tactics and mechanisms such as essentialist framing and post-truth epistemology to respond to the alleged crisis of hegemonic masculinity. As this chapter has demonstrated, these rhetorical strategies rely on simplification, vilification and antagonistic scapegoating enacted through post-truth epistemologies and essentialist fixation of opponents' positions. They perpetuate the "us versus them" divide and vilify opponents as enemies, negating any possibility for pluralism tolerance, reason, deliberation and truth-seeking. It is in this narrative ecology where the rising anti-gender mobilization enacts a ruthless performance of hypermasculine discourse in Turkey, pushing the AKP to an "uncompromised" masculinist policy vision.

BIBLIOGRAPHY

Acar, Feride, and Gülbanu Altunok. 2013. "The Politics of Intimate at the Intersection of Neo-liberalism and Neo-conservativism in Turkey." *Women's Studies International Forum* 41 (1): 14–23.

Adak, Sevgi. 2020. "Expansion of the Diyanet and the Politics of the Family in Turkey under AKP Rule." *Turkish Studies.* https://doi.org/10.1080/14683849. 2020.1813579.

Ahvalnews. 2020. "Turkey Will Review Measures in Women's Rights Convention." February 19, 2020. https://ahvalnews.com/women/turkey-will-review-measures -womens-rights-convention-erdogan-says.

Akkan, Basak. 2018. "The Politics of Care in Turkey: Sacred Familialism in a Changing Political Context." *Social Politics: International Studies in Gender, State & Society* 25 (1): 72–91.

Aksoy, Hurcan Aslı. 2018. "Gendered Strategies between Democratization and Democratic Reversal: The Curious Case of Turkey." *Politics and Governance* 6 (3): 101–111.

Akyuz, Selin, and Ferda Sayan Cengiz. 2016. "Overcome Your Anger if You Are a Man: Silencing Women's Agency to Voice Violence Against Women." *Women's Studies International Forum* 57: 1–10.

Altan-Olcay, Özlem. 2009. "Gendered Project of National Identity Formation: The Case of Turkey." *National Identities* 11 (2): 165–186.

Aslanidis, Paris. 2018. "Populism as a Collective Action Master Frame for Transnational Mobilization." *Sociological Forum* 33 (2): 443–464.

Atasoy, Yıldız. 2009. *Islam's Marriage with Neoliberalism*. London: Palgrave Macmillan.

Ayhan, Tutku. 2017. "Protecting the Woman or the Family? Contradiction between the Law and its Practice in Violence Against Women Cases in Turkey." *Siyasal Bilimler Dergisi* 5 (1): 137–162.

Bachetta, Paola, and Margaret Power (eds.). 2013. *Right Wing Women: From Conservatives to Extremists around the World*. New York: Routledge.

BBC. 2012. "Erdogan Sparks Row over Abortion." June 1, 2012. https://www.bbc.com/news/world-europe-18297760

BBC. 2016. "Turkey's Erdogan Warns Muslims Against Birth Control." May 30, 2016. https://www.bbc.com/news/world-europe-36413097.

Benford, Robert, and David Snow. 2000. "Framing Processes and Social Movements: An Overview and Assessment." *Annual Review of Sociology* 26 (1): 611–639.

Bianet. 2018. "153 Kadın Örgütünden Haklarımızdan Vazgeçmeyeceğiz." https://m.bianet.org/bianet/toplumsal-cinsiyet/199623-153-kadin-orgutunden-haklarimizdan-vazgecmeyecegiz.

Blais, Melissa, and Francis Dupuis-Déri. 2012. "Masculinism and the Antifeminist Countermovement." *Social Movement Studies* 11 (1): 21–39.

Çağatay, Selin. 2019. "Varieties of Anti-Gender Mobilizations: Is Turkey A Case?" *LSE Gender Blog*. https://blogs.lse.ac.uk/gender/2019/01/09/varieties-of-anti-gender-mobilizations-is-turkey-a-case/.

Candas, Aysen, and Yıldız Silier. 2014. "Quietly Reverting Public Matters into Private Troubles: Gendered and Class Based Consequences of Care Policies in Turkey." *Social Politics* 21 (1): 103–123.

Cindoglu, Dilek, and Didem Unal. 2017. "Gender and Sexuality in the Authoritarian Discursive Strategies of New Turkey." *European Journal of Women's Studies* 24 (1): 39–54.

Corredor, Elizabeth. 2019. "Unpacking Gender Ideology and the Global Right's Anti-Gender Counter Movement." *Signs: Journal of Women in Culture and Society* 44 (3): 613–638.

Council of Europe. 2020. "Chart of Signature and Ratifications." March 21, 2010. https://www.coe.int/en/web/conventions/full-list/-/conventions/treaty/210/signatures.

Coşar, Simten, and Aylin Özman. 2004. "Centre-right Politics in Turkey after the November 2002 General Election." *Contemporary Politics* 10 (1): 57–74.

Coşar, Simten, and Metin Yeğenoğlu. 2011. "New Grounds for Patriarchy in Turkey? Gender Policy in the Age of AKP." *South European Society and Politics* 16 (4): 555–573.

D'Ancona, Matthew. 2017. *Post-Truth: The New War on Truth and How to Fight Back*. New York: Random House.

Darakchi, Shaban. 2019. "Western Feminists Want to Make Us Gay: Nationalism, Heteronormativity and Violence Against Women in Bulgaria." *Sexuality and Culture* 23: 1208–1229.

Diken. 2020. "Metropoll Anketi: 10 Kişiden 6'sı İstanbul Sözleşmesi'nden Çekilmeyi Onaylamıyor." July 26, 2020. http://www.diken.com.tr/metropoll-anketi-on-kiside n-altisi-istanbul-sozlesmesinden-cikmayi-onaylamiyor/.

Diyanet-sen. 2020. "Istanbul Convention Should Be Abolished Before It Destroys the Family." May 17, 2020. http://www.diyanetsen.org.tr/istanbul-sozlesmesi-aileyi -yok-etmeden-feshedilmelidir.

Doyle, Jessica. 2018. "Government Cooptation of Civil Society: Exploring the AKP's role within Turkish Women's CSO's." *Democratization* 25 (3): 445–463.

Eksi, Betül, and Elizabeth Wood. 2019. "Right-wing Populism as Gendered Performance: Janus-Faced Masculinity in the Leadership of Putin and Erdogan." *Theory and Society* 48: 733–751.

Eraslan, Sibel. 2019. "Istanbul Sözleşmesinin Ağır Yükü." *Star*, December 4, 2019. https://www.star.com.tr/yazar/istanbul-sozlesmesinin-agir-yuku-yazi-1498177/.

Esen, Berk, and Sebnem Gumuscu. 2016. "Rising Competitive Authoritarianism in Turkey." *Third World Quarterly* 37 (9): 1581–1606.

Eslen-Ziya, Hande. 2020. "Right-wing Populism in Turkey: Leading to all New Grounds for Troll Science in Gender Theory." *HTS Theological Studies* 76 (3): 1–9.

Foroughi, Hamid, Yiannis Gabriel, and Marianna Fotaki. 2019. "Leadership in a Post-Truth Era: A New Narrative Disorder." *Leadership* 15 (2): 135–151.

GazeteDuvar. 2019. "Turkish Family Platform against 8 March." March 8, 2019. https://www.gazeteduvar.com.tr/gundem/2019/03/08/turkiye-aile-meclislerinden -8-mart-karsiti-cagri/.

Gotell, Lise, and Dutton, Emily. 2016. "Sexual Violence in the Manosphere: Antifeminist Men's Rights Discourses on Rape." *International Journal for Justice, Crime and Social Democracy* 5 (2): 65–80.

Graff, Agniezska, and Elzbieta Korolczuk. 2018. "Gender as "Ebola from Brussels": The Anti-colonial Frame and the Rise of Illiberal Populism." *Signs, Journal of Women in Culture and Society* 43 (4): 797–821.

Graff, Agnieszka, Ratna Kapur, and Suzanna Danuta Walters. 2019. "Introduction: Gender and the Rise of the Global Right." *Signs: Journal of Women in Culture and Society* 44 (3): 541–560.

Güneş-Ayata, Ayse, and G. Doğangün. 2017. "Gender Politics of the AKP: Restoration of a Religio-conservative Gender Climate." *Journal of Balkan and Near Eastern Studies* 19 (6): 610–627.

Guardian. 2014. "Erdogan: Women not Equal to Men." November 24, 2014. https://www.theguardian.com/world/2014/nov/24/turkeys-president-recep-tayyip-erdogan-women-not-equal-men.

Guardian. 2016. "Turkish President Says Childless Women are Deficient, Incomplete." June 6, 2016. https://www.theguardian.com/world/2016/jun/06/turkish-president-erdogan-childless-women-deficient-incomplete.

Habervakti. 2020. "Turkish Family Assembly Will Organize a Panel about Family in Istanbul." February 17, 2020. https://www.habervakti.com/kadin/turkiye-aile-meclisi-istanbul-da-aile-konulu-panel-h95799.html.

Harsin, Jayson. 2018. "Post Truth Populism: The French Anti Gender Theory Movement and Cross-Cultural Similarities." *Communication Culture and Critique* 11 (1): 35–52.

Iğsız, Aslı. 2008. "Documenting the Past and Publicizing Personal Stories: Sensescapes and the 1923 Greco Turkish Population Exchange." *Journal of Modern Greek Studies* 26 (2): 451–487.

Independent Türkçe. 2019. "The Debate on KADEM on Social Media is Getting Tense." July 9, 2019. https://www.independentturkish.com/node/49646/haber/sosyal-medyadaki-kadem-tart%C4%B1%C5%9Fmas%C4%B1-b%C3%BCy%C3%BCyor-aile-yap%C4%B1s%C4%B1na-ters-mi-de%C4%9Fil-mi.

Johnson, Paul Elliot. 2017. "The Art of Masculine Victimhood: Donald Trump's Demagoguery." *Women's Studies in Communication* 40 (3): 229–250.

Kadıoğlu, Ayse. 2010. "The Pathologies of Turkish Republican Laicism." *Philosophy and Social Criticism* 36 (4): 489–504.

Kadın Cinayetlerini Durduracağız Platformu. 2020. "Veriler." April 1, 2020. http://kadincinayetlerinidurduracagiz.net/kategori/veriler?sayfa=6.

Kandiyoti, Deniz. 2013. "Fear and Fury: Women and Post-revolutionary Violence." January 10, 2013. https://www.opendemocracy.net/en/5050/fear-and-fury-women-and-post-revolutionary-violence/.

Kandiyoti, Deniz. 2016. "Locating the Politics of Gender: Patriarchy, Neoliberal Governance and Violence in Turkey." *Research and Policy on Turkey* 1 (2): 103–118.

Kaplan, Hilal. 2020a. "Istanbul Sözleşmesi Yaşatır mı?" *Sabah*, August 7, 2002. https://www.sabah.com.tr/yazarlar/hilalkaplan/2020/08/07/istanbul-sozlesmesi-yasatir-mi.

Kaplan, Hilal. 2020b. "Feminizim ve Eşcinsellik." *Sabah*, May 1, 2020. https://www.sabah.com.tr/yazarlar/hilalkaplan/2020/05/01/feminizm-ve-escinsellik-aileyi-tahribinbaslangicnoktasi.

Kaya, Ayhan. 2015. "Islamization of Turkey under the AKP Rule: Empowering Family, Faith and Charity." *South European Society and Politics* 20 (1): 47–69.

Kocamaner, Hikmet. 2019. "Regulating the Family Through Religion: Secularism, Islam and the Politics of the Family in Contemporary Turkey." *American Ethnologist*. https://doi.org/10.1111/amet.12836.

Korkman, Zeynep. 2015. "Blessing Neoliberalism: Economy, Family and the Occult in Millennial Turkey." *Journal of the Ottoman and Turkish Studies Association* 2 (2): 335–357.

Kováts, Ezster. 2017. "The Emergence of Powerful Anti-Gender Movements in Europe and the Crisis of Liberal Democracy." In *Gender and Far Right Politics in Europe*, edited by Michaela Köttig, Renate Bitzan, and Andrea Petö, 175–189. Basingstoke: Palgrave Macmillan.

Kováts, Ezster, and Maari Põim (eds). 2015. *Gender as Symbolic Glue: The Position and Role of Conservative and Far Right Parties in the Anti-gender Mobilization in Europe*. Brussels: Foundation for European Progressive Studies and Friedrich-Ebert-Stiftung Budapest.

Koyuncu, Berrin, and Aylin Özman. 2019. "Women's Rights Organizations and the Turkish State in the post-2011 Era: Ideological Disengagement versus Conservative Alignment." *Turkish Studies* 20 (5): 728–753.

Kuhar, Roman, and David Paternotte. 2017. *Anti-gender Campaigns in Europe: Mobilizing against Equality*. London: Rowman & Littlefield.

Lüküslü, Demet. 2016. "Creating a Pious Generation: Youth and Education Policies of the AKP in Turkey." *Southeast European and Black Sea Studies* 16 (4): 637–649.

Maraşlı, Sema. 2018. *Güçlü Kadınlar Neden Mutlu Değil?* (Why are Powerful Women not Happy?) Istanbul: Motto Yayınları.

Maraşlı, Sema (@Semamarasli). 2020a. *Twitter*. March 8, 2020, 9:17 pm. https://twitter.com/Semamarasli/status/1236732902676869123.

Maraşlı, Sema (@Semamarasli). 2020b. *Twitter*. March 24, 2020, 5:54 pm. https://twitter.com/Semamarasli/status/1242479848431308801.

Maraşlı, Sema (@Semamarasli). 2020c. *Twitter*. August 11, 2020, 5:51 pm. https://twitter.com/Semamarasli/status/1293198355145928705.

Marwick, Alice, and Robyn Caplan. 2018. "Drinking Male Tears: Language, the Manosphere and the Networked Harassment." *Feminist Media Studies* 18 (4): 543–559.

Mayer, Stefanie, and Birgit Sauer. 2017. "Gender Ideology in Austria: Coalitions around an Empty Signifier." In *Anti-gender Campaigns in Europe: Mobilizing against Equality*, edited by Roman Kuhar, and David Patternote, 23–40. London: Rowman & Littlefield.

Mellström, Ulf. 2018. "In the Time of Masculinist Political Revival." *NORMA* 11 (3): 135–138.

MepaNews. 2020. "NGO Statements: The Istanbul Convention is not Binding." February 22, 2020. https://www.mepanews.com/stklardan-ortak-bildiri-istanbul-sozlesmesi-nas-degildir-feshedilebilir-34090h.htm.

Milliyet. 2019. "Erdogan Announced Revision of Alimony in the Legal Reform." October 6, 2019. https://www.milliyet.com.tr/siyaset/cumhurbaskani-erdogan-kizilcahamamda-acikladi-nafaka-2-yargi-paketine-giriyor-6047406.

Mutluer, Nil. 2019. "The Intersectionality of Gender, Sexuality and Religion: Novelties and Continuities in Turkey during the AKP Era." *Southeast European and Black Sea Studies* 19 (1): 99–118.

Nicolas, Lucy, and Christine Agius. 2017. *The Persistence of Global Masculinism: Discourse, Gender and Neocolonial Articulations*. New York: Palgrave.

Norris, Pippa, and Ronald Inglehart. 2019. *Cultural Backlash: Trump, Brexit and Authoritarian Populism*. Cambridge: Cambridge University Press.

Ozbay, Cenk, and Ozan Soybakis. 2020. "Political Masculinities: Gender, Power and Change." *Social Politics* 27 (1): 27–50.

Özkazanç, Alev. 2019. "The New Episode of Anti-gender Politics in Turkey." *LSE Engenderings*. https://blogs.lse.ac.uk/gender/2019/05/20/new-episode-anti-gender-turkey/.

Paternotte, David, and Kuhar, Roman. 2018. "Disentangling and Locating the "Global Right": Anti-Gender Campaigns in Europe." *Politics and Governance* 6 (3): 6–19.

Saresma, Tuija. 2018. "Gender Populism: Three Cases of Finns Party Actors' Traditionalist Antifeminism." In *Populism on the Loose*, edited by Urpo Kovala, Emilia Palonen, Maria Ruotsalainen, and Tuija Saresma, 177–200. Jyväskylä: Jyväskylän Yliopisto

Sivilsayfalar. 2018. "Family Platform: No Penalty for Throwing out the Father." August 2, 2018. http://www.sivilsayfalar.org/2018/08/02/aile-platformu-kediyi-attiginizda-bile-cezasi-var-babayi-attiginizda-yok/.

Snow, David, Robert D. Benford, Holly J. McCammon, Lyndi Hewitt, and Scott Fitzgerald. 2014. "The Emergence, Development, and Future of the Framing Perspective: 25+ Years Since Frame Alignment." *Mobilization: An International Quarterly* 19 (1): 23–46.

Sönmez, Berrin. 2019. "Erken Evlilik Değil o, Çocuk Istismarı." *GazeteDuvar*, January 17, 2019. https://www.gazeteduvar.com.tr/yazarlar/2019/01/17/erken-evlilik-degil-o-cocuk-istismari.

Star. 2020. "Istanbul Sozlesmesi Güven Verecek Hale Getirilmeli." July 18, 2020. https://www.star.com.tr/guncel/tgtv-baskani-akbulut-istanbul-sozlesmesi-guven-verecek-hale-getirilmeli-haber-1468096/.

T24. 2019a. "Erdogan Said Istanbul Convention is not Binding." January 4, 2019. https://t24.com.tr/haber/muslumanlara-tehdit-oldugu-savunulan-istanbul-sozlesmesi-icin-erdogan-feshedilebilir-dedi,824334.

T24. 2019b. "'Feministler teröristlerden daha tehlikeli' diyen Sema Maraşlı'yı Akit TV önünde protesto eden kadınlar adli kontrol şartıyla serbest." October 17, 2019. https://t24.com.tr/haber/feministler-teroristlerden-daha-tehlikeli-diyen-sema-marasli-yi-akit-tv-onunde-protesto-eden-kadinlara-tutuklama-talebi,844129.

T24. 2020. "Istanbul Sozleşmesi çok Kan Dökecek." August 10. https://t24.com.tr/haber/prof-ebubekir-sofuoglu-istanbul-sozlesmesi-cok-kan-dokecek-cinsiyet-degistirmek-isteyen-cocuklar-ailelerinden-zorla-alinabilecek,895908.

Tansel, Cemal Burak. 2018. "Authoritarian Neoliberalism and Democratic Backsliding in Turkey: Beyond the Narratives of Progress." *South European Society and Politics* 23 (2): 197–217.

Tokdoğan, Nagehan. 2020. "Reading Politics Through Emotions: Ontological Resentment as the Emotional Basis of Current Politics in Turkey." *Nations and Nationalisms* 26 (2): 388–406.

Unal, Didem. 2019. "The Abortion Debate and Profeminist Coalition Politics in Turkey." *Politics & Gender* 15 (4): 801–825.

Unal, Didem, and Dilek Cindoglu. 2013. "Reproductive Citizenship in Turkey: Abortion Chronicles." *Women's Studies International Forum* 38: 21–31.

Verloo, Mieke, and Paternotte, David. 2018. "The Feminist Project Under Threat in Europe." *Politics and Governance* 6 (3): 1–5.

Yarar, Betül. 2020. "Neoliberal-Neoconservative Feminisms in Turkey: Politics of Female Bodies/Subjectivities and the Justice and Development Party's Turn to Authoritarianism." *New Perspectives on Turkey*. https://doi.org/10.1017/npt.2020.18.

Yeniakit. 2019a. "Sema Maraşlıdan Başörtülü Feministler Çıkışı." May 2, 2019. https ://www.yeniakit.com.tr/haber/yazar-sema-Maraşlıdan-basortulu-feministler-cikisi-bu-kadinlar-muslumanlara-din-karsitlarindan-daha-fazla-zarar-veriyorlar-735234 .html.

Yeniakit. 2019b. "Istanbul Convention is Assassination of the Family." August 27, 2019. https://www.yeniakit.com.tr/haber/istanbul-sozlesmesi-aileye-suikasttir-902 514.html.

Yılmaz, Zafer. 2017. "The AKP and the Spirit of New Turkey: Imagined Victim, Reactionary Mood and Resentful Sovereign." *Turkish Studies* 18 (3): 482–513.

Yinanç, Barçın. 2017. "Turkey Should Stick to Istanbul Convention on Violence Against Women." *Hurriyet Daily News*, July 31, 2017. https://www.hurriyetdaily news.com/turkey-should-stick-to-istanbul-convention-on-violence-against-women -116127.

Young, Iris Marion. 2003. "The Logic of Masculinist Protection: Reflections on the Current Security State." *Signs* 29 (1): 1–25.

Chapter 5

Nature Lovers and Fuzzy Headed Thinkers

Emotion, Outdoors Masculinity, and the Birth of Anti-Environmentalism

Nicholas Blower

One summer morning in 1952, several hundred people gathered near the edge of the Colorado River to see Michael Straus open the Granby Pumping Plant. The plant was a technical achievement: a vast complex that would fill a reservoir large enough to sustain half the state of Colorado. Yet Straus— the commissioner of major hydroelectric developer the US Bureau of Reclamation—did not linger on Granby as an engineering feat. Instead, he used his pulpit to warn the crowd about activists seeking to stall the region's hydrological development. He characterized these groups as lounging in "air-conditioned caves overlooking Central Park in New York, Lincoln Park in Chicago, and Boston Commons" (as sited in Powell 2008, 107). These men were the "transplanted westerner who has a tendency to forget his heritage" (107). Conjuring visions of a domesticated foe unable to overcome Western hardships, Straus depicted early environmentalism as effeminate.

Environmental historians have referenced Straus's speech many times. It has been identified as a contentious moment in a greatly scrutinized battle-ground: the hydroelectric development of the Colorado River. This conflict, in its most intense form, lasted from the early-1950s to the early 1970s. Yet existing scholarly investigations have focused on the activities of conservation groups: how their campaigns against hydroelectricity helped broaden recreational agendas and produced the modern environmental movement (Farmer 1999; Gottlieb 2005, 76–77, 80–82; Martin 1989; Nash 2001). Few have explored the *reception* of these organizations by a dubious public (Harvey 2000). By contrast, this chapter traces the evolving rhetoric critics deployed to discredit early American environmentalists. It explores how this discourse engaged with contemporary fears about masculinity to reinforce a persuasive, populist narrative.

The model of populism examined in this chapter had little contemporary analogue within the United States. Mid-century anti-conservationists did not consider themselves populists. They influenced audiences that would have only been able to offer a general definition of the term, or that considered populism the practice of grassroots movements that collapsed at the end of the nineteenth century (Nugent 2013, 4). The populism practiced by these critics was, therefore, largely embryonic, and it targeted a comparatively nascent environmental movement. As such, it was diffuse and lacked any formal political allegiance, though its intellectual descendants would be almost uniformly drawn toward anti-statist, right-wing activism. That said, mid-century anti-conservationists clearly fit definitions that conceive of populism as a political strategy (Dorraj and Dodson 2009; Woods 2014, 15–16). Key orators were typically regional politicians, newspaper editors, and engineering executives that sought to stoke the anger of grassroots workers, without being "grassroots" themselves. Their rhetoric, too, anticipated later US populist movements that sought to frame complex political issues as a conflict between two homogeneous groups, one a "pure" working class and one an antagonistic "elite" (Mudde and Kaltwasser 2017, 5–6). Collectively, these critics reframed the Colorado hydroelectric conflicts into a tale of hardscrabble Western laborers versus a corrupt environmental movement.

Wealth and class frequently made nature's protectors a "corrupt elite" in 1950s and 1960s anti-conservationist narratives about the Colorado River, but not as frequently as their failed masculinity. The chapter begins by examining how satirical and serious portraits alike relied on the idea that conservationists deviated from contemporary white masculine norms. Populist anti-conservationist rhetoric drew upon wider debates that believed American masculinity was in crisis (Schlesinger 1958; Gilbert 2005, 61). Preservationists were identified as prepubescent, infirm, or housebound; they did not meet masculine criteria physiologically or psychologically. These standards of male appearance and behavior were themselves shaped by frontier narratives and histories that had occurred in Western environments similar to where many Southwestern hydroelectric conflicts played out. The ideal Westerner was muscular, vital, strong, decisive, and emotionally reserved. Conservationists by contrast were portrayed as old, soft bodied, emotional, indecisive, and irrational. They possessed traits typically considered feminine.

The chapter then turns to assessing how conservationists sought to reject this critical rhetoric by promoting their own masculine integrity. Conservationists recognized that populist attacks focused on their *identity* rather than their philosophical underpinnings or political allegiances. They responded with their own media campaigns, publicizing their capacity to endure Western, "frontier" hardships. Rather than offering a new vision of manhood when definitions of masculinity were in flux, they sought to show the ways they belonged to a masculine orthodoxy that cultural critics feared was in decline.

Finally, the chapter explores the contradictions encountered by populist *and* environmentalist arguments when they related to masculine ideals. Populist rhetoric collided with debates about hydroelectricity and gender; whether dams produced new opportunities for manly, grassroots labor, or hastened the explosion of suburbia where male authority was eroded. By contrast, conservationists resisted this hydraulic society—and increasingly, the consumer culture that many saw as threatening masculinity at mid-century. Yet while they articulated a brand of conservation rooted in masculine athleticism, they failed to do so without implicating themselves as the elitist group of populist rhetoric. Month-long hiking expeditions and mountainous ascents promised male rejuvenation in an age of consumerism but were economically far beyond the reach of the American middle class.

In the wider sense, this study also provides insight into how potent populist critiques of masculinity could be when other elements of difference were harder to identify. Both pro- and anti-environmental groups operating in 1950s and 1960s Utah and Arizona were overwhelmingly white, male, middle- or upper-middle class, Republican, and from the trans-Mississippi region. Race, seen as a reliable differentiating factor by many Americans in the period, and a frequent cause of social discord, was almost entirely absent in these conflicts. Class emerges as the most prominent secondary critique here, though its presence ebbs and flows, and was typically marshalled to support attacks on environmentalist masculinity.

CONSERVATIONISTS AND MASCULINE NORMS

Critics of American conservation had presented its followers as failing to adhere to normative masculine behavior long before the Colorado conflicts began. The *San Francisco Call* had pioneered this approach in the 1910s by caricaturing preservationist forefather John Muir as a crossdresser. The paper placed him in elaborate women's attire, complete with dress, apron, and flowered bonnet. Using a broom, Muir "fussily and fruitlessly" attempted to sweep away the floodwaters of O'Shaughnessy dam (Rome 2006, 441–442; Unger 2008, 5). San Francisco engineer Marsden Manson similarly argued Muir's writings were full of "verbal lingerie," "feathers," "plumes," and "embroideries" (Righter 2005, 90). To environmental historian Adam Rome, early critics reenvisioned conservationists as "political hermaphrodites" (2006). Though these writers never precisely defined what they felt was normative male behavior, they recognized accusations of femininity and androgyny were an effective political strategy in an industrial development conflict.

Michael Straus's 1952 speech at Granby Pumping Plant similarly invoked the specter of gender ambiguity. In the early 1950s, conflict loomed within Dinosaur National Monument on the Utah-Colorado border, where the Bureau of Reclamation planned two structures: a high-wall dam at Echo Park, where the Green and Yampa Rivers met, and a smaller downstream dam at Split Mountain. For conservationists, any dam within the borders of Dinosaur risked the sanctity of the wider National Park System. Many spoke out in emotionally charged language. The most famous of these responses was a 1950 *Saturday Evening Post* article with the incendiary title "Shall We Let Them Ruin Our National Parks?" (DeVoto 1950, 17; see also Maher 2008, 224; Scheffer 1991, 118). Written with vivid prose by popular Western historian Bernard DeVoto, the piece asked if Americans, "wanted their sovereign rights, and those of their descendants . . . wiped out" (DeVoto 1950, 17; see also Wehr 2004, 197).

The sense of an impending conservation crisis in the early 1950s was broadly paralleled by more widespread concerns about a crisis of masculinity. By 1955, a "chorus of prophets" blamed aggressive women, a centralizing society, the monotony of office jobs, and a range of other ills for uncertainty about the "correct" way to be male (Gilbert 2005, 62). For many in the West, DeVoto's calls for aesthetic landscape protection further muddied these waters; he challenged the long-standing view that Western masculinity was synonymous with natural conquest. A Pulitzer Prize-winning scholar, he was already infamous within his home state of Utah for his criticism of Mormon culture (Stegner 1985, 153–154). DeVoto was certainly aware of debates about manhood in the American Southwest. He noted in 1946 that a post-war proliferation of beards and cowboy hats revealed that "anxious" Westerners were terrified they had "not inherited *all* the frontier masculinity," and argued these symbols were hollow bluster (DeVoto 2005, 55). Still, the vociferous reaction against his *Saturday Evening Post* article surprised him. One incendiary attack on the writer by *The Denver Post* infantilized DeVoto and started to call him and his followers the "nature boys" for their resistance (Harvey 2000, 98). Such critiques drew upon elements of the decade's sense of "male panic" (Thomas 2008, 19; Moss 2011, 107). Cultural observers increasingly expressed fears about the post-war extension of adolescence, which social scientists increasingly connected to rising homosexual behavior (Lunbeck 1997, 231–232).

Allusions to homosexuality were not the only ways in which conservationists were presented as threatening the normative boundaries of white mid-century masculinity. While some newspapers identified conservationists as adolescent and psychologically stunted, others used age to imply physical weakness and infirmity. Northern Utah's *Vernal Express* published what it called a "humorous skit" about visiting Dinosaur and listening to the "old, whiskered" members of the Wilderness Society offer a rambling and incoherent lecture (Cochran 1954, 13). The *Tucson Daily Citizen* argued that conservationists should not seek to visit the wilderness as they were "not so hardy" ("Douglas Leads Hike" 1954, 3). Even in age, the implication of adolescence or emotional immaturity remained. Columnist Clark Smith of the *Arizona Republic* described movement members as stuck in rocking chairs, angry at the world but no longer able to affect it (1953, 2). By 1954, the idea of an impotent (and often elderly) male fuming about nature from his home became the predominant image of Echo Park's defenders.

These emasculating portraits further revealed their populist impulses by simultaneously branding conservationists as part of a distant elite. To be male yet housebound not only implied a feminine preference for the domestic; conservationists' homes were simultaneously framed as expansive, urban abodes with air conditioning and several creature comforts. Accusations of wealth seemed to reinforce masculine failings, and these arguments proved remarkably persuasive. Populist regional commentary about cloistered conservationists graduated to the national stage in less than two years. An article in *Time* referred to conservationists as "professional nature lovers . . . all of whom wear shoes and live in houses while writing about the great outdoors" ("Old Car Peddler" 1954, 16). A piece six months earlier in *Life* linked "nature lovers" to an image of Washington's political elite ("Sounds of Anguish" 1954, 46). That representation was typical for articles that sporadically updated readers on the Echo Park conflict. Photography presented conservationists as elderly, stooped men in claustrophobic and privileged settings.

The term used by *Life* and *Time*—"nature lovers"—was particularly prevalent in Western presses as the anti-activist machinery accelerated in 1951. Many recognized the term as a gendered insult used by ardent industrial developers like Straus, fellow bureau leader Floyd Dominy, and Utah representative William A. Dawson, who feared American preservationism's growing political clout (Harvey 2000, 194). In 1962, Joseph Wood Krutch, a Western naturalist, argued that the phrase evolved during the Echo Park conflict into a "contemptuous epithet" (Krutch 1962, 338). One Utahn hunter felt it desperately unfair he and his friends had been branded "'nature lovers' in such a derogatory fashion" ("Outdoor Roundup" 1951, 9). "The Old Nature Lover is a dramatic-type character, so you'll have to forgive his fancy talk," wrote one columnist, before bemoaning that such individuals acted as the "self-appointed handmaidens of spring" (Smith 1953, 2). A cartoon that ran in a number of regional Western papers prominently depicted US Forest Service Icon Smokey the Bear finding a still-lit campfire (and littered camping ground) and angrily exclaiming "NATURE LOVERS!" The

accompanying text simply stated, "A *queer* way of showing appreciation for
. . . man's handiwork!" ("Smokey Says" 1953, 8).

What specific insult was meant by the phrase was a little harder to parse.
Elite, urbane authors had sporadically called writers of the American West
and Southwest "nature lovers" since the 1930s. Often used in tandem with the
then-pejorative "regionalist," the accusation implied an author offered a pro-
vincial perspective and exhibited questionable intellectual ability (Davidson
1991, 65–66). Many of those initially branded as "nature lovers" were female
writers who anticipated the concerns of post-war conservation, writing
critically of technology and contesting the ingrained ideology of progress
(Schaefer 2004, 7). In essence, "nature lovers" was veiled shorthand used
to attack feminine perspectives that male critics saw as overly emotional.
Its transformation into anti-environmentalist slogan did little to change this.
When DeVoto and others were feminized into "nature lovers," critics argued
their temperaments made them ignorant of broader societal affairs. It was a
way of declaring they should not comment on the traditionally male discourse
of a region's water and power needs, and a way of reinforcing gender boundaries many felt were collapsing (Righter 2005, 90).

RE-MASCULINIZING CONSERVATION

Members involved in the conservation coalition to save Echo Park recognized the battle over Dinosaur National Monument was more than a conflict
to preserve the sanctity of the National Park System. Several groups saw the
national and regional media's new interest in preserving nature as a chance
to achieve popular support. This awareness was particularly keen for David
Brower, executive director of Californian conservation group the Sierra Club
(Dunaway 2005, 117–118). Most of Brower's daily efforts in the 1950s went
toward establishing a publishing program for the Club. Going to work in
downtown San Francisco each morning in a suit and tie, and surrounded by
images of distant landscapes, he often appeared more as wilderness salesman
than wilderness warrior. In this respect, Brower embodied the very model
of the urban, elite, domesticated environmentalist derided in populist anti-
conservationist commentary.

David Brower neither saw himself nor his fellow conservationists in these
terms. He had learned about conservation by reading back issues of the *Sierra
Club Bulletin*, devouring the exploits of his predecessors—who were overwhelmingly male—the way "one would read the Bible" (Brower 1980, 12).
The mountaineering accounts of early Sierra Club hikers certainly evoked the
American West entrenched in the national imagination—a pungently rough
space of hypermasculine achievement. Brower was seduced by the idea of

conservationists as explorers and pioneers. He believed they could be sold to the public in the same way, and that this image would be more powerful than critical portraits that characterized movement members as feminine shut-ins. By 1952, he planned to salvage conservation's image not by articulating a new model for masculinity, but by associating it with the traditions of an idealized American Western past. It was a model of conservation that was still fundamentally about recreation, based on male decisiveness and action, though it further emphasized those mid-century masculine tropes praised by those fearing "manly" decline.

The two Club publications seeking to illustrate this vision were the short film *Wilderness River Trail* (1953) directed by Charles Eggert, and the book *This is Dinosaur* (1955), edited by Western author Wallace Stegner. In publicizing Dinosaur National Monument, both texts were successful, but when it came to selling a masculine image of conservation, both Eggert and Stegner struggled. There were clear tensions between envisioning environmentalists as self-sufficient outdoorsmen and promoting conservation as a popular movement. Prior to the Echo Park campaign, the Club were known for climbing California's Sierra Nevada range, but presenting Dinosaur as a challenging wilderness marked it as a landscape for the few—and played into populist narratives of conservation elitism. When questions of physical fitness entered the equation—Dinosaur had no formal roads—the tensions between expanding popular appeal and restoring masculine reputation were even more keenly illustrated. For Eggert's part, he presented the monument as a remote wilderness that invited masculine challenge, but not one that required herculean effort. It was a difficult middle ground to tread. The film interspersed male action scenes of white-water rafting with families enjoying the quieter spaces of the monument.

This is Dinosaur, edited by Western naturalist Wallace Stegner, fared less well as it pursued similar aims. It too presented conservation as a masculine endeavor, but in doing so subscribed to a vision of Dinosaur more starkly divided by gender. Combining written responses to the monument with an extensive photographic element, all the book's essays were written by men. Its visuals further promoted clear gender distinctions. In *This is Dinosaur*, most photography features men—alone or in small groups—traversing an expansive wilderness. Women appear rarely, and then typically shepherded by husbands or perhaps fathers. The sole image in the text that includes a woman without her spouse is simply titled "Sand Canyon." It depicts what is likely club member Martin Litton's wife guiding her children through the monument (Stegner 1955, n.p.)

These choices reflected that despite populist narratives about effeminate conservationists, many movement members remained allied to mid-century conservative conceptions about gender propriety (Gilbert 2005, 65). Sierra

Club editors and trip-leaders desired to maintain clear cultural and social distinctions between men and women. In aiming to reclaim a masculine image for conservation, they transplanted contemporary gender divisions into the wilderness, presenting what some contemporary observers would have considered a gendered utopia. Women appeared in images to provide a passive contrast to male activity. *This is Dinosaur*'s visual selections are entirely in keeping with historian Susan Schrepfer's assessment of the Club in the 1950s: an organization where activities deemed "masculine" were reserved for male members. Female masculinity had no place in the Club during this decade: women were expected to pursue appropriately "feminine" pursuits. They were expected to remain at camp, look after children while husbands hiked, or pick wildflowers (Schrepfer 2005, 121–125).

VAGUE EMOTIONS

When conservationist Richard Bradley reflected upon successfully blocking the Echo Park project, he mentioned a curious benefit to its outcome. In addition to noting the increased professional competency and lobbying experience that conservation groups acquired, Bradley remarked that success during the project's congressional hearings meant movement members were suddenly taken seriously by the national press. He noted the political impediment caused by the nicknames "nature lovers, bird watchers, wildlifers, self-appointed dogooders, so-called conservationists, [and] fuzzy-headed thinkers" (Bradley 1964, 340).

Conservationist success at Dinosaur National Monument changed popular gendered criticisms. On some level, the "nature lover" caricature that had become entrenched by 1955 was comical rather than threatening. That bumbling, almost satirical portrait became harder for critics to sustain as the ranks of conservation groups swelled after 1960. Westerners saw a broader agenda developing for conservationists. They became involved discussions about chemical fertilizers, pesticides, energy, and overpopulation, even as they sought to prevent further hydroelectric development in Arizona, at Glen Canyon and the Grand Canyon (Wyss 2016, 183). Anti-conservationists, therefore, witnessed a movement undergoing rapid expansion but lacked the vocabulary to articulate what they saw; the term "environmentalist" would not enter common usage until 1970 (Heberlein 2012, 178). As a result, "nature lovers" was increasingly replaced with a more general—and at times frustratingly unclear—critique of conservationist emotion.

What specific emotion was so repellent in conservationists was never quite clear. It was more likely that expressing an arbitrarily determined degree of "excessive" emotion was still deemed a female practice in the mid-1960s. In

1966, *Arizona Daily Star* columnists condemned dam opponents for clouding the issue of Grand Canyon development with "emotional factors" (Humphries 1966, 9). Bureau leader Floyd Dominy also criticized what he called "emotional appeals" the same year ("Dam Foes Accused" 1966, 5). The *Arizona Daily Sun* told subscribers that preservationist resistance to hydroelectric construction in the Grand Canyon was "couched in the same appeal to emotion rather than logic" ("Last Word" 1966, 4). In 1968, the *Tucson Daily Citizen* featured a letter that characterized conservationists as "hysterical and irresponsible" ("Sierra Club's Ad" 1968, 12). One wife, writing to her local paper's advice column in 1965, asked what to do with her husband, who having joined a "nature lovers club" at sixty-one, was experiencing "his second childhood." Disliking his changed personality, she complained: "I am so disgusted with him I could throttle him . . . I don't know what's gotten into him" (Buren 1965, 32). Conservation continued to pervert, for many, the most valued aspects of traditional American Western masculinity. It warped a regional character that many believed had been historically measured and taciturn (Anahita and Mix 2006, 334).

Did the assertion that male conservationists exhibited a greater degree of emotion than was "normal" have much basis? Hydroelectric conflict at Glen and the Grand Canyon occurred in the early and mid-1960s, as urban America began to rethink gender norms, but these debates were barely evident around proposed dam sites in rural Arizona. Vocal conservationists like David Brower and Edward Abbey publicly grieved as Glen Canyon Dam began to fill Lake Powell in 1963, but they were not representative examples of conservationist behavior (Turner 2015, 76–80; Morris 2004, 104–105). Most members of the Sierra Club, Wilderness Society, and other conservation groups bound to these conflicts did not reveal their emotions as readily. Indeed, many privately chafed at the loud public personas of these individuals (Cohen 1988, 412–434; Dunaway 2005, 189–192; Turner 2012, 131).

THE CULT OF THE WORKER

There was also the question of whether more generalist attacks on conservationist emotionality caused these critiques to lose some of their populist character. In one sense, the critical portraits of the 1960s failed to explicitly present conservationists as part of an elite group in the way the previous decade's complaints had. Yet even as gender increasingly seemed the sole point of attack, many Utahns and Arizonans dubious of conservation understood masculinity to be inextricably enmeshed with class. Particularly in rural communities, normative manliness involved working-class professions that environmental activism often opposed. These included, most significantly, infrastructural development jobs, such as construction and road building.

Such pursuits were typically viewed as one of the only remaining ways of honing masculinity in the West in the post-war period (Anahita and Mix 2006, 334). Taxing work remained integral to the construction of rural Western masculinity in the mid-1960s, especially when it was physically arduous. When preservationists sought to prevent *all* development in an area, they not only deprived rural working-class Westerners of employment; they frustrated attempts to construct a meaningful masculine self-image (White 1996, 181). Therefore, as "feminine" environmentalists celebrated nature around southern Utah and northern Arizona in the 1960s, rural residents continued to celebrate the efforts of male labor. In the most remote parts of each state, roads remained symbols of transformative growth well into the late-1960s. This amplified the celebration of infrastructural, working-class masculinity. As historian Jared Farmer notes in a southern Utah context "supplies, medicine, mail, family—all of these were only as close as the roads were passable" (Farmer 1999, 43).

Yet just as conservationists struggled to resolve masculine endeavor with broad appeal, anti-conservationist beliefs about labor and masculinity exhibited their own inconsistencies. The infrastructural jobs that 1960s critics praised were often idealized. Commenters often discounted the engineering degrees many associated careers now required, instead imagining them to be largely outdoors occupations that only demanded strenuous physiques and psychological fortitude (Hultgren 2018, 21). Dams were similarly viewed as populist projects in the 1950s and 1960s because they were linked to expanding the "manly," outdoor professions of farming, logging, and ranching. This was a compelling image that many Westerners found deeply seductive, and the US Bureau of Reclamation eagerly presented the agency's mission as deeply enmeshed with expanding the opportunities of the common worker (Espeland 2000, 1086; Molle et al. 2009, 338). Their outcomes often starkly diverged from this rhetoric, and the egalitarian potential of dams was rarely achieved in practice. Increasingly, water allotments were consumed by large agribusinesses and other Western power projects; bureau leaders were predominantly technocrats that had little kinship with Southwestern laborers (Worster 1992, 102).

Simultaneously, populist rhetoric that supported Southwestern hydroelectric development failed to notice that these superstructures often facilitated suburban lifestyles that many identified as a threat to clearly defined gender roles and male identity. Suburban living—with its reliance on time-saving electronic gadgets and a culture of consumption—intensified the notion of a "male panic" in the 1950s and 1960s. A range of intellectuals feared suburbia encouraged men to be lazy and soft, and that it removed men from their previously strenuous lives where they lived with energy, integrity, and authority (Gilbert 2005, 66).

Some of these intellectuals found a voice within the conservation movement, such as environmental journalist William H. Whyte and Southwestern author Edward Abbey. Abbey opposed dams in part because he believed the conveniences of hydroelectricity encouraged sedentary life and eroded masculinity. He noted that "in the modern techno-industrial culture, it is possible to proceed from infancy to senility without ever knowing manhood" (Kord and Krimmer 2013, 221). Abbey differed starkly from many "environmental" actors that resisted hydroelectric development, being far more cognizant of the challenges faced by Western laborers. Yet he shared the belief of Wilderness Society and Sierra Club leaders that the conservation of nature would perpetuate a traditional form of American Western masculine individualism, rather than erode it.

POPULAR CRITICISM IN THE ENVIRONMENTAL DECADE

Southwestern critics stung by a second conservationist success in 1968 with the abandonment of two more dam projects in the Grand Canyon soon saw the national apotheosis of popular environmentalism. They received scenes of mass participation during America's first "Earth Day" in April 1970 with dismay. The environmental ethic appeared to have thoroughly embedded itself across the nation (Rome 2014; Kennedy, Chok, and Lui 2012, 78). Though scholars have noted strategies of resistance political and economic opponents of environmentalism began to develop during the "environmental decade," popular critics in the American Southwest were lost in an unfamiliar and hostile landscape (Boynton 2015, 8–9). One Utahn columnist expressed it best when he remarked: 'it has come to appear that anyone who is not an "environmentalist" is some kind of public enemy' ("Concern" 1973, 2).

The widespread marches of Earth Day suggested that gender and class critiques had been limited in their ability to stymie environmentalism's growth. Yet as early critics of the movement became more cautious with their rhetoric, national media coverage internalized their arguments. Television interviews and magazine articles involving the environment focused on distraught women, resurrecting earlier perceptions of the cause as a predominantly female and emotional issue. ABC News, covering the fallout of the 1969 Santa Barbara oil spill, filmed a young woman crying about an America she believed was imploding (Dunaway 2015, 35). *Life* magazine quoted another female protestor "quietly weeping," and who said to her interviewer, "I feel as though . . . everyone was murdered" (Dunaway 2015, 41). Rather than focusing on long-standing environmental groups who had become hardened political campaigners, media outlets prioritized those who further linked natural preservation to a loss of emotional control.

Memorable male environmental icons appeared less frequently in the decade, but they were similarly defined by their sensitivity. In 1971, the Keep America Beautiful campaign against littering introduced viewers to Iron Eyes Cody, a "Native" that emerged from a bucolic wilderness and was brought to tears by industrial America. Cody was not remembered for his ideal embodiment of the traits that white society ascribed to manliness. His lone tear for modern pollution reduced him to the "Crying Indian" (Klopotek 2001, 252). Cody's status as an emotive environmental icon isolated him from his masculinity, and from a long Euro-American tradition that used Native imagery to foster outdoors manliness in adolescents (Willow 2010, 70).

Films fictionalizing environmental crises in the decade also depicted a form of male emotionality in line with early anti-environmental critique. Bruce Dern and Michael Douglas won praise for their performances in two "environmental" feature films, the futuristic *Silent Running* (1971) and contemporary nuclear industry critique *The China Syndrome* (1979) (Shapiro 2002, 222). These films were—perhaps subconsciously—deeply critical of male environmentalists. In *Silent Running,* Dern's character Freeman Lowell tends the world's last forest in a space station orbiting earth. He exists in a state of childlike wonder and possesses "not terribly acute intelligence" (Ebert 2016). When the station's crew threaten the woodland, Lowell kills his fellow shipmates, then himself. Viewers are left to question the proportionality of his response. In a similar vein, Michael Douglas's character in *The China Syndrome* is an environmental activist whose presence proves harmful during a looming nuclear disaster. He is "too hotheaded, too quick to . . . challenge authority figures . . . his 'hysterical' reactions appear juvenile, based solely on feeling and not on fact" (Dunaway 2015, 130).

These depictions attempted to articulate environmentalism's evolving relationship with class and populism. The notion of all-encompassing ecological threats animated the environmentalism of 1970 more than natural aesthetics. The apocalyptic rhetoric of Earth Day encouraged Americans to think they had a decade left to save the Earth, and that as a result, environmentalism was a movement for everyone (Nelson 1970; Dowie 1996, 33). This belief temporarily obscured the historic failure of environmental groups to reach beyond their remarkably narrow class and racial boundaries. Additionally, it obfuscated mainstream environmentalism's ignorance of minority and poor communities that had long suffered disproportionately from air and water pollution, chemical dumping, and other environmental concerns (Gottlieb 2005, 323, 328; Leeman 2016, 339–341; Ray 2013, 90–92).

Fears of pervasive environmental disaster similarly had implications for environmentalism and manhood. Increasingly, environmental concern meant recognizing personal vulnerability and rejecting the post-war masculine ideal of invulnerability (Dunaway 2008, 76). To supporters, some degree of emotion was a rational response to a growing body of scientific literature that offered dismal forecasts about environmental health. While environmentalism's critics continued to downplay these warnings, they still underlined that a movement lacking emotional control was dangerous. If environmentalists were right, then this was a time for pragmatism, not histrionics.

CONCLUSION

Male conservationists saw various negative gendered characterizations as they began to contest industrial development in the post-war period: that they were boys, that they were elderly and infirm, and that they lacked the constitution for Western living. These critiques linked the nascent environmental movement to a failure of manhood and fears about the erosion of Western masculinity. Simultaneously, critics sought to feminize environmentalist identity by presenting their positions as overly emotional. In doing so, they relied upon gender stereotypes that conceived of women as inherently more hysterical and less rational than men.

How many critics of early environmentalism genuinely believed their rhetorical attacks is questionable. In the case of government officials like Michael Straus, Floyd Dominy, and William A. Dawson, economic and institutional incentives were more likely explanations for gendered critiques than any real fear about the trajectory of American masculinity. The same holds true for other bureau employees, engineers, and technicians. Uncomfortable with debates about wilderness and the natural sublime, they only engaged in similarly abstract, identity-based attacks as a matter of last resort. Less certain are the motivations of newspaper columnists and Intermountain residents who maintained that environmentalism was an effeminate practice in the years following the Echo Park conflict. As the environmental movement developed and grew, gendered attacks were less likely to be uniformly economic in impetus.

Regardless of underlying belief, these rhetorical battles reveal a widespread feeling among critics that questioning environmentalist masculinity was an effective tool of delegitimization. Early environmental groups countered this by selling an orthodox vision of male identity that presented conservationists as athletic climbers, explorers, and river-runners. The intent of each faction was similar, though not identical, as they pursued the support of different groups. Critics mocked environmentalist masculinity to stoke populist anger;

conservationists reconstructed their male credentials in pursuit of national support. In tandem, these efforts illustrated how important masculinity was to both factions. Criticisms of class, though often secondary, were increasingly inextricable from gendered attacks, as environmental resistance to infrastructural development progressively alienated more Western laborers.

Though the groups in the Colorado River conflicts of the 1950s and 1960s were largely homogenous, an unexamined element of this conflict that invites further research is the role played by Mormonism. Scholars have typically overlooked how the verbal exchanges that cemented environmentalism's Intermountain reputation played out near the epicenter of the Mormon culture region. While the initial gendered criticisms of conservationists were delivered by officials who had little personal connection to the area, these portraits found particularly fertile soil in which to grow, and it is worth considering how Mormonism influenced this growth. While Mormon environmental history has traditionally noted the paradoxical elements between the Mormon faith and environmentalism, more recent work has begun to challenge this, highlighting Mormonism's conservation ethic (Rogers and Godfrey 2019). Considering this research, it is worth considering what forms of environmentalist identity were celebrated within this tradition, and the role masculinity played in this.

The Intermountain West has, in the decades since 1970, produced a series of grassroots anti-environmental movements—from the Sagebrush Rebellion (1980s) to the Bundy family (2010s)—that have eagerly deployed the language of masculinity and class in their critiques of the modern environmental movement (Boggs 2019, 293; McNall 2018, 136–149). These groups have offered a more definable form of populism—explicitly anti-statist and deeply connected to a range of other grassroots and militia movements that have rallied around the Republican right. Yet their beliefs about environmentalism as culturally corrosive to trans-Mississippi masculine and democratic traditions are clearly rooted in the warped images critics pinned on citizen conservation groups in the 1950s and 1960s. Early populist critiques of environmentalist masculinity have, therefore, proven virulent in how they fed into the beliefs of more explicitly populist groups that have influenced a subsequent generation of relations between environmental groups and rural Westerners. Gendered portraits of emotional and irrational environmentalists began in the realm of representation, but in parts of the rural Southwest, these images have graduated to entrenched belief.

BIBLIOGRAPHY

Anahita, Sine, and Tamara L. Mix. 2006. "Retrofitting Frontier Masculinity for Alaska's War against Wolves." *Gender and Society* 20 (3): 332–353.

Boggs, Kyle. 2019. "The Rhetorical Landscapes of the 'Alt Right' and the Patriot Movements: Settler Entitlement to Native Land." In *The Far Right and the Environment: Politics, Discourse and Communication*, edited by Bernhard Forchtner, 293–309. Abingdon: Routledge.

Boynton, Alex. 2015. "Formulating an Anti-Environmental Opposition: Neoconservative Intellectuals During the Environmental Decade." *The Sixties* 8: 1–26.

Bradley, Richard. 1964. "Damming the Colorado River." In *Voices for the Earth: A Treasury of the Sierra Club Bulletin, 1893–1977*, edited by Ann Gillam, 337–341. San Francisco: Sierra Club Books, 1997.

Brower, David. 1980. "Environmental Activist, Publicist, and Prophet." *The Bancroft Library*. https://bancroft.berkeley.edu/ROHO/collections/subjectarea/natres/ sierraclub.html.

Buren, Abigail Van. 1965. "Suddenly Gramps is Nature Lover; is that Natural?" *Ogden Standard-Examiner*, August 1, 1965: 32.

Cochran, Clay L. 1954. "Economist Writes Satire on Nature Lovers Plea." *Vernal Express*, April 15, 1954: 13.

Cohen, Michael P. 1988. *The History of the Sierra Club: 1892–1970*. San Francisco: Sierra Club Books.

"Concern, But Let's Compromise." 1973. *Color Country Spectrum*, August 9, 1973: 2.

"Dam Foes Accused of Scare Tactics." 1966. *Arizona Republic*, June 29, 1966: 5.

Davidson, Donald. 1991. *Regionalism and Nationalism in the United States: The Attack on Leviathan*. New Edition. New Brunswick: Transaction Publishers.

DeVoto, Bernard. 1950. "Shall We Let Them Ruin Our National Parks?" *Saturday Evening Post*, July 22, 1950.

DeVoto, Bernard. 2005. *DeVoto's West: History, Conservation, and the Public Good*. Athens: Ohio University Press.

Dorraj, Manochehr, and Michael Dodson. 2009. "Neo-Populism in Comparative Perspective: Iran and Venezuela." *Comparative Studies of South Asia, Africa, and the Middle East* 29 (1): 137–151.

"Douglas Leads Hike to Save Nature Outpost Near Capital." 1954. *Tucson Daily Citizen*, March 20, 1954: 3.

Dowie, Mark. 1996. *Losing Ground: American Environmentalism at the Close of the Twentieth Century*. Cambridge: MIT Press.

Dunaway, Finis. 2005. *Natural Visions: The Power of Images in American Environmental Reform*. Chicago: University of Chicago Press.

Dunaway, Finis. 2008. "Gas Masks, Pogo, and the Ecological Indian: Earth Day and the Visual Politics of American Environmentalism." *American Quarterly* 60 (1): 67–99.

Dunaway, Finis. 2015. *Seeing Green: The Use and Abuse of American Environmental Images*. Chicago: University of Chicago Press.

Ebert, Robert. 2016. "Silent Running." RogerEbert.com. First published 1971 in *Chicago Sun-Times*. https://www.rogerebert.com/reviews/silent-running-1971.

Eggert, Charles, dir. 1953. *Wilderness River Trail*. San Francisco: Dawson Productions.

Espeland, Wendy Nelson. 2000. "Bureaucratizing Democracy, Democratizing Bureaucracy." *Law & Social Inquiry* 25 (4): 1077–1109.

Farmer, Jared. 1999. *Glen Canyon Dammed: Inventing Lake Powell & the Canyon Country.* Tucson: University of Arizona Press.

Gilbert, James. 2005. *Men in the Middle: Searching for Masculinity in the 1950s.* Chicago: University of Chicago Press.

Gottlieb, Robert. 2005. *Forcing the Spring: The Transformation of the American Environmental Movement.* Washington, DC: Island Press.

Harvey, Mark W. T. 2000. *A Symbol of Wilderness: Echo Park and the American Conservation Movement.* Seattle: University of Washington Press.

Heberlein, Thomas A. 2012. *Navigating Environmental Attitudes.* New York: Oxford University Press.

Hultgren, John. 2018. "Those Who Bring From the Earth: Anti-Environmentalism and the Trope of the White Male Worker." *Ethics, Policy & Environment* 21 (1): 21–25.

Humphries, Harrison. 1966. "Conservationists vs. Dambuilders: Canyon Issue Clouded by Emotional Factors." *Arizona Daily Star*, August 19, 1966: 9.

Kennedy, Mark Thomas, Jay Inghwee Chok, and Jingfang Liu. 2012. "What Does It Mean to be Green? The Emergence of New Criteria for Assessing Corporate Reputation." In *The Oxford Handbook of Corporate Reputation*, edited by Michael L. Barnett and Timothy G. Pollock, 69–93. Oxford: Oxford University Press.

Klopotek, Brian. 2001. "'I Guess Your Warrior Look Doesn't Work Every Time': Challenging Indian Masculinity in the Cinema." In *Across the Great Divide: Cultures of Manhood in the American West*, edited by Matthew Basso, Laura McCall, and Dee Garceau, 251–273. Abingdon: Routledge.

Kord, Susan, and Elisabeth Krimmer. 2013. *Contemporary Hollywood Masculinities: Gender, Genre, and Politics.* New York: Palgrave Macmillan.

Krutch, Joseph Wood. 1962. *More Lives Than One.* New York: William Sloane Associates.

"The Last Word on Birds." 1966. *Arizona Daily Sun*, December 12, 1966: 4.

Leeman, Richard W. 2016. "Environmental Racism and Environmental Justice: Benjamin Chavis Jr. and Issues of Definition and Community." In *Green Voices: Defending Nature and the Environment in American Civic Discourse*, edited by Richard D. Besel and Bernard K. Duffy, 325–352. Albany: State University of New York Press.

Lunbeck, Elizabeth. 1997. *The Psychiatric Persuasion: Knowledge, Gender, and Power in Modern America.* Princeton: Princeton University Press.

Maher, Neil M. 2008. *Nature's New Deal: The Civilian Conservation Corps and the Roots of the American Environmental Movement.* New York: Oxford University Press.

Martin, Russell. 1989. *A Story That Stands Like A Dam: Glen Canyon and the Struggle for the Soul of the West.* New York: Henry Holt and Company.

McNall, Scott G. 2018. *Cultures of Defiance and Resistance: Social Movements in 21st Century America.* Abingdon: Routledge.

Molle, François, Peter P. Mollinga, Phillippus Wester. 2009. "Hydraulic Bureaucracies and the Hydraulic Mission: Flows of Water, Flows of Power." *Water Alternatives* 2 (3): 328–349.

Morris, David Copland. 2004. "Traversing the Timelines." In *Eco-man: New Perspectives on Masculinity and Nature*, edited by Mark Christopher Allister, 98–110. Charlottesville: University of Virginia Press.

Moss, Mark. 2011. *The Media and Models of Masculinity*. Lanham: Lexington Books.

Mudde, Cas and Cristóbal Rovira Kaltwasser. 2017. *Populism: A Very Short Introduction*. New York: Oxford University Press.

Nash, Roderick Frazier. 2001. *Wilderness & the American Mind*. New Haven: Yale University Press.

Nelson, Gaylord. 1970. *America's Last Chance to Preserve the Earth*. Waukesha: Country Beautiful Corporation.

Nugent, Walter. 2013. *The Tolerant Populists: Kansas Populism and Nativism*. Chicago: University of Chicago Press.

"The Old Car Peddler." 1954. *Time*, August 23, 1954: 16.

"Outdoor Roundup with Casey." 1951. *Daily Herald*, June 3, 1951: 9.

Powell, James Lawrence. 2008. *Dead Pool: Lake Powell, Global Warming, and the Future of Water in the West*. Berkeley: University of California Press.

Ray, Sarah Jaquette. 2013. *The Ecological Other: Environmental Exclusion in American Culture*. Tucson: University of Arizona Press.

Righter, Robert W. 2005. *The Battle Over Hetch Hetchy: America's Most Controversial Dam and the Birth of Modern Environmentalism*. New York: Oxford University Press.

Rogers, Jedediah S. and Matthew C. Godfrey. 2019. *The Earth Shall Appear as the Garden of Eden: Essays on Mormon Environmental History*. Salt Lake City: University of Utah Press.

Rome, Adam. 2006. "'Political Hermaphrodites': Gender and Environmental Reform in Progressive America." *Environmental History* 11 (3): 440–463.

Rome, Adam. 2014. *The Genius of Earth Day: How a 1970 Teach-In Unexpectedly Made the First Green Generation*. New York: Hill & Wang.

Schaefer, Heike. 2004. *Mary Austin's Regionalism: Reflections on Gender, Genre, and Geography*. Charlottesville: University of Virginia Press.

Scheffer, Victor B. 1991. *The Shaping of Environmentalism in America*. Seattle: University of Washington Press.

Schlesinger Jr., Arthur. 1958. "The Crisis of American Masculinity." Accessed August 13, 2020. https://classic.esquire.com/article/1958/11/1/the-crisis-of-american-masculinity.

Schrepfer, Susan R. 2005. *Nature's Altars: Mountains, Gender, and American Environmentalism*. Lawrence: University Press of Kansas.

Shapiro, Jerome F. 2002. *Atomic Bomb Cinema: The Apocalyptic Imagination on Film*. Abingdon: Routledge.

"Sierra Club's Ad Brings Warning." 1968. *Tucson Daily Citizen*, January 23, 1968: 12.

Smith, Clark. 1953. "As I See It." *Arizona Republic*, March 9, 1953: 2.

"Smokey Says: Nature Lovers!" 1953. *Orem-Geneva Times*, June 11, 1953: 8.

"Sounds of Anguish From Echo Park." 1954. *Life*, February 22, 1954: 45–46.

Stegner, Wallace. 1985. "Bernard DeVoto." *Western American Literature* 20 (2): 151–164.

Stegner, Wallace, ed. 1955. *This is Dinosaur*. New York: Alfred A. Knopf.

Thomas, Harry. 2008. "Good Old Boy Masculinity and Same-Sex Desire in *Cat on a Hot Tin Roof* and *The Bitterweed Path*." In *Invisible Suburbs: Recovering Protest Fiction in the 1950s United States*, edited by Josh Lukin, 3–22. Jackson: University Press of Mississippi.

Turner, James Morton. 2012. *The Promise of Wilderness: American Environmental Politics Since 1964*. Seattle: University of Washington Press.

Turner, Tom. 2015. *David Brower: The Making of the Environmental Movement*. Berkeley: University of California Press.

Unger, Nancy. 2008. "The Role of Gender in Environmental Justice." *Environmental Justice* 1 (3): 115–120.

Wehr, Kevin. 2004. *America's Fight Over Water: The Environmental and Political Effects of Large-Scale Water Systems*. Abingdon: Routledge.

White, Richard. 1996. "Are You an Environmentalist or Do You Work for a Living?" In *Uncommon Ground: Rethinking the Human Place in Nature*, edited by William Cronon, 171–185. New York: W.W. Norton & Company.

Willow, Anna J. 2010. "Images of American Indians in Environmental Education: Anthropological Reflections on the Politics and History of Cultural Representation." *American Indian Culture and Research Journal* 34 (1): 67–88.

Woods, Dwayne. 2014. "The Many Faces of Populism: Diverse but Not Disparate." In *The Many Face of Populism: Current Perspectives*, edited by Dwayne Woods and Barbara Wejnert, 1–26. Wingley: Emerald Group Publishing.

Worster, Donald. 1992. *Rivers of Empire: Water, Aridity, and the Growth of the American West*. New York: Oxford University Press.

Wyss, Robert. 2016. *The Man Who Built the Sierra Club: A Life of David Brower*. New York: Columbia University Press.

Part II

POPULIST MASCULINITIES

Chapter 6

The Primogeniture of the White Man

Land and Trumpian Populism

Juho Turpeinen

In this chapter, I investigate a white masculinity that Trumpian populism subjectivizes as "the people." I argue that Trumpian rhetoric—which constructs a notion of the American people that is shot through with race, gender, and class—draws on a well-established political culture that predates any supposed turn to "Trumpism." As such, it is important to not only analyze Trumpian rhetoric,[1] but to investigate a political culture that such populism feeds on and bolsters. We can explain some of the power of Trumpian populism through what I term here the primogeniture of the white man. Although the constitutive elements of this concept are shared to varying degrees by different local and transnational movements and phenomena, the primogeniture of the white man is ultimately highly contextual. As such, I approach the matter by means of a case study: I thematically analyze online comment sections related to news stories on the reduction of Bears Ears National Monument.[2] While the case of Bears Ears is not essential to studying the primogeniture of the white man, it serves as an illustrative example of it.[3]

On December 4, 2017, President Donald J. Trump arrived in the overwhelmingly Republican state of Utah (Jones 2016) to declare an 85 percent reduction of Bears Ears National Monument, located in the state.[4] This was only some eleven months after the Republican president's Democratic predecessor had, as one of his final actions as the chief executive, created the monument through presidential proclamation.[5] Indeed, overturning Barack Obama's public lands policy was among President Trump's early efforts to undermine his predecessor's legacy. In Utah, the media reported on the event extensively.[6] The issue became a nation-wide media event, with outdoor clothing companies and celebrities chiming in on the matter (Alberty 2017; Landrum Jr. 2017). The reduction of Bears Ears was proposed and supported by the Utah state government, and vehemently opposed by the

Native American tribes who originally campaigned for the monument and were involved in its management. *The New York Times* reported that the issue divided locals (Turkewitz 2017b), and according to *Deseret News*, "both sides in the monument debate claim[ed] support from local tribal members or grass-roots people" (O'Donoghue 2017). It was later reported in *The New York Times* that emails between the office of Utah senator Orrin Hatch and an Interior Department official indicated that potential for energy development—which in Utah is connected to the funding of public schools—was behind the decision to reduce the size of the monuments, and thus federal environmental protections in the area (Lipton and Friedman 2018).[7]

In what follows, I argue that not only does the online commentary supportive of Trump's reduction of Bears Ears exemplify the primogeniture of the white man, but it shows the potential for using such a conceptual toolkit for analyzing a specific kind of white masculinity that responds to Trumpian populism. In the Laclauian sense, populism is a rhetorical means of politics. Through a set of common demands, it is used to construct a people, a unity of identity that does not exist prior to its articulation. The "people" is posited against some elite political force—in this case the federal government. This process relies on the use of empty or floating signifiers, rhetorical devices that do not constitute a coherent and complete set of ideas, but onto which an array of referents can be attached and linked together in pursuit of hegemony (Laclau 2005). In the context of this study, Trumpian rhetoric consist of signifiers like "states' rights" and "federal overreach." I argue that a discursive white masculinity attaches meanings to these signifiers and that we can make these meanings intelligible by means of three interwoven concepts constitutive of the primogeniture of the white man: anti-statism, pastoralism, and liberalism.

ANTI-STATISM

Anti-statism is a broad term that can refer to various anti-government movements and ideologies. In the United States, anti-federal government sentiments can be tracked back to the founding of the nation. The current movement to transfer federal lands to the states continues land rights activism that saw its revival in the Sagebrush Rebellion, a movement that right-wing politicians tapped into in the 1970s and early 1980s (White 1991, 567–568). The state of Utah lent the movement credibility in 2012, when it, as the first state to do so, passed a law that demanded the federal government cede lands to the state, although this was to no effect (Healy and Johnson 2016).

In the conservative online narrative, Trump's reduction of Bears Ears is generally assumed to mean that the land no longer part of the monument goes "back" to the state of Utah or its people (Anonymous 1),[8] or that the "federal government doesn't and will never have rights to own states land per the constitution" (Anonymous 2).[9] Either way, Trump is undoing federal tyranny:

> I live in Utah and this was a huge issue when Obama made them national monuments. He took away so much land for hunting, camping and hiking and a lot of people were really upset. So this is a wonderful thing that our POTUS has done for our state! Thank you President Trump!! (Anonymous 3)

Rather than grabbing land from the states, Obama designated extant federal land to create the monument (Obama 2016). In the conservative narrative, however, the monument is federal theft of state property: "It's the very definition of a federal land grab by Obama from the state of Utah. BLM [Bureau of Land Management] is trying to expand it's power even on state owned land" (Anonymous 4). States' rights and state sovereignty are cited as reasoning against the monument and in favor of Trump's reduction: "The land belongs to Utah, and to Utah's sovereignty" (Anonymous 5). This positioning of states against the federal government can be found in both national and local conservative media sources—represented in this study by *Fox News* and *Deseret News* (see table 6.1). The dividing line is between liberal and conservative narratives: The liberal narrative, strongest in the *New York Times* comments, frames Bears Ears as property common to all Americans and as worth protecting, while in the conservative narrative, strongest in the *Fox* comments, Bears Ears is a symbol of federal oppression.

The United States government has in recent decades tended to reduce, rather than increase, the amount of federal lands. Nevertheless, the goal of Sagebrush rebels—transferring federal lands to the states—has not been realized (Hardy Vincent, Hanson and Argueta 2017, 15–20). With Trump's reduction, the land remained federal, rather than being transferred to the state of Utah (Trump 2017a). This was even mentioned in the *Fox News* article posted on *Fox News*' Facebook page to which some of these commenters were replying (Chakraborty 2017). These commenters either ignored this information, or, more likely, did not read the article to begin with—but this is exactly the point. Aggrieved white masculinity "does not need to be addressed by policy producing its concrete betterment," as political theorist Wendy Brown (2018, 75) argues, "because it seeks mainly psychic anointment of its wounds." Performance and rhetoric appear to be enough, and information that might undermine "psychic anointment" is ignored, even if immediately available.

The conservative narrative in the online comments reflects Trump's rhetoric. In Trump's speech in Salt Lake City, he framed the reduction as a states' rights issue—a long-standing signifier in conservative legal rhetoric with racist and classist implications (e.g., Schwartz 2001; Pearcy and

Clabough 2019)—and a win for the state of Utah and its citizens, against an oppressive federal government:

> I've come to Utah to take a very historic action to reverse federal overreach and restore the rights of this land to your citizens. . . . With the action I'm taking today, we will not only give back your voice over the use of this land, we will also restore your access and your enjoyment. Public lands will once again be for public use. (Trump 2017b)[10]

Trump's rhetoric here is populist. It implies that "the people" is white and masculine as he articulates the reduction itself as enabling access to land on the grounds of white, masculine activity. This populism plays out in the context of Trump's established performance of masculinist white privilege (Brown 2019, 173–174).

Drawing on a long history of anti-statism, Trumpian populism links the people with the local state government in a chain of equivalences, and, in another, the federal government with its exterior, one that is foreign at best and an enemy at worst. The claim that federal lands are theft of the people's lands is an articulation of these linkings: "He [Trump] isn't destroying anything, just keeping the fed from stealing land from people" (Anonymous 6). These linkings are reinforced by the institutional makeup of the country. Constitutional scholar Sanford Levinson (2014) argues that while the constitution nominally frames the government and the people as the same entity, the founders held a particularly low opinion of "the people" and set out to build an inherently elitist form of government (2658). "Disillusionment with the actual workings of representative democracy" led to democratic developments in the western states (Levinson 2014, 2671), and compared to the constitution, many state constitutions allow for greater participatory power (Levinson 2014, 2661). This experience lends credence to an interpretation of the government as elitist—an interpretation that reflects the design of the country's political system. As a constitutive element of the primogeniture of the white man, anti-statism shapes the form of white masculinity analyzed in this study by defining it through its other, the federal government, which it by implication casts as non-white, effeminate, and undeserving or incapable of owning land, to which the white man always has the first right.

PASTORALISM

In the context of this study, anti-statism is closely linked to pastoralism. By pastoralism, I do not only refer to an ideology that promotes the culture of "pastoralists"—that is, mobile livestock-keepers (Scoones 2020, 2)—nor do

I imply that pastoralism is wholly reflective of how rural America thinks and feels (cf. Wuthnow 2018). Rather, I draw on what literary critic Leo Marx describes in *The Machine in the Garden* as a "popular and sentimental pastoralism," one that is "an expression less of thought than of feeling" (2000, 11). Pastoralism romanticizes rural life, and whether "genuine or spurious," it is motivated by "the yearning for a simpler, more harmonious style of life, an existence 'closer to nature'" (Marx 2000, 11). While pastoralism is not unique to the United States, it shapes the American experience with particular intensity, its range of influence running the gamut from electoral systems to public policy to leisure activities (Marx 2000, 11).

The "American" culture that Marx's concept of pastoralism describes is, however, inflected by gender, race, and class. Following historian Bruce Kuklick's (1972) influential critique of Marx and other "Myth and Symbol" scholars as mistaking a part for the whole, a host of scholars have—rightfully, as Marx concedes—criticized *The Machine in the Garden* and the paradigm it represents as "the expression of a timid, elitist, white male mentality in the service of an entrenched establishment" (Marx 2000, 208–209). In the context of the primogeniture of the white man, however, the narrow applicability of these persistent notions of "American" culture is precisely the point. Rural life is associated with notions of masculinity, such strength, hardiness and industriousness, exemplified by farming and ranching. As cultural geographers Joshua Inwood and Anne Bonds note, in American culture, the "racialized and gendered . . . figure of the rugged frontiersman is routinely positioned as the central character in the patriarchal taming of the savage West" (2017, 261).[11] Pastoralism is also culturally opposed to urbanism (Marx 2000, 11), and this divide is historically contoured by a racial and political division; rural areas are mostly white and more conservative than cities (Wuthnow 2018, 1–2, 5). Moreover, as sociologist Robert Wuthnow notes, the rural "'moral order' is . . . predicated on 'white-ness'" (2018, 11). Pastoralism, then, is linked to the idea of a ruling class that is masculine and white, even if in populist rhetoric this ruling class is termed "the people" and its other "the elite." Far from timid, perched at the top of the social hierarchy but wounded by social changes, white masculinity has transformed into a rancorous monster (Brown 2018). Pastoralism functions as both palliative nostalgia for its mental pain and a justification for the primogeniture of the white man.

In Trump's rhetoric the reduction of Bears Ears guaranteed previously prohibited, traditionally masculine activities like hunting and ranching, linking these to aesthetic beauty and divinity, while reserving conservation for individual responsibility beyond the remit of the government:

Families will hike and hunt on land they have known for generations, and they will preserve it for generations to come. Cattle will graze along the open range.

Sweeping landscapes will inspire young Americans to dream beyond the horizon. And the world will stand in awe of the artistry God has worked right here
in your great state. (Trump 2017b)

This masculine activity is reflected in how many commenters defend Trump's
decision:

So the president just backed up a huge federal land restriction. Gave me hunting access to two million more acres of PUBLIC land. Reduced restrictions on
uses such as hunting and fishing. Removed mandates such as road removal, cut
bureacracy and saved a few hundred million dollars and I'm supposed to be
upset about it? (Anonymous 7)

In addition to "again" allowing hunting and fishing, the "return" of land is
assumed to go to the "rightful" owners: ranchers and farmers, with white,
masculine implications: "Will the EO return the land to the Ranchers it
legally belongs to? Clinton and Obama both stripped land from families that
had worked the lands for several generations. So it would be only right to
return it to them" (Anonymous 8). This is even posited against recreational
use, particularly that of out-of-staters (Anonymous 9). Obama and the federal
government are understood as the enemy of ranchers and farmers:

That's your perspective isn't it, screw you Americans we are the government
and we don't care if your Cattle can't graze or the farmer can't farm, because
I'm obama and I want to EO this land because i want to regulate how you farm
and ranch. (Anonymous 10)

According to the BLM and the US Forest Service, hunting, fishing,
and grazing were always allowed inside the monument (Bureau of Land
Management 2016; US Forest Service). Nor did the monument designation affect private property rights (US Forest Service). Instead, the designation "would prohibit new mineral leases, mining claims, prospecting or
exploration activities, and oil, gas, and geothermal leases" (Bureau of Land
Management 2016). Once again, in order to be effective, populist rhetoric
that promises to soothe aggrieved white masculinity does not require tangible
change in the realm of public policy.

Moreover, pastoralism is understood to have been threatened by the federal
government and now liberated by Trump:

Thank you for rolling back federal land grabs! They were put in place to destroy
rural communities and rural life! I have always wondered if the place is so beautiful after 250 plus years since the country became the USA why would it need
to be locked away from the public now? It would seem they have done a good
job WITHOUT making it off limits to everyone! (Anonymous 11)

This sentiment reflects a rural-urban cultural divide between "land as a source of economic activity" and "wildlife as a place of purity to be set aside" (Eisenberg 2017, 129). Despite anger rooted in economic precarity, the spatial dimension of this tension does not lend it to simple class analysis. Rather, it is contoured by racial and gender difference. The concept of the American working class is often presumptively interpreted as white, while, in fact, "a substantial proportion of American workers today are women, and particularly women of color, in the service industry" (Eisenberg 2017, 141), and compared to the experience of whites, "neoliberalism, and post-Fordism before it, have been far more devastating to the Black American working class" (Brown 2018, 60). The tension, then, is between white, rural, masculine identity and its urban other. Indeed, some of the online commenters interpret the monument reversal as undoing a racially understood Obama presidency. Obama is accused of having "set race relations back 50 years" (Anonymous 12) and that "yall say whites are land theives lmao. Bamas black he stole land from utah wasnt it a million acres?" (Anonymous 13). Racist undertones are also expressed without directly referencing race. As a *Fox* Facebook commenter demonstrates:

> Radical liberals fear any instance of Trump succeeding. If Trump continues to win and it continues to benefit America and Americans, Democrats will keep losing seats. All they have left are welfare recipients, inmates, illegal immigrants, and Islamic terrorists. The Democrat party has abandoned law-abiding citizens, especially working Americans. (Anonymous 14)[12]

Here, the constituency of the Democratic Party is described in stereotypically racialized terms, while the "America" and "Americans" that benefit from Trump's "continued winning" are perceived as its inverse and understood by implication as white. The narrative of undoing the Obama presidency is present across the sources but shaped by the liberal-conservative-divide. In the liberal narrative, most evident in the *Times* comments, the unmaking of Obama's legacy is a negative, while in the conservative narrative, strongest in the *Fox* comments, it is a positive. Even when ostensibly devoid of racial or ethnic reference, the very ideological underpinnings of the rural-urban divide are racially and ethnically informed.

Quite separate from the masculinist and white supremacist implications of the movement to transfer federal lands to the states, one can empathize with anti-statist anger rooted in a rural discontent with cultural changes brought on by a politically regulated economy. As environmental law scholar Ann M. Eisenberg points out, decreasing rural populations and diminishing opportunities for those who stay have made for fertile ground for anti-statist anger. A suitable target is the federal government whose regulatory practices have the potential of shifting the economy away from traditional rural jobs based on resource extraction. This sentiment needs to be understood spatially, as it is rooted in a regional identity defined in part by an unfamiliarity with a distant and seemingly uncaring federal government. Here, identity-based anger is compounded by federal policy, which may alter local economic practices and curtail political power in areas where it traditionally has not done so (Eisenberg 2017, 158–159). These passions that are tapped into by political and business elites and "questionable media sources," fueling "anti-environmental, anti-federal alienation" (Eisenberg 2017, 159). This abandonment of environmentalism by the Right was largely a reaction to cultural changes that began in the 1960s, followed by a related shift in political allegiances. By the 1980s, the Right had come to value anti-statism more than the environment, reinterpreting conservation of nature as part of the welfare state and the liberal agenda (Drake 2013, 179–184). Commenters that are anti-statist to this degree reject the conservation mandate of the government: "The Feds shouldn't be in the business of land ownership" (Anonymous 15). Here, anti-statism and conservatism[13] may conflict with pastoralism by valuing "states' rights" and energy development more than they do the rural landscape. This tension is exemplified by a *Fox* Facebook comment that attempts to reconcile these seemingly dissonant elements:

People it is not up to the Federal Government to take land from a state. Federal government is not in the business for them selves. The state can now think for themselves and if they chose to use it for oil than be it. When will people learn if you give the Feds anything they will take more advantage of the state. Trump is correct Obama forced and took land as he did from many ranchers and farmers. Liberals I understand your feeling how ever when will you quit thinking the Feds should be in your life. So far what do you have High taxed liberal states to support welfare programs government telling you cant buy a large soda cant use a gas lawn mower, Please read the Constitution and you will find your Officals have been lying to you. (Anonymous 18)

The favoring of localism—flawed as it may be—over distant, urban notions of federal conservation, is rooted in what Wuthnow calls as the "moral order" of rural culture (2018). While the romanticizing of local sovereignty may turn out be corrosive of the landscape that sustains rural—and, indeed, all—life, American pastoralism, as Marx (2000, 129) notes, rhetorically reconciles industrial development and nature as a benign "middle landscape." The white man gets to have his land and devour it too.[14] Pastoralism shapes white masculinity as a constitutive element of the primogeniture of the white man. Where anti-statism defines white masculinity by casting the federal government as the other, as non-white, effeminate, and propertyless, pastoralism casts in these terms its urban other.

LIBERALISM

The terms "liberal" and "conservative" used in this study, as well as in American political discourse at large, refer to different ends of the overall "liberal" spectrum of mainstream politics in the United States. Although liberalism and conservatism have diverged in the United States to emphasize, for example, civil rights and property rights, respectively, both are rooted in classical liberalism (Starr 2012). Classical liberalism interprets private property and freedom as essentially the same thing. The government, and by extension anything public, is a tyrannical perversion of democracy that undermines freedom. Moreover, the white, masculine interpretation of history assumes that the land was terra nullius before European arrival in America. In Lockean liberalism, the legitimation of private property comes from labor: labor transforms the commons into property (Locke 1982, V. 27).[15] However, Locke's contention that property is a natural right secured by the state also retains wealth inheritance (1982, VII. 87, VIII. 120), an aristocratic remnant that was never eradicated in the ostensibly republican revolution of 1776.[16] This ideology was born in a colonial context: For Locke, America was unused and available, to be transformed into private property by working the land (1982, V. 26–27, V. 36). The Founding Fathers of the United States "thoroughly embraced Lockean labor theory as the basis for a right of acquisition because it affirmed the right of the New World settlers to settle on and acquire the frontier" (Harris 1993, 1727–1728). In other words, white labor makes land property, and this frontiersman imagery is positioned against the federal government:

> The citizens of Utah wanted and petitioned for this change . . . they didn't want bureaucrats in Washington controlling local lands . . . please do a little research before spreading anything the NY Times prints . . . mostly affects grazing rights for local cattlemen. (Anonymous 19)

Perhaps it is the colonial heart of liberalism that explains why advocates of white masculinity fail to recognize the legitimacy of Native American claims to land, but understand the white, masculine activity of ranching to have granted title to it, even while denying federal legitimacy:

> The land belongs to the people of Utah. Obama should have never expanded the Parks in the first place. It's called less federal government action for those who believe big government is the be all, end all. There are actually people in these

United States who think less federal government intrusion is a good thing. AND, get over the idea that indians were here when the continent formed. They are immigrants just like everyone else. (Anonymous 20)

One commenter makes this connection explicit, claiming that "it is not land that belongs to Native American's. It has been used as recreation farming and ranching by all for 150+ years" (Anonymous 21).

The colonial legacy of liberalism runs deeper still. Legal scholar Cheryl I. Harris argues that in the United States, whiteness as property—"affirmed, legitimated, and protected by the law" (1993, 1713) in numerous ways—is rooted "in the parallel systems of domination of Black and Native American peoples out of which were created racially contingent forms of property and property rights" (1993, 1714). Slavery, in part, linked property to whiteness (see also Finkelman 2012), but it was the conquest of Native American lands that connected land and whiteness within the concept of property (Harris 1993, 1721). Moreover, Harris attributes the lasting influence of whiteness as property in the law, in part, to Lockean liberalism's favoring of the individual over social groups (1993, 1761–1762). Political theorist Mark Devenney takes the argument further, arguing that all hegemonic orders are rooted in the logics of property, and are, as such, territorial and exclusionary (2020).

In the comments, the linking of whiteness to land and property rights is opposed by conflicting narratives: There is support for Bears Ears as a Native project (Anonymous 22) and for Native sovereignty and land rights in opposition to the federal government—it is even suggested by one *Indian Country Today Media Network* Facebook commenter that Native American sovereignty is an issue akin to states' rights (Anonymous 23). Thus, Native American advocacy narratives—ingenuous or not—do not fit neatly within the liberal or conservative narrative and warrant further research. It is clear, however, that the narrative of white ownership of land is part of historical struggles to control or sever Native Americans' traditional relationships to land—and related tribal sovereignty. Following terra nullius, European colonization of the North American continent was justified in the nineteenth century with a divinely ordained "manifest destiny" that promoted, but not necessarily motivated, white settler expansion (White 1991, 73–75), and was legislated by means such as the Dawes Act of 1887 that forced Native Americans into an oppressive system of land ownership that undermined Native sovereignty (Genetin-Pilawa 2012, 134–155).

Moreover, the racially hierarchical, liberal welfare state makes some subsidies visible and others invisible (Disch 2011). The subsidies of the rancher are invisible, in contrast to the visible welfare of the racialized other in the form of food stamps and other handouts: "Just cut their welfare payments, that is how they got into their present predicament anyway, relying on the Great White Father in Washington for handouts" (Anonymous 24). According to the US Department of the Interior, state and private grazing fees can cost nearly ten times as much as federal ones, although private leases may contain some additional services, like fencing, and rights to timber, hunt, and fish (2017, 3). Thus, invisibly subsidized "rights" are juxtaposed with "unearned" benefits.

Liberalism and anti-statism find their ultimate form in neoliberalism (Brown 2019). Political theorist Wendy Brown argues that neoliberalism conceptualizes morality, ostensibly rooted in tradition, as a marketplace of ideas. Regulation of that market is necessarily a limitation on freedom and, thus, all social justice becomes fascist coercion that delimits freedom. Where Friedrich Hayek, perhaps the most notable of neoliberalism's founding fathers, saw tradition as a condition of freedom, neoliberal nihilism has forged it into a weapon in white man's battle to maintain supremacy (Brown 2019, 89–122). Brown's approach attempts to reconcile neoliberalism with "affectional investments in privileges of whiteness and First World existence in the nation and national culture or in traditional morality" (2019, 182). This trend merely comes to a head with Trump:

> Thank God we have a common sense President that will roll back these liberal feel good land grabs and make the land accessible to everyone again. No more keep out signs, no more closed roads. Hunting and off road vehicles will be welcomed back for everyone not just park officials. New Yorkers may love experiencing the outdoors thru their tv documentaries but some of us want unfettered access to our public lands again. Keep the federal govt out of our states! (Anonymous 25)

Nihilistic inability to care for anything but the self—and even then, only in an immediate sense—justifies white male supremacy. Its masculinity may be impotent but is enhanced by all-terrain vehicles—the use of which, damaging to the environment as it may be, is valorized by neoliberalism's conception of liberty.

Trump, who "built his own political career" on racist "birtherism"[17] (Pearcy and Clabough 2019, 386), is understood as the messianic savior of white masculinity from the tyranny of effeminate black otherness: "Under racist obumma it was the largest Land Grab in the history of the USA" (Anonymous 26). In this comment, a national monument campaigned for by Native Americans and designated by the first black president of the country is "racist" and unprecedented, because it is perceived as an attack on the primogeniture of the white man by a constellation of non-white racial otherness. Much like Native American land rights, American history is undergirded by struggle for and against the rights of African Americans, including land rights. This struggle is rooted in slavery, and despite the Civil War and the civil rights movement, has resulted in the enduring social construction of white landownership and black landlessness—even making invisible the history of, however limited, black land ownership (Reid 2012, 1–16). Ultimately, the attack on the primogeniture of the white man by non-white otherness is coercive of freedom, because in the liberal tradition, property, perceived as rightfully belonging to white masculinity, its subsidization made invisible by the liberal welfare state, is freedom, and because a nihilistic neoliberal reason has made the property owner hostile to all social justice. Where anti-statism and pastoralism contour white masculinity by casting the federal government and the urban as non-white, effeminate, and propertyless, the third constitutive element of the primogeniture of the white man, liberalism, links property to freedom. Liberalism, thus, casts the other of white masculinity as not only non-white, effeminate, and propertyless, but as unfree.

CONCLUSION

For political philosophers Michael Hardt and Antonio Negri, right-wing populist movements are rooted in love of racialized identity and "behind identity lurks property," especially land rights (Hardt and Negri 2017, 51–53). In Trump's populist framing, property and land rights rightfully belong to the people—and not to a distant, elitist, federal government. Trump's appeals to whiteness and masculinity resonate with a conservative narrative—analyzed in this chapter in the form of online commentary surrounding the reduction of Bears Ears National Monument—linking white, masculine identity, right-wing populism, and land rights together. Thus, in Trump's right-wing populism, racialized hierarchy takes on a masculine character through its masculine male appearance and emphasis on traditionally masculine activities like ranching. Trumpian populism appeals to white masculine passions through signifiers like "states' rights" and the reduction of a national monument speaks to white masculine anxiety on a rhetorical level. Trump is perceived as a messianic figure, promising to right the wrong of oppressive "federal overreach," bringing freedom to the people. While this narrative, on its face, often has little to do with observable empirical reality, it can be made intelligible through the concept of the primogeniture of the white man.

This white title to land, more often implicit than explicit, and justified on the grounds of masculine activity, undergirds a racial hierarchy whose roots reach all the way back to the beginnings of the nation. Trumpian populism constructs "the people" as white and masculine, propertied and free, against a black, effeminate, propertyless and unfree "elite." Indeed, Trump's populist appeal can be read as a continuation of a long historical tendency of resistance to non-white land ownership in the United States. This resistance is fueled by a political culture that, despite its changes, legitimizes white supremacy and patriarchy. Moreover, we can read the Obama presidency as emasculating the white man. Commenters feel, regardless of veracity, that masculine activities were prohibited by Obama, that the lands belonged to ranchers and farmers, and that Trump gave this power back. The federal government—the other, the black—has no place owning land, because it does not perform property in white, masculine terms. Undoing the Obama presidency and federal tyranny must mean that land is returned to the states.[18] This meaning is linked, along a chain of equivalences, to an appreciation of racially understood, masculine uses of land, and to a concept of freedom that is intimately linked to property.

Trumpian populism, then, does not appear in a vacuum, but functions by appeals to popular discontent. It draws and builds on existing political ideologies and notions of identity through the rhetorical use of signifiers. The signifiers of Trumpian populism can be read along an equivalential chain of anti-statism, pastoralism, and liberalism. While in terms of political theory these approaches are not all commensurate, they constitute a constellation of populist rhetoric that subjectivizes masculine, white conservatism. Reading these concepts alongside each other helps us understand what fuels white populist masculinity: It is not mere misunderstanding of capitalism to assume that the rancher has rights to land on which his cattle grazes, or simple ignorance of history to presume that the frontiersman has original title to lands in the West. In the United States, property rights and racial hierarchy are intimately linked, and secure each other (Inwood and Bonds 2017, 255–256). "Whiteness," as Inwood and Bonds explain the Harrisian concept, "is not just a social identity, but also something that secures power and dominance and can be possessed, protected, and invested in" (2017, 255; see also Harris 1993). Compounded by a felt sense of place in society, a spatialized hierarchy, land becomes the primogeniture of the white man who is primus inter pares to inherit the American Dream. As Trumpian populism draws on and constructs narratives of white supremacy and masculinity rooted in a relationship between land and identity, it becomes part of a long history of racial oppression and conflict in America.

In the primogeniture of the white man, identity as property can be inherited; the conflation of identity and property produces ethnicity as property and retains property-as-freedom as something that is inherited. Ideology secures property, property secures identity, and this identity, inflected by the colonial racializations of modernity, functions both as a path to property and as a kind of property itself, one that must be defended from the other. In this zero-sum game, loss of the primogeniture of the white man would mean loss of not only first right to property secured by white masculinity, and the privileged position of white masculinity secured by property, but of freedom. As such, justice hinges on property and racialized, gendered identity as the means by

Table 6.1

News source	Number of articles/ posts	Total number of comments analyzed
The Salt Lake Tribune	17	2,925
The Salt Lake Tribune Facebook page	1	205
Deseret News	14	458
Deseret News Facebook page	6	331
The New York Times	1	1,752
The New York Times Facebook page	3	3,259
Fox News	1	1,521
Fox News Facebook page	2	5,758
Indian Country Today Media Network Facebook page	1	363

which the enduring ills of our conjuncture could and should be redressed. It is this identity and its subjectivation, its sense of freedom and justice that we must learn to read and understand if we wish to engage it and the world so troubled by its ascendance.

NOTES

1. For an analysis of Trump's populism, see Joshua Martin's chapter in this collection.

2. The online comments thematized in this study have been selected from Utah-based and national news sources that reflect editorial values along the liberal-conservative spectrum (see the section on liberalism in this chapter). I have limited the selection to online versions and Facebook pages of these news sources based on the availability of news stories and posts published online between December 4 and 5, 2017. These articles and posts contain explicit reference to Bears Ears National Monument and have user comments attached to them. For a breakdown of the sources, see table 6.1.

3. The reduction of Bears Ears has generated interest among scholars on a host of issues, such as the legality of the reduction (Yoo and Gaziano 2018; Hein 2018), the moral facets of regulating public lands "with cultural significance" (McBrayer and Roberts-Cady 2018), Native American literary activism (Smith 2020), and the reduction's effects on the politics of Indigenous knowledge (Higgins 2018).

4. Salt Lake City, the capital of the state of Utah where President Trump made his announcement, is more Democratic than the rest of the state, however. For example, the plurality of Salt Lake County voted for a Democratic presidential candidate in 2008 and 2016 (Swensen 2020).

5. Trump also reduced the size of the Clinton-designated Grand Staircase-Escalante National Monument (Turkewitz 2017a).

6. According *The Salt Lake Tribune*, the reduction of Bears Ears and Grand Staircase-Escalante National Monuments was among the newspaper's most read

stories in 2017 (Weber 2017). *Deseret News'* news directors voted the monument reduction the top story of 2017 (Leonard 2017).

7. In addition to the oil and gas industry influence uncovered by the *Times*, the uranium industry was also implicated in lobbying for the reduction (Brunvand 2020).

8. Although the online user comments cited in this study have been publicly available at the time of citation, and some of them have been written under obvious pseudonyms, I have chosen to anonymize the sources here to protect the privacy of these commenters, as my intent is not to criticize individual commenters. I have numbered the anonymous comments here not in reference to their place in the data sets I have analyzed, but in reference to their order of appearance in this chapter. I have provided the editors of this collection with the full, original citations of the material.

9. I present quotations from the online comments here as they originally appear, including typographic and grammatical errors.

10. The language about people being "locked out" of land and land being "arbitrarily" taken by the federal government is also present in the language of secretary of the Interior Ryan Zinke (Maffly 2017).

11. Historically, environmentalists in the West have attempted to appeal to pastoralist white masculinity by promoting federal lands, including national monuments, as platforms for masculine performance. See Nicholas Blower's chapter in this collection.

12. The comment was cited March 22, 2018, but has since been removed and is not available online as of October 28, 2020.

13. The aforementioned rural-urban divide in how land is viewed (Eisenberg 2017, 129) parallels that of the conservative-liberal one, in which conservatives favor energy development as a pragmatic solution (e.g., Anonymous 16), while liberals condemn it on the grounds of its social harm and environmental impact (e.g., Anonymous 17).

14. Although Marx ends *The Machine in the Garden* with the argument that this reconciliation has become archaic and ineffective (2000, 199–200) he later contends that his judgment had proven too hasty (2000, 209–210).

15. Incidentally, this has been a failed legal strategy of the Sagebrush Rebels (Blumm and Jamin 2016, 812–814).

16. While the United States retained inheritance, revolutionaries like Thomas Paine and Thomas Jefferson had advocated an end to it, which, according to Alice Lerud, Jefferson felt produced an "artificial aristocracy, founded on wealth and birth, without either talent or virtue" (Carter 2012, 197).

17. "Birtherism" refers to the baseless accusation or belief that Barack Obama was not born in the United States.

18. See also Lawrence Grossberg's argument that in right-wing populism "the state is constructed as the enemy of the nation (the sovereign people)" (Grossberg 2018, 881).

BIBLIOGRAPHY

Alberty, Erin. 2017. "'The President Stole Your Land': Outdoor Gear Merchants Push Back Against Trump's Order to Shrink Two Utah Monuments." *The Salt*

Lake Tribune, December 5, updated December 6, 2017. https://www.sltrib.
com/news/2017/12/05/recreation-industry-leaders-launch-campaigns-against-utah-
monument-reductions/.

Blumm, Michael C., and Olivier Jamin. 2016. "The Property Clause and Its
Discontents: Lessons from the Malheur Occupation." *Ecology Law Quarterly*
43 (4): 781–826.

Brown, Wendy. 2018. "Neoliberalism's Frankenstein: Authoritarian Freedom in
Twenty-First Century 'Democracies.'" *Critical Times* 1 (1): 60–79.

Brown, Wendy. 2019. *In the Ruins of Neoliberalism: The Rise of Antidemocratic
Politics in the West*. New York: Columbia University Press.

Brunvand, Amy. 2020. "Researching Bears Ears: Reference Practice for Civic
Engagement." *Reference Services Review* 48 (1): 49–61. https://doi.org/10.1108/
RSR-09-2019-0061.

Bureau of Land Management. 2016. *Bears Ears National Monument Fast Facts and
Q&A*. December 28, 2016. https://www.blm.gov/programs/national-conservation
-lands/national-monuments/utah/bears-ears/fast-facts.

Carter, Elizabeth R. 2012. "New Life for the Death Tax Debate." *Denver University
Law Review* 90 (1): 175–211.

Chakraborty, Barnini. 2017. "Trump Shrinks Utah Monuments Created by Obama,
Clinton." *Fox News*, December 4, 2017. http://www.foxnews.com/politics/2017
/12/04/trump-shrinks-utah-monuments-created-by-obama-clinton.html.

Devenney, Mark. 2020. *Towards an Improper Politics*. Edinburgh: Edinburgh
University Press.

Disch, Lisa. 2011. "Tea Party Movement: The American 'Precariat'?" *Representation*
47 (2). https://doi.org/10.1080/00344893.2011.581057.

Drake, Brian Allen. 2013. *Loving Nature, Fearing the State: Environmentalism and
Antigovernment Politics before Reagan*. Seattle: University of Washington Press.

Eisenberg, Ann M. 2017. "Alienation and Reconciliation in Social-Ecological
Systems." *Environmental Law* 47 (1): 127–178.

Finkelman, Paul. 2012. "Slavery in the United States: Persons or Property?" In *The
Legal Understanding of Slavery: From the Historical to the Contemporary*, edited
by Jean Allain, 105–134. Oxford: Oxford University Press.

Genetin-Pilawa, C. Joseph. 2012. *Crooked Paths to Allotment: The Fight over
Federal Indian Policy After the Civil War*. Chapel Hill: The University of North
Carolina Press.

Grossberg, Lawrence. 2018. "Pessimism of the Will, Optimism of the Intellect:
Endings and Beginnings." *Cultural Studies* 32 (6): 855–888. https://doi.org/10.1
080/09502386.2018.1517268.

Hardt, Michael, and Antonio Negri. 2017. *Assembly*. New York: Oxford University Press.

Hardy Vincent, Carol, Laura A. Hanson, and Carla N. Argueta. 2017. *Federal Land
Ownership: Overview and Data*. CRS Report R42346. Library of Congress,
Congressional Research Service, March 3, 2017. Federation of American Scientists.
https://fas.org/sgp/crs/misc/R42346.pdf.

Harris, Cheryl I. 1993. "Whiteness as Property." *Harvard Law Review* 106 (8):
1707–1791.

Healy, Jack, and Kirk Johnson. 2018. "The Larger, but Quieter Than Bundy, Push to Take Over Federal Land." *The New York Times*, January 10, 2016. https://www .nytimes.com/2016/01/11/us/the-larger-but-quieter-than-bundy-push-to-take-over-federal-land.html.

Hein, Jayni Foley. 2018. "Monumental Decisions: One-Way Levers Towards Preservation in the Antiquities Act and Outer Continental Shelf Land Acts." *Environmental Law* 48 (1): 125–166.

Higgins, Margot. 2018. "From a National Monument to a National Disgrace." *Ethics, Policy & Environment* 21 (1): 9–12. https://doi.org/10.1080/21550085.2018.14478.

Inwood, Joshua F. J., and Anne Bonds. 2017. "Property and Whiteness: The Oregon Standoff and the Contradictions of the U.S. Settler State." *Space and Polity* 21 (3): 253–268. https://doi.org/10.1080/13562576.2017.1373425.

Jones, Jeffrey M. 2016. "Red States Outnumber Blue for First Time in Gallup Tracking." *Gallup*, February 3, 2016. https://news.gallup.com/poll/188969/red-states-outnumber-blue-first-time-gallup-tracking.aspx.

Kuklick, Bruce. 1972. "Myth and Symbol in American Studies." *American Quarterly* 24 (4): 435–450.

Laclau, Ernesto. 2005. *On Populist Reason*. London: Verso.

Landrum Jr., Jonathan. 2017. "Mark Ruffalo is 'Disgusted' with Trump's Monument Decision." *The Salt Lake Tribune*, December 13, updated December 14, 2017. https ://www.sltrib.com/news/nation-world/2017/12/14/mark-ruffalo-is-disgusted-with -trumps-monuments-decision/.

Leonard, Wendy. 2017. "Trump's Monumental Decision Tops Beehive State's Biggest Stories of 2017." *Deseret News*, December 30, 2017. https://www. deseretnews.com/article/900006590/trumps-monumental-decision-tops-beehive-states-biggest-stories-of-2017.html.

Levinson, Sanford. 2014. "Popular Sovereignty and the United States Constitution: Tensions in the Ackermanian Program." *Yale Law Journal* 123 (8): 2644–2674.

Lipton, Eric, and Lisa Friedman. 2018. "Oil Was Central in Decision to Shrink Bears Ears Monument, Emails Show." *The New York Times*, March 2, 2018. https:// www.nytimes.com/2018/03/02/climate/bears-ears-national-monument.html.

Locke, John. 1982. *Second Treatise of Government: An Essay Concerning the True Original Extent and End of Civil Government*. Edited by Richard H. Cox. Wheeling: Harlan Davidson.

Maffly, Brian. 2017. "Here's a Look at Key Lands Left Out of Trump's New Monuments—and What Areas Remain Protected." *The Salt Lake Tribune*, December 4, updated December 8, 2017. https://www.sltrib.com/pb/news/2017/12 /05/trump-turned-two-vast-utah-national-monuments-into-five-smaller-ones-heres -a-look-at-the-new-sites-and-key-lands-that-got-left-out.

Marx, Leo. 2000. *The Machine in the Garden: Technology and the Pastoral Ideal in America*. New York: Oxford University Press.

McBrayer, Justin, and Sarah Roberts-Cady. 2018. "The Case for Preserving Bears Ears Ethics." *Policy & Environment* 21 (1): 48–51. https://doi.org/10.1080/215500 85.2018.144803.

Obama, Barack. 2016. "Establishment of the Bears Ears National Monument. By the President of the United States. A Proclamation." *The White House*, December 28, 2016. https://obamawhitehouse.archives.gov/the-press-office/2016/12/28/proclamation-establishment-bears-ears-national-monument.

O'Donoghue, Amy Joi. 2017. "Utah Legislature Votes to Shed Bears Ears Monument Designation." *DeseretNews*, February 3, 2017. https://www.deseretnews.com/article/865672545/Utah-Legislature-votes-to-shed-Bears-Ears-monument-designation.html.

Pearcy, Mark and Jeremiah Clabough. 2019. "Discussing the Elephant in the Room: The Republican Party and Race Issues." *Social Studies Research and Practice* 14 (3): 377–390. https://doi.org/10.1108/SSRP-03-2019-0019.

Reid, Debra A. 2012. "Introduction." In *Beyond Forty Acres and a Mule: African American Landowning Families Since Reconstruction*, edited by Debra A. Reid, and Evan P. Bennet, 1–18. Gainesville: University Press of Florida.

Schwartz, Herman. 2001. "The Supreme Court's Federalism: Fig Leaf for Conservatives." *The ANNALS of the American Academy of Political and Social Science* 574 (1): 119–131. https://doi.org/10.1177/000271620157400109.

Scoones, Ian. 2020. "Pastoralists and Peasants: Perspectives on Agrarian Change." *The Journal of Peasant Studies*. https://doi.org/10.1080/03066150.2020.1802249.

Smith, Laura. 2020. "The Quiet Politics and Gentle Literary Activism Behind the Battle for Utah's Bears Ears National Monument." *Area* 00: 1–5. https://doi.org/10.1111/area.12609.

Starr, Paul. 2012. "Liberalism, Center-Left." In *The Oxford Companion to American Politics*, Vol. 2, edited by David Coates, 68–76. Oxford: Oxford University Press.

Swensen, Sherrie, and Salt Lake County Clerk. 2020. "Salt Lake County Election Results and Archives." *Salt Lake County Clerk*. https://slco.org/clerk/elections/election-results/.

Trump, Donald J. 2017a. "Presidential Proclamation Modifying the Bears Ears National Monument." *The White House*, December 4, 2017. https://www.whitehouse.gov/presidential-actions/presidential-proclamation-modifying-bears-ears-national-monument/.

Trump, Donald J. 2017b. "Remarks by President Trump on Antiquities Act Designations." *The White House*, December 4, 2017. https://www.whitehouse.gov/briefings-statements/remarks-president-trump-antiquities-act-designations/.

Turkewitz, Julie. 2017a. "Trump Slashes Size of Bears Ears and Grand Staircase Monuments." *The New York Times*, December 4, 2017. https://www.nytimes.com/2017/12/04/us/trump-bears-ears.html.

Turkewitz, Julie. 2017b. "Battle Over Bears Ears Heats Up as Trump Rethinks Its Monument Status." *The New York Times*, May 14, 2017. https://www.nytimes.com/2017/05/14/us/bears-ears-ryan-zinke.html.

U.S. Department of the Interior. 2017. *Department of the Interior Office of Policy Analysis, U.S. Department of the Interior Economic Report FY 2016*. September 25, 2017. https://www.doi.gov/sites/doi.gov/files/uploads/fy_2016_doi_economic_report_2017-09-25.pdf.

U.S. Forest Service. *Bears Ears National Monument: Questions & Answers*. January 15, 2019. https://www.fs.fed.us/sites/default/files/bear-ears-fact-sheet.pdf.

Weber, Sara. 2017. "The Salt Lake Tribune's Most-Read Stories of 2017." *The Salt Lake Tribune*, December 30, 2017, updated January 4, 2018. https://www.sltrib.com/news/2017/12/30/the-salt-lake-tribunes-most-read-stories-of-2017/.

White, Richard. 1991. *"It's Your Misfortune and None of My Own": A New History of the American West*. Norman: University of Oklahoma Press.

Wuthnow, Robert. 2018. *The Left Behind: Decline and Rage in Rural America*. Princeton: Princeton University Press.

Yoo, John C., and Todd Gaziano. 2018. "Presidential Authority to Revoke or Reduce National Monument Designations." *Yale Journal on Regulation* 35 (2): 617–665.

Chapter 7

The Populist Body at Work (and War)

Fascism, Conspiracism, and Idealized White Heroism in Falling Down *(1993),* Forrest Gump *(1995), and* Fight Club *(1999)*

Christian Jimenez

This chapter studies three Hollywood films, *Falling Down* (Schumacher 1993), *Forrest Gump* (Zemeckis 1995), and *Fight Club* (Palahniuk 1999), that evoked populism, especially a hyper-masculine form of populism, and provided room for a radical, right-wing political message, including references to fascist and neofascist ideologies. Populists use the quotes and even myths from these films—the hard-working white male versus lazy non-white, an aggressive foreign policy protecting the nation versus a cosmopolitan foreign policy seeking peace—and their popularity makes them worthy of analysis.

Several studies have focused on populism and fascism (Berlet and Lyons 2000; Diamond 1995; Mulloy 2018). Yet the literature on both populism and fascism have concentrated on how reactionaries mainly wish to protect their wealth and income (Mayer 2016; Monbiot 2010). Right-wing populist activists are assumed to be mainly pawns of the wealthy. Recent work on social movement theory, however, alerts us to how powerfully symbols and ideals drive social movements at both the elite and grassroots level (Blee 2002; Dobratz and Shanks-Meile 1997; Snow, Rochford, Worden, and Benford 1986). This chapter acts as a bridge to past and new research on the radical right and its deployment of populism as a mobilizing "frame."

POPULISM VERSUS FASCISM?

Populism, according to Michael Kazin, is a rhetorical "language whose speakers conceiv[ing] of ordinary people as a noble assemblage not bounded by class" (1995, 1). Fascism is no less contested than populism. Roger Griffin defines it "as a revolutionary form of nationalism" (1991, xi). Fascism for Griffin

> sets out to be a political, social and ethical revolution, welding the "people" into a dynamic national community under new elites infused with heroic values. The core myth that inspires this project is that only a populist, trans-class movement of purifying, cathartic national rebirth (palingenesis) can stem the tide of decadence. (Griffin 1991, xi)

Griffin's definition fits the first film, *Falling Down*, almost exactly. The United States is depicted as being in a state of deep decline. Only a heroic "cathartic national rebirth" can save it. *Forrest Gump* has less graphic violence than *Falling Down*, but it also mythologizes "the people" into patriotic whites and blacks "infused with heroic values" (xi). Finally, *Fight Club*'s plot posits precisely a "populist, trans-class movement of purifying" (xi), a corrupt society led by white male terrorist Tyler Durden.

Griffin's definition is powerful, yet it ignores fascism as a gendered discourse. National birth and rebirth are puzzlingly assumed to be a non-gendered narrative used by populist fascists. In practice, fascist populism often excludes people based on race and gender. As Suvi Keskinen puts it: "whiteness is the implicit and taken for granted norm . . . against which 'others' are defined" (2014, 483). In US populist politics, George Wallace and Ronald Reagan, for example, idealized white America as hard-working people (Mulloy 2018, 110). While populism formally is race-neutral, in reality, populism was aimed mainly at middle-class whites to mobilize them on behalf of reactionary movements. However, not every form of whiteness is acceptable; populism applauds whiteness, highlighting masculine energy, honor, honesty, integrity, and willingness to self-sacrifice.

The white (male) hero who embodies these characteristics is often portrayed as the victim of vast conspiracies driven by Jews, feminists, and others (McDonald 1978). It might be that ironic populist movements mobilize followers using conspiracy theories. Still, as Sasson notes, "conspiracy theories flourish, in part, because they are ways to foster solidarity and collective action" (1995, 278). Even if a conspiracy is untrue, it helps to bind people. While conspiracism has obvious appeal in promoting solidarity, the populist tendency of idealizing masculine heroism limits the possible appeal of fascist discourse.

Both in populist and fascist discourses, women are given a limited and inactive role—they need to be protected, and in exchange, they ought to support (not challenge) the male activity. As Teitelbaum notes: "[a]ssociations with tradition, the home, spirituality, and emotionalism have marked women as vessels of national essence in varied historical and geographic contexts" (2014, 415). Reactionary discourse tends to idealize and demonize womanhood simultaneously. For example, the threat of sexual violence is used to justify reactionary politics. Hence Trump claimed Mexico was "bringing drugs [in the US]. They're bringing crime. They're rapists," and nothing less than physical separation from Mexico was necessary (Mulloy 2018, 173). This claim pinpoints the racial politics of populism and fascism, and shows how populists use the gendered trope of defending and obtaining women. The films examined in this chapter reject this outright racist frame, yet they follow a consistent populist strategy of showing white womanhood threatened by feminists, leftists, bureaucrats, and/or politicians. The white hero is motivated by wanting to save a white woman in danger in each narrative.

CONSPIRACISM AND HYPER-MASCULINITY

Many films can be said to explore American populism. These three films are selected because of their relevance and time-frame—all films were released in the 1990s and influenced future events. Films as cultural products help legitimize some voices and silence others. A third reason is how gender is rarely the explicit subject of a film and is often used as a plot device, not as the narrative's central myth. These films examine gender thoroughly and how it is racialized and stylized explicitly. Overall, these films helped idealize and normalize two particular attitudes in their populist narratives: conspiracism and hyper-masculinity.

Conspiracism is usually assumed to be pervasive among people who hold little societal power (Mirowsky and Ross 1983; Sasson 1995). This chapter demonstrates this is untrue. Even elites who have substantive power can be drawn to conspiracy theories. While media and academic scholarship might be dismissive of conspiracy theories, conspiracy theorizing is a popular pastime for elite and non-elite alike. While both *Falling Down* and *Fight Club* feature conspiracism strongly, *Forrest Gump* references them only in passing (e.g., the Watergate conspiracy).

The masculine discourses in these films are complex because, in Foucauldian terms, sexual discourse includes moments of agency and structure (Foucault 1978). In the conspiracism context, the masculine is dominant for two reasons. One is the sheer popularity of it in popular and elite magazines, novels, and music. For instance, Ayn Rand's conspiratorial pro-masculine novel *Atlas Shrugs* (1957) has sold twenty *million* copies. Another is that pro-feminine forces are structurally weaker and need the help of the state, and when the state is hostile, it is harder for pro-feminine policies and rhetoric to resonate.

All the examined films reflect a pro-masculine frame and treat it as the norm. Forrest Gumb, a naïf main character, is driven mainly by a need to help others. Yet he is no less a masculine hero than Tyler Durden, the rebellious warrior of *Fight Club*. Connell argued that masculinity is "simultaneously a place in gender relations, the practices through which men and women engage that place in gender, and the effects of these practices on bodily experience, personality and culture" (1995, 71). Hyper-masculinity exaggerates these practices. If masculinity makes femininity and the feminine subordinate, hyper-masculinity drives such subordination to such an extreme it parodies normal masculinity. Hyper-masculinity sometimes exposes masculinity's weaknesses in paradoxical ways (Brookey and Westerfelhaus 2002; Peele 2001). In *Falling Down*, *Forrest Gump*, and *Fight Club*, gender is posited as a hyper-masculine arena the physically able and determined must survive in. Nevertheless, this forces the viewer to wonder if this form of masculinity is worth preserving.

These three films, in many ways, question the Reagan rhetoric about the hard-working white man. For example, with the exception of *Forrest Gump*, military veterans are not as idealized as they are routinely in right-wing films. Yet, these films are also suspicious of "pro-feminist," metro-sexual male of the 1990s who downplays his masculinity, and feminism is often shown to have a negative force linked to consumerism, conformity, and lack of self-control (Wang 1995). While each film embodies a masculine mythology, there are also key differences, with some accommodating racial diversity and others glorifying a past where white men were dominant.

THE ANGRY WHITE MALE STRIKES BACK: SCHUMACHER'S ANTI-REAGAN SATIRE

Falling Down depicts a stiff, white-collar worker called D-FENS (Michael Douglass) who goes on an urban rampage. D-FENS begins the film by leaving behind his car and venturing into an urban space filled with dangerous (often non-white) men testing his masculinity. Director Schumacher frames D-FENS as more than an individual gone berserk: the end of the Cold War has rendered him jobless. Once lucrative defense contracts have ceased, and while the rich in America remain comfortable, the middle class is symbolized as being in decline. Schumacher depicts Los Angeles as filled with African American homeless men, poor Latino immigrants desperately selling goods, and various white veterans begging for food (Davies 1995). Schumacher does not demonize these people; the American people are shown as being victimized by the Reagan administration's policies.[1] Thus, the film situates its white hero amid problems of structural unemployment, crime, and homelessness, which shows capitalism in a negative light. Yet, D-FENS, the protagonist, is not shown as solely good and noble; the audience soon realizes he is a flawed man in many ways.

In the narration, Schumacher frames blacks mainly in a sympathetic light. Asians, however, are a different matter. The first obstacle D-FENS faces is a greedy Korean store clerk refusing to give him change. Schumacher is careful to have the Korean initiate aggression by reaching for a phallic-shaped bat. As Mahoney notes, Schumacher wants us to see "the violence ('real' and epistemological) that is *done* to [Will] Foster (D-FENS)" (Mahoney 1997, 176). D-FENS's real name, Will, refers to his ironic lack of agency.

Will has a will only in a nominal sense at the start of the narrative. He is white and male but has little control over his life. As the narrative progresses, he gains agency by asserting his masculinity. In the Korean shop scene, a key scene in the film, American flags fall to the floor, and Will successfully wrests the bat and begins to destroy the shop. Will only acts violently, however, because the Korean clerk has been overcharging him with exploitative prices. Some non-white immigrants (but not all) have exploited the white man, and now the working-class white man is fighting his enemies, from Latino gangsters to rich white golfers, to reclaim his masculinity. While Schumacher denied he made a racist film, race was indeed intentionally made use of. Schumacher lamented Hollywood films showing Americans fed up with the system mostly were angry men played "by African-Americans. Well, they're not the only angry people in the United States" (Davies 1995, 214).

Will needs to forge a highly pro-American class-based populism to save America. While not a fascist himself, Will is alarmingly close to the classic fascist hero destroying a corrupt society to initiate the nation's rebirth. For instance, Will has a run-in with a neo-Nazi who talks loudly and disparagingly about two male customers that are coded as gay. The neo-Nazi also uses offensive slurs freely when referring to racial or sexual minorities. D-FENS is recognized by the neo-Nazi, who promises to protect him, much to D-FENS's puzzlement. The Nazi says he and D-FENS are the same. Will is shocked—he is unable to imagine how his (justified) white "American" rage can slide into pro-Hitler fascism of white supremacy. Despite mainly terrorizing non-whites, Will sees himself as not trying to hurt anyone.

It is understandable hearing about Will's rampage why the neo-Nazi would think his (pro-Hitler, fascist) ideology and Will's (all-American, victimized) populism are identical. Will rebuffs the neo-Nazi, who is angered and tries to apprehend Will at gunpoint. Will successfully resists and shoots the Nazi, whose body crashes into the mirror where we see Will's fractured reflection. Most of *Falling Down* sympathizes with Will and his plight, but the encounter with the Nazi shows a point where the earlier identification with Will's anger at racial minorities and the authorities has lessened. Will's killing the Nazi goes uncriticized: the Nazi is the extreme racist and sexist populism should reject. After killing the Nazi, Will abandons his stale, middle-class (literally white) clothes and puts on black army fatigues becoming an urban guerilla. The film tells us that while Will started with legitimate grievances, he has pushed his masculinity into dangerous fascist areas and should not be applauded.

Schumacher argues Reagan essentially exploited white rage to get himself into power but did not substantially help the working class once in office (Mulloy 2018). Yet the critique of Reagan goes further and blames feminism for Will's troubles and, by extension, all men. Even though Schumacher depicts D-FENS's ex-wife, Beth (Barbara Hershey), being justifiably worried about her ex-husband's violent temper, Beth herself simultaneously is portrayed as irrational, selfish, and mean-spirited. Thus, while Will should be angry at Reagan and the capitalist class that have betrayed the working class masses, politically correct ideologies like feminism and multiculturalism are also rendered suspect. As Beth tells him: "This isn't your home anymore" (Schumacher 1993).

Schumacher condemns both conservative trends (Reagan-style economics) and liberal ones (post-Sixties feminism). When Will tries reconnecting with Beth, police officer Prendergast (Robert Duvall) is there to intervene.[2] Will is shocked to learn that he himself is the villain of the story: "I'm the *bad* guy? How'd that happen?" (Schumacher 1993). Will is not a Nazi or a greedy capitalist. He just wants to see his child but as reasonable as his demands seem, they are putting others in danger. As Kennedy notes, the filmmakers "acknowledge race and class antagonisms while privileging the perspectives of a (de)centered white male subjectivity" (1996, 95). Ultimately, Will must die because his politics have become too extreme, but his death in a shootout is framed as tragic. Prendergast reluctantly plays the role of executor yet acknowledges the system has lied to everyone, including himself. Yet Will's death will financially benefit his small daughter. "I'm obsolete—not economically viable," D-FENS notes sadly before dying (Schumacher 1993). The film begins with a highly racialized message but ends with a more universal, class-based message for all Americans to challenge the system and insist on being justly treated.

Schumacher's conspiracism assumes the system has failed all men in America. As Kennedy argues: "*Falling Down* may parody the imperial individualism of white American manhood but it does not negate it, rather it retells . . . [its story] as a morality tale for multiracial, late imperial America" (Kennedy 1996, 99). By mythologizing Will's plight, all men can wake up and see that they must unite despite their differences. Ideally, Will might be part of a multiracial coalition. But in this particular story, he has pushed his populist masculinity into a dangerous form of neo-fascism. *Falling Down* leaves us in a critical gap. Neither fascism nor feminism will help Will or working-class America. But beyond organizing together across racial lines, the film does not propose how angry American men can change the system democratically or progressively. It may only be by dying that white men can help inspire a pro-democratic populist revolt.

THE MODERATE SOLUTION?
GUMP AS MYTHIC WHITE SAVIOR

Robert Zemeckis's *Forrest Gump* attempts to minimize racial and class tensions as virtually absent in American history. The titular character is a mentally defective naïf who selflessly helps everyone he encounters. A Southerner, devout Christian, and son of a single mother, Forrest Gump (Tom Hanks), unlike Will, has no flaws and is nearly invincible facing rednecks, Vietnamese guerillas, and other malcontents. While Gump fights in the Cold War, he hates no one. He is just "a saintly fool" who is uniquely good (Rosenbaum 1997, 166). Even admirers of the film do not deny Forrest is an idealized form of white manhood. On the contrary, admirers blatantly admit: "Forrest is our Everyman, that populist fellow who watches events like assassinations, wars, and political outrages with the unthinking aplomb of someone with no historical comprehension of the profound significance of what he is witnessing" (Early 2010, 217). Here, Forrest becomes a symbol for all Americans.

Forrest deeply believes in God and American ideals, and if these feel too absurd, then that the fault is on our (alleged) postmodern cynicism. Whereas *Falling Down* covers only one day in early 1990s Los Angeles, *Forrest Gump* ambitiously tries to cover American life from the 1950s to the 1980s by focusing on major historical events: from the rise of Rock & Roll to the Kennedy assassinations and from the Vietnam War to drug culture, ending on a thinly veiled AIDS metaphor. Forrest interacts with these events both in small and large ways, for example, by visiting a number of US presidents.

Signing up for Vietnam, Forrest befriends a black man, Bubba (Mykelti Williamson), and the two remain close until Bubba's death. He also meets a gritty (and white) Lieutenant Dan Taylor (Gary Sinise). The focus is on how white, black, and Latino soldiers suffer by constantly walking in the Vietnamese landscape. Forrest, for example, never comes face-to-face with the Vietnamese Communists. He merely runs to save his comrades from gunfire where the Communists are framed as the aggressors—in their own native country. To Rosenbaum, "*Forrest Gump* depicts Vietnam as a tragedy only for Americans" (1997, 169). For example, Forrest never saves any Vietnamese civilians; his concern is his fellow American soldiers.

When he returns home, Gump is surprised that his hometown crush, Jenny (Robin Wright), has joined the anti-war movement. Whereas the black and white soldiers are shown to be brave and good, most anti-war protestors are violent drug-using hypocrites. Forrest even beats up a white male anti-war activist who slaps Jenny. Tellingly, the white man is unkempt, thin, non-muscular, and physically powerful against a woman, but Gump quickly beats him. Thus, Gump exposes the hypocrisy of "anti-war" leftists who talk about anti-imperialism yet tolerate violence—against women. Almost all anti-war activists are depicted as "spoiled, self-centered and misguided" (Arnold 2006, 166). Violence against civil rights and anti-war activists is ignored—though Zemeckis did originally film scenes showing some activists being violently assaulted, this was ultimately cut from the theatrical version ("Gump Mania" 1995).

The major causes of the anti-war movement are solved in a privatized manner. Forrest accidentally helps put away Nixon by alerting hotel staff to the Watergate break-in: conspiracies exist, but the likes of Forrest expose them. A similar argument regarding faith and capitalism occurs with Dan, who is injured in Vietnam, loses his legs, and winds up as a wino. When Dan and Forrest reunite, Dan has lost his faith in God. Dan tells Forrest how a priest advised him, "God is listening, but I have to help myself" (Zemeckis 2001). Eventually, Dan joins Forrest in his shrimp business—as a way to honor Bubba. Once Dan becomes rich, he regains his faith. Dan is redeemed, as is Bubba's sacrifice when Forrest shares his wealth with Bubba's family.

Zemeckis also makes curious racial differentiations. While the Vietnamese are shown as either hapless villagers or enemies, the Chinese are depicted as mere curiosities or inferior. Forrest, as part of his armed service, becomes a master ping-pong player defeating Chinese players easily. Forrest becomes a minor celebrity and endorses ping-pong paddles bearing the likeness of Mao. While Zemeckis parodies some extremities among anti-Communists, the viewer is never left in doubt that capitalism and Christianity are superior to godless Communism.

Forrest's very name comes from "General Nathan Bedford Forrest, who founded the Ku Klux Klan, in the 1860s. As Gump narrates this background, we see footage of the general leading the Klan. Gump . . . [as] redeemer of the nation . . . can transcend the ugly aspects of its past" (Chumo 1995, 3). Native Americans, African Americans, and non-white immigrants should not look to the government for help. They should not organize for revolution but rededicate themselves to the myth of American self-help and patriotic, religious charity. Regarding this, the film has one moment of radicalism. After Bubba's mother is rich, we see explicitly a white woman serving her as she sits in a mansion. The black woman now has power; she controls her wealth—but it was only due to Forrest's generosity.[3] Thus as mythic, as *Forrest Gump* is, it touches on a reality that some non-whites have succeeded in capitalist America. Whether this success is enough is not addressed by the narrative.

As Wang notes, the film creates a binary between good, patriotic non-whites and dangerous dark-skinned men. When Gump tries to see alerted

Jenny in Washington, DC, she has become a radical anti-war activist and is working with the Black Panthers. During his encounter with the Black Panthers, Wang comments how the film shows "the danger of black autonomy to a white woman and by giving voice to the threats of Black Nationalism, *Forrest Gump* emphasizes the need to keep these bodies under white America's control" (Wang 2000, 98). At the Black Panther meeting, an image of Argentine revolutionary Communist Che Guevara is clearly visible in the background.

While Gump mainly helps people one-on-one like Jenny, he does sometimes help people en masse. Spontaneously, Gump runs cross-country in the 1970s, and people follow him. He doles out platitudes to his followers, who find profound meaning in them, like an odd mixture of populist politician and a messiah. Gump's life is heroic, but paradoxically he is also a victim.

Near the conclusion, Gump reunites with Jenny, and they marry. The reunion, including the meeting with his (normal) child and his cumulated wealth, rewards Gump's choices to follow the mythic code of being a strong patriotic white man and rich beyond measure. Yet, he is too late to save Jenny. She, followed the anti-war movement, had uninhibited sex, subscribed to radical politics, and embraced feminism, has become infected with a mysterious disease (AIDS) and is condemned to death. The pro-conservative message was so clear that Patrick Buchanan, who ran for president in 2000, accepted the film as reflecting a pro-Reagan, pro-patriotic message (Buchanan 1994).

Symbolically, the 1960s is framed as a lost period where America was torn by "extremists" on both sides—the KKK and racists, and unpatriotic protestors. Only Gump, and some decent non-whites and whites, succeeded and survived. Gump is denied a loving wife (like Will), but he has a small boy he can love and raise. Similarly, Dan has been on trial due to his disability, yet his faith is rewarded. At Gump's wedding, he is walking on (metal) legs and is accompanied by a wife, an attractive Asian woman, Susan (Teresa Denton). Brave white men, while victimized by unpatriotic elites, survived and have overcome the legacies of racism and classism. Despite racists and feminists' efforts—shockingly equated as equally evil and culpable—Gump is the moderate non-racist white who served his country. While he lost many people, he gained a child to raise, and valuable friends, black and white.

BACK TO THE URBAN:
FANTASIES OF CHALLENGING THE MAN

In many ways, *Fight Club* is an update of *Falling Down*. However, Director David Fincher parodies, in key respects, the urban thriller Schumacher created. *Falling Down* offers an affirming message that a patriotic populism may triumph over Reaganism. *Fight Club* is much more cynical and argues that if men are to find a healthy masculinity, it may only be among a select group of friends who reject both feminism but traditional forms of authority. If *Forrest Gump* is pure fantasy, *Fight Club* moderates the fantasy of the violent male. It also eliminates the pro-capitalist, conservative message Zemeckis had. *Fight Club* is a straightforward appeal to men that they need to rethink what being a masculine male means and not necessarily accept what the American army or mainstream media think men should do.

In the beginning, the narrator (Edward Norton) is held at gunpoint. He has the gun in the mouth as if performing fellatio. A major terrorist attack is about to occur when the narrator breaks the fourth wall and tells us how he got into such a weird situation. Through flashbacks, he tells the audience about himself. The narrator admits he is a well-paid white-collar worker. Stressed by boredom and ethical compromises that his work as a corporate employee entails, the narrator laments becoming "a slave" to "the Ikea nesting instinct. We [presumably the narrator means men] used to read pornography. Now it was the Horchow Collection. I . . . [e]ven [had] the glass dishes . . . crafted by the . . . hard-working indigenous peoples of wherever" (Fincher 2002).

The narrator finds momentary relief by infiltrating support groups for bowel and brain cancer. The narrator enjoys listening to other people's traumas, calling the support group "my vacation" (Fincher 2002). However, a sexy smoker, Marla (Helena Botham Carter), intrudes into his groups, and her obvious lies about having cancer anger him. Insomnia from which the narrator had been suffering from returns, for which he blames Marla. The narrator meets Tyler Durden, a salesman, by chance and is attracted to Tyler's easy-going attitude and devil-may-care philosophy.

Whereas the narrator is often nervous and anxious, Tyler is confident that he is right and modern society is corrupt and decadent. The narrator moves in with Tyler, who slowly persuades him to accept his hyper-masculine philosophy and for men to reclaim their primal nature and reject consumer society as false. The narrator accepts Tyler's idea they need to create an army. The narrator goes from a puny, weak white-collar worker to a chiseled masculine warrior. He stops sleepwalking and becomes an active, engaged man.

While the narrator enjoys a sense of belonging to a group with the men in fight club, the dynamic remains exclusionary. For instance, after the fight club has begun, the narrator and Tyler walk down the street; they talk with one another and then hop onto a bus. The narrator sees an advertisement for underwear and says in voiceover how he felt "sorry for all the guys packing into gyms, trying to look like what Calvin Klein and Tommy Hilfiger said they should" (Fincher 2002). The narrator does not notice or care that Tyler's own stylish clothes, indebted to "grunge," is no less superficial

(Bedford 2011). Furthermore, the narrator looks at an advertisement featuring a male model in his underwear and another male model showing off his naked buttocks. The narrator mockingly asks Tyler: "Is that what a man looks like?" (Fincher 2002). Only the upper classes can afford to become male models, and Tyler mocks the upper classes as unmanly. "Self-improvement is masturbation," Tyler snidely remarks (Fincher 2002). Men trying to look like models are not real men but too sensitive about their looks. Tyler's words add a neofascist subtext. The male models are symbols of (bad) male "queerness." Tyler never explicitly attacks homosexuality but the only queer images explicitly in the film are of naked lesbians.[4] In short, homosexuality is to be tolerated; it has to suit white men's interests and desires. Likewise, while the fight club is ostensibly multiracial and non-hierarchical, the narrator is the presumptive (white) leader.

The film also uses a differentiation of the (white) male body conforming to a certain pattern. For instance, during the support groups, the narrator meets Bob (Marvin "Meatloaf" Aday), whose male breasts have become female-like and large due to the misuse of steroids. Bob, in the support group, hugs the narrator into his breasts. When he reappears later, it turns out Bob is in fight club. Fight club's strange rules include the rule that during a fight, men cannot wear shirts or shoes (Fincher 2002). But when the narrator fights Bob, the viewer sees the narrator's bare chest. Bob, however, keeps his shirt on. Presumably, a man with woman-like breasts showing off his body would be excessive and is thus never shown. This visual and plot contradiction is never addressed. The narrator says Tyler's rules, such as not talking about fight club, are to be followed without exception. Either the narrator is simply lying, or the extradiegetic narrator allows a sole exception to Tyler's rules in order to create an exclusionary understanding of the masculine.

Treatment of the effeminate males and the female characters makes it reasonable to argue that in the film, "women, *in general,* constitute the problem" to be solved by the narrator and Tyler (Wager 2009, 108 emphases added). In the bathroom of their broken-down house, Tyler speaking to the narrator makes this sexism explicit, speaking of how disappointing his mother has been. Tyler says: "I'm wondering if another woman is really the answer we need" (Fincher 2002). To be sure, one can read the text against Tyler's intent and argue the bathroom-scene implies homosexuality. Tyler's populism is *potentially* pro-queer, even when Fincher does not follow up on this. Scholars have noted how the narrative continually works to normalize heterosexism and put down homosexuality (Brookey and Westerfelhaus 2002). The feminine is consistently devalued. Even the female body is devalued. Tyler and the narrator steal women's fat dumped in the garbage to produce soap and sell it to pay for the fight club. The premise is played for laughs, but the fact remains men are using women's body parts for profit.

Asian, Latin, and African American members in the fight club show that it is racially inclusive. But this inclusiveness is deceptive. When Tyler goes to sell his soap, he goes to a plush beauty shop, he chats with and charms a young African American woman, Susan (Valerie Bickford), he looks like a "neo-70s pimp . . . with buzz-cut hair and big dark sunglasses" (Greven 2009, 162). The film taps into black sexuality, but only Tyler is shown engaged in possible interracial romance. The narrator never sees a sexual interest in non-white women. Indeed, except for Susan, non-white women are framed as civilians the narrator speaks to and sees but takes no interest in.[5]

The unreliable narration of the Norton-narrator in no way blocks the central message that "white men . . . [are] victims of society and, at the same time, adequately strong, virile, tough, and in control of their lives" (Kusz 2002, 469). The toughness white men demand is realized by Tyler having the men in fight club dressed in lookalike black clothes and act like robots obeying him. The extradiegetic narrator may not openly accept Tyler's crazed philosophy but provides non-diegetic music to make Tyler's terrorism appear just and good.

As with the other two films selected, Fincher inserts moments of anti-capitalism and anti-authoritarianism to try to distance the film from fascism. When the police attempt to investigate the fight club, Tyler grabs an (old) white police chief and orders him "to call off your rigorous investigation." Otherwise, Tyler's men will "take your balls." As Tyler warns him: "The people you are after are the people you depend on. We cook your meals, we haul your trash. . . . We guard you while you sleep" (Fincher 2002). The upper classes are weak, old, even white. Tyler's men, white and black, are young, tough, and courageous. In short, the upper classes survive on Tyler's sufferance, and the men of the fight club do not need them. Tyler sees his men as victims of capitalism, "slaves with white collars" (Fincher 2002). Nevertheless, Fincher presents Tyler's motives as non-racial: That the men of fight club are sometimes non-white and come to worship him appears as a coincidence.

Nevertheless, one scene is racial and anticipates Trump's anti-Chinese ideology. The narrator and Tyler go late at night to a liquor store. Tyler goes and finds an Asian clerk, Raymond Hessel (Joon Kim)—who in the DVD is designated as "Human Sacrifice." The words do appear in the source novel where Tyler is talking about soap (Palahniuk 1997, 75) and where Hessel is explicitly called "Caucasian" (Palahniuk 1997, 152). It is Fincher's decision to draw on the stereotype of the physically weak Asian clerk in a number of films from *Menace II Society* (Hughes and Hughes 1993) to Michael Bay's *Bad Boys* (1995) as well as Schumacher's film with its greedy Korean clerk.

Also, Hessel has done nothing to provoke Tyler, unlike Schumacher's Korean clerk. Tyler still initiates aggression, grabs Hessel, and forces him outside the store to a dirty yard. Hessel falls to the ground and is turned into a stuttering, crying coward. Like Bob, Hessel "acts as one of a series of foils that designate the lower extreme of masculinity" (Locke 2014, 65). Hessel admits (*at gunpoint*) that he studied to be a veterinarian but quit school. Tyler has Hessel promise he will go back to school or die. As Hessel scurries off, Tyler mockingly yells: "Run Forrest! Run!" (Fincher 2002). The narrator is shocked and demands to know why Tyler almost killed Hessel. However, Tyler was merely bluffing, and the gun was empty. Tyler is a terrorist, but instead of cruelty Tyler has engaged in, at worst, "benevolent paternalism" (Locke 2014, 62). Tyler makes these pleas sound non-racial, but a racial tinge persists. Asian men need to be terrorized into embracing their masculinity, while whites, as well as black and Latino, men need only Tyler's verbal support to become real men. Norton-narrator even jokes that Tyler would like to fight Gandhi.

Whether the Norton-narrator really was a mere bystander to Tyler's terrorizing Hessel is not clarified even at the conclusion. It could be the narrator is simply recalling events favorable to him—he might have actually enjoyed Tyler's torturing Hessel—yet the question as to why the extradiegetic narrator is allowing the Norton-narrator to present himself as an innocent is not answered. Fincher might be mocking the narrator's naïve nature, or more disturbingly, Fincher differentiates Tyler as the bad (white) fascist taking his ideology too far and the narrator as the good (white) populist male who wakes up to the evils of consumerist capitalism.

Project Mayhem is highly decentralized—fight clubs have spontaneously appeared in many major cities—but Tyler never loses control. Near the end, Tyler is revealed as a full-blown fascist and his populism as a lie. He promised to liberate the men from a feminized consumer society, yet his highly masculine fascist cult enslaves them. The men even wear similar black shirts like uniforms (a reference to Mussolini and Hitler) and practice military drills. Unlike in *Forrest Gump*, where the military is idealized, the fight club men use military tactics but hate patriotism and mock the American flag. The terror they practice is organic and direct. All men must band together to fight feminism, capitalism, and consumerism. Yet Fincher complicates the populist message. When Tyler, however, kidnaps Marla, the narrator takes the extreme step of shooting himself, and the narration circles back to the beginning.

Vanquished, the narrator embraces Marla as both look to the night skyline as buildings collapse. Project Mayhem has not been stopped; corporate buildings collapse. In the final frames, a male penis, fully erect, appears for a moment. The deep questions of how power, class, race, and sex work in modern society are tossed out for a conclusion featuring an "orgy of male violence and racism, male homosocial and erotic couplings, and misogyny" (Wager 2009, 113). The revolutionary message turns out to be a joke.

Despite Fincher's satirical tone, the populist anger he focuses on was all too real. The film's producers wanted to have Tyler destroy a specific target their audience would cheer being destroyed in the form of credit card companies (Raftery 2019, 219). Even with a booming economy and a pre-9/11 America, many men gravitated to *Fight Club* and literally created fight clubs in their communities. While some non-whites have also celebrated *Fight Club*, its main fan base has been white men who feel alienated and want to reclaim a masculinity they see as being repressed.

From beginning to end, the film is about how a white male deals with power and politics. Women play only a peripheral role. Whereas Palahniuk's Marla is tough and independent, Marla in the film repeatedly needs saving having little independent willpower.[6] Nevertheless, Marla is the agent who awakens the narrator to the secret of who Tyler really is. But she is punished and not rewarded for helping the white hero. Hence Grønstad may be right and Fincher is (mostly) satirizing fascism, but it is not true that the film is "admitting that masculinity is . . . an empty signifier" (2008, 175). On the contrary, the narrator and Tyler have privileged status because they are men. With the exceptions of Hessel and Bob, virtually all men have agency while women are inactive. Whereas Forrest copes with his male pain with God's help, in *Fight Club*, there is no God. The men in fight club want the world to change to accommodate their displays of masculinity in their self-inflicted wounds.

The dilemma is that *Fight Club* moves beyond simply tolerating other genders into actively devaluing other than heterosexuality and force conflict on unsuspecting men (and women) to better themselves. *While* it retains the notions of heterosexuality, toughness, and victimhood, *Fight Club* redefines victimhood as simply being intolerant to lower forms of masculinity—especially those of Asian men. The narrative does reject Tyler's fascist purity as too dangerous, but it provides no roadmap on how the populist anger it alludes to is to be solved. At least, *Falling Down* hints that white men must join with other classes, and even genders, if American democracy is to be saved. Fincher only gives the audience a private romance. The larger fate of other people is not of much concern to the narrator. He has become a populist, but his politics will apparently be confined to be a good husband to Marla and nothing more.

CONCLUSION: MYTHS OF THE PAST, POLITICS OF THE NOW

Having analyzed these three films, several conclusions can be made. One is that populism as a discourse operates at multiple levels. Its appeal is to not one race or one class alone. It seeks to both unify and divide. The good people unite against the bad, and people are judged by being virtuous, tough, honest, and sincere. While Communism is never embraced, populists offer a class-based critique. But class is defined not as income or even wealth but as a set of attitudes and virtues. What makes Will and the narrator good men is that they are honest, compassionate, and virile—they are also violent, aggressive, and assertive. But such violence is legitimized, being used again by those trying to constrain their masculinity.

In American right-wing populist imageries, tough white and black men can come together, but women are perennially suspicious. Women's roles are mainly as romantic partners. In Trump's case, the anti-feminist populism is taken to an extreme with him admitting as a white man with wealth that all women were mere objectives. "You can do anything [to them]. . . . Grab them by the pussy" (Mulloy 2018, 176). In contrast, Tyler and Will try to avoid physically assaulting women. A marriage with a loving woman is idealized in all these films. Trump's hyper-masculine populism has a strong sense of sexism, and the filmmakers reject that. But they idealize a moderate form of sexism where the men have power over women. In *Forrest Gump*, Jenny tragically dies because Forrest lets Jenny choose to become a protest singer and be involved in the anti-war movement. The implication being that if only Forrest had forced Jenny to marry him early in the narrative, she might have been saved.

Fight Club, in particular, also anticipates Trump's love of militarism and violence but mocking of American soldiers. Tyler is a Nietzschean who sees himself as a powerful male warrior. However, he joins no army and is no soldier. The militarism and warrior ethic are raw and direct. Warriors (especially if they succeed) and touch men are applauded. But Trump has little real belief in traditional patriotism. The real populist sees through the illusions of capitalism, feminism, and even patriotism. It is not by some cosmopolitan abstractions that society can be saved but through a direct (violent) bonding of white men and non-white men joining in overthrowing a decadent elite and seizing power directly. Will no less than Tyler expose the very real hypocrisies of the media, the political elite, and the capitalist class promising rewards for hard work and good behavior.

The answer is not to reject the messages in these films wholesale. Populism has a dimension amenable to pro-democratic reform. As Kazin advises, "when a new breed of inclusive grassroots movements does arise, intellectuals should contribute their time, their money, and their passion for justice. They should work to stress the harmonious, hopeful, and pragmatic aspects of populist language and to disparage the meaner ones" (1995, 284). Populism as a discourse is not predestined to be a reactionary force only. Populism is "more an impulse than an ideology" and can shift from left to right quickly (Kazin 1995, 3). What is necessary is to be aware that right-wing populist images do resonate with a large part of the public (if not the majority).[7] Movements on the left from labor to the anti-war movement have also been marked by conspiracism (and, unfortunately, racial and gender exclusion) and populist language. But whereas left-wing movements have a self-critical dynamic, right-wing movements tend to be less prone to internal self-correction, and reform is often superficial.

The point of the analysis has not been to malign all populists (even conservative ones) as sexist neo-fascists. Populism has democratic potential, but a consistent theme in these films is that others must be excluded for (some white) heroes to triumph. Ironically, some of those excluded are rich white men like Trump. But for the most part, the excluded include white criminals, Latino gangsters, Asian men, and feminists. This may seem to narrow populism only to white men, but this is untrue. However, narrow, Trump's populism promises to empower non-white men as well (though only to a certain degree). The appeal of populism is that it legitimizes reactionary attitudes and arguments as authentic, real, wholesome, even natural. For instance, African American boxing star Floyd Mayweather Jr. defended Trump's sexist remarks as an example of how "a real man" talks (Bieler 2017). In other words, Trump's demonization of women, the Chinese, and others is normal. America should defend itself from enemies, foreign and domestic. Men should assert their masculinity. A normative attitude is naturalized as what should be expected among people.

This chapter has tried to show attitudes embodied in popular culture that helped normalize attitudes that paved the way for Trump's hyper-masculine populism. Cultural symbols are difficult to interpret, must be integrated into a broader research strategy of how fascists can appropriate popular culture to their cause (Teitelbaum 2014). In that respect, the analysis is cautionary. Popular culture both reflects but also helps define attitudes political elites use and manipulate. Films like novels and television shows are not one-way devices but can offer dynamic dialogue. However, the conclusion reached here is that popular culture's dominant themes can legitimize and glorify an exclusionary form of populism. Those seeking to understand how fascism quickly has gained power would do well to study how the attitudes giving rise to the reactionary right have been with us and widely celebrated for some time.

NOTES

1. According to Robert Pollin, even aside from government debt, corporate debt was so high by the end of the 1980s that "by the time the recession began in July 1990,

corporate interest rates were absorbing 44 percent of pretax profits" (gdt. in Chomsky 1993, 111).

2. Schumacher does not idealize the police either. One black police officer, in fact, arrests an African American protestor. Prendergast appears to be an exception in a corrupt system.

3. It is true some non-whites like Oprah Winfrey have even become billionaires but the film avoids how even with substantial wealth minorities are nowhere close to the wealth of rich whites like Bill Gates. "Wealth" is treated as a good Americans should pursue but how much is not specified by Zemeckis tellingly.

4. Fincher could be mocking pornography more than enacting it. There are no explicit references to lesbianism in the other films analyzed but Fincher allows lesbians some (albeit troublesome) representation.

5. One single shot shows a non-white woman at the support group, but we learn nothing about her or her pain.

6. Richard Schickel, for instance, blamed Marla's dullness on "feminism's [!] failures" (qdt. in Wager 2009, 105). A stunning conclusion but one *Fight Club* does indeed hint at.

7. While this chapter is self-consciously written to aid comparative analyses of populism, there is one key issue—God—which probably matters less in other contexts; with the possible exception of Russia, populists in other countries appeal to the people's xenophobia and fears notably with no message about God as they do in the United States.

BIBLIOGRAPHY

Arnold, Gordon. 2006. *Afterlife of the Vietnam War: Changing Visions in Politics and on Screen*. Jefferson: McFarland & Co.

Bay, Michael, dir. 1995. *Bad Boys*. Columbia Pictures.

Bedford, Mark. 2011. "Smells Like 1990s Spirit: The Dazzling Deception of *Fight Club*'s Grunge-Aesthetic." *New Cinemas* 9 (1): 49–63.

Berlet, Chip, and Lyons, Matthew. 2000. *Right-Wing Populism in America: Too Close for Comfort*. New York: Guilford Press.

Bieler, Des. 2017. "Floyd Mayweather Says Trump's 'Locker-Room Talk' is How 'Real Men' Speak." *Washington Post*, September 14, 2017. https://www.washingtonpost.com/news/early-lead/wp/2017/09/14/floyd-mayweather-says-trumps-locker-room-talk-is-how-real-men-speak/.

Blee, Kathleen. 2002. *Inside Organized Racism: Women and the Hate Movement*. Berkeley, CA: University of California Press.

Brookey, Robert, and Robert Westerfelhaus. 2002. "Hiding Homoeroticism in Plain View: *The Fight Club* DVD as Digital Closet." *Critical Studies in Media Communication* 19 (1): 21–43.

Buchanan, Patrick J. 1994. "Hollywood Surprise. 'Hello, I'm Forrest Gump and I'm a Conservative.'" *The Pittsburgh Post-Gazette*, August 8, 1994: B3.

Chomsky, Noam. 1993. *Year 501*. Boston: South End Press.

Chumo, P. N. 1995. "'You've Got to Put the Past behind You Before You Can Move On': Forrest Gump and National Reconciliation." *Journal of Popular Film and Television* 23 (1): 2–7.

Connell, R. W. 1995. *Masculinities*. Berkeley, CA: University of California Press.

Davies, Jude. 1995. "Gender, Ethnicity and Cultural Crisis in *Falling Down* and *Groundhog Day*." *Screen* 36 (3): 14–32.

Diamond, Sara. 1995. *Roads to Dominion: Right Wing Political Movements and Political Power in the United States*. New York: Guildford.

Dobratz, Betty A., and Stephanie L. Shanks-Meile. 1997. *The White Separatist Movement in the United States: "White Power, White Pride!"* Baltimore: John Hopkins University Press.

Early, Emmett. 2003. *The War Veteran in Film*. Jefferson, NC: McFarland & Sons.

Fincher, David, dir. 1999. *Fight Club*. Los Angeles: 20th-Century Fox. DVD, 2002.

Foucault, Michel. 1978. *The History of Sexuality Volume I: An Introduction*. New York: Vintage.

Greven, David. 2009. *Manhood in Hollywood from Bush to Bush*. Austin: University of Texas Press.

Griffin, Roger. 1991. *The Nature of Fascism*. New York: Routledge.

Grønstad, Asbjørn. 2008. *Transfigurations: Violence, Death and Masculinity in American Cinema*. Amsterdam: Amsterdam University Press.

"Gump Mania." 1995. *Spy*. February 1995: 46.

Hughes, Albert, and Allen Hughes, dir. 1993. *Menace II Society*. New Line Cinema.

Kazin, Michael. 1995. *The Populist Persuasion: An American History*. New York: Basic Books.

Kennedy, Liam. 1996. "Alien Nation: White Paranoia and Imperial Culture in the U.S." *The Journal of American Studies* 30 (1): 87–100.

Keskinen, Suvi. 2014. "Re-constructing the Peaceful Nation: Negotiating Meanings of Whiteness, Immigration and Islam after a Shopping Mall Shooting." *Social Identities: Journal for the Study of Race, Nation and Culture* 20 (6): 471–485.

Kusz, Kyle W. 2002. "*Fight Club* and the Art/Politics of White Male Victimization and Reflexive Sadomasochism." *International Review for the Sociology of Sport* 37 (3–4): 465–470.

Locke, Brian. 2014. "'The White Man's Bruce Lee': Race and the Construction of White Masculinity in David Fincher's *Fight Club*." *Journal of Asian American Studies* 17 (1): 61–89.

Mahoney, Elizabeth. 1997. "The People in Parentheses: Space Under Pressure in the Post-Modern City." In *The Cinematic City*, edited by David Clarke, 168–185. London: Routledge.

Mayer, Jane. 2016. *Dark Money: The Hidden History of the Billionaires Behind the Rise of the Radical Right*. New York: Doubleday.

McDonald, Andrew [William Pierce]. 1989 [1978]. *The Turner Diaries*. Hillsboro, WV: National Vanguard Books.

Mirowsky, John, and Catherine E. Ross. 1983. "Paranoia and the Structure of Powerlessness." *American Sociological Review* 48 (2): 228–239.

Monbiot, George. 2010. "The Tea Party Movement: Deluded and Inspired by Billionaires." *The Guardian*, October 25, 2010. www.guardian.co.uk/commentisfree/cifamerica/2010/oct/25/tea-party-koch-brothers.

Mulloy, D. J. 2018. *Enemies of the State: The Radical Right from FDR to Trump.* Lanham: Rowman & Littlefield.

Palahniuk, Chuck, dir. 1997. *Fight Club.* New York: Vintage.

Peele, Thomas. 2001. "*Fight Club*'s Queer Representations." *JAC: Journal of Advanced Composition Theory* 21 (1): 862–869.

Raftery, Brian. 2019. *Movie. Year. Ever.: How 1999 Blew Up the Big Screen.* New York: Simon & Schuster.

Rand, Ayn. 1957. *Atlas Shrugged.* New York: Random House.

Rosenbaum, Jonathan. 1997. *Movies as Politics.* Berkeley, CA: University of California Press.

Sasson, Theodore. 1995. "African American Conspiracy Theories and the Social Construction of Crime." *Sociological Inquiry* 65 (3–4): 265–268.

Snow, David, E. Burke Rochford, Steven K. Worden, and Robert D. Benford. 1986. "Frame Alignment Processes, Micromobilization, and Movement Participation." *American Sociological Review* 51: 464–481.

Schumacher, Joel, dir. 1993. *Falling Down.* Los Angeles: Warner Brothers. DVD, 2009.

Teitelbaum, Benjamin R. 2014. "Saga's Sorrow: Femininities of Despair in the Music of Radical White Nationalism." *Ethnomusicology* 58 (3): 405–430.

Wager, Jans B. 2009. *Dames in the Driver's Seat: Rereading Film Noir.* Austin: University of Texas Press.

Wang, Barbara. 2000. "A Struggle of Contending Stories: Race, Gender, and Political Memory in *Forrest Gump*." *Cinema Journal* 39: 92–115.

Zemeckis, Robert, dir. 1994. *Forrest Gump.* Hollywood, CA: Paramount Pictures. DVD, 2001.

Chapter 8

Hypermasculine Images and the Hindu Identity in Malayalam Cinema

Swapna Gopinath

Indian society has been in a state of flux since the 1990s, post-globalization and the subsequent transformations in Indian sociopolitical, economic, and cultural discourses. The transition from a welfare state to a neoliberal one, which began with the opening up of the markets in the 1990s, is still in progress, while the shift to a right-wing Hindu political power is shaping the nation's identity in multifarious ways. To embrace these changes in India's social scenario, visual cultural practices have evolved over the past decades. Similarly, cinema has responded to these changes in Indian society in fascinating ways. A popular form of entertainment, cinema has captured the shifting paradigms of social sensibility, ranging from earlier films of patriotic fervor to later transnational cinema and to movies for urban multiplex audiences.

Since its inception as a free nation, India as a democracy has negotiated sociocultural and political meanings by means of cinema. Cultural production and practices have addressed issues of nationalism and identities. In recent times, the hegemonic power centers, particularly the politically defined religious group identity of the dominant Hindu, who have acknowledged cinema's uncontested influence among the populace, have closely monitored and censured the politics of representation in films. Hence, the dialectics at work between social realities and cinema ought to be critically studied. Through a reading of Malayalam films, a regional Indian film industry, this chapter provides insight into the altered realities of social living, especially since neoliberal practices and the Hindutva politics of identity have emerged as key components in Indian social discourses.

Apart from Bollywood, the Hindi film industry, which is popular nationwide and internationally, India has regional film industries in respective vernacular languages. The Malayalam film industry, or Mollywood, belongs to one of the southern states, Kerala. Mollywood has a rich film tradition, including prominent filmmakers of experimental cinema who have adopted techniques and stylistic patterns from such world cinema traditions as Italian neorealism. For example, auteurs like Adoor Gopalakrishnan have brought in laurels internationally and paved the way for greater experimentation with techniques and themes. Since 1928, the Malayalam cinema industry has grown steadily, and it has attracted the attention of the dominant Hindi Bollywood industry, which has remade several Malayalam films in Hindi. Kerala, where Malayalam movies are produced, has burgeoning film societies in rural and urban areas, creating an audience that appreciates both artistic and commercial cinema. Additionally, the films have a diaspora audience with the Malayalee population in the Gulf countries and other parts of the world.

Malayalam cinema since its beginning has flourished with the presence of talented artists and technicians. Since the 1980s, two male actors, Mohanlal and Mammootty, have dominated the industry and both still enjoy huge popularity as iconic images of Malayalam cinema. Neelima Menon (2019) has observed that in 1986, both actors emerged as superstars with the release of *Rajavinte Makan* (Kannanthanam 1986) and *Aavanazhi* (Sasi 1986), thereby establishing their formidable presence. They remained commercially viable stars capable of consecutive solo hits in the decades to follow, and won laurels and innumerable awards for their roles.

By mid-1990s and early 2000s, the rise of a new protagonist with a toxic male identity had slowly begun to evolve. This trend also transformed the stardom of Mammootty and Mohanlal. Mohanlal had begun his career by playing villains, such as in the film *Manjil Virinja Pookkal* (*Flowers that bloomed in the snow*, Fazil 1980). Later he shifted to the roles of major protagonists and gained immense popularity as a superstar. Mammootty, on the other hand, had started by playing lead roles, and he had established his popularity with family drama roles of a sophisticated elite individual. Since the late 1980s up until the present day, they have made more than thirty films. Since most of them have Hindu male protagonists, these films demonstrate the remarkable shift in the understanding of masculinity that has been happening in contemporary India. I will indicate the patterns of masculine identities portrayed by these two prominent actors during the period of an ideological shift that has happened in India throughout the late twentieth and early twenty-first centuries.

MASCULINITIES

R. W. Connell (1987, 16), one of the pioneers in masculinity studies, observes that we cannot have a unitary concept about masculinity, since there are multiple masculinities. Masculinity, therefore, is a complex range of identities, or as Philippa Gates (2006, 29) comments: "the reality is that masculinity is not homogeneous and consists of an array of multiple masculinities differentiated by class, race, ethnicity, sexual orientation, age, and other social determinants." Although not all masculine identities are toxic or aggressive, traditional, hegemonic masculinity often strives to be assertive, aggressive, and dominating (Butler 1990, 25). Many of the Mohanlal and Mammootty films choose to adopt a masculine representation that is endorsed by patriarchal hegemonic structures.

Masculinities are always bound to social structures, which shape subjectivities. As Bourdieu (2001, 11) observes: "The social world constructs the body, both as gendered reality and as depository of the categories of gendering perception and appreciation." Hegemonic masculine identities are constructed similarly, and they tend to be toxic, patriarchal, influential, and idealized (Tosh 1999). Hegemonic masculinity also strives to remain as the dominant or normative one, and display certain characteristic features. Manliness in this context is often defined as being physically strong, ready for combat, and sexually virile. Furthermore, hypermasculine selves are those where "three behavioral dispositions are justified by beliefs: entitlement to callous sex, violence as manly and danger as exciting" (Mosher and Tomkins 1988, 61).

The notion of symbolic violence is particularly important in the context of cinematic representations of masculinities where violence is endorsed in multifarious ways. Symbolic violence is considered "the essential part of masculine domination" (Bourdieu 1990, 11), which also translates into hypermasculinity as the "masculinity of protection" (Young 2003, 6). This symbolic violence legitimates inequality and structural violence aimed at women and other marginalized groups in society. Young (2003, 6), drawing on Foucault, argues that: "Masculinist protection is more like pastoral power . . . than dominative power that exploits those it rules for its own aggrandizement." Similarly, films, where the male protagonist who rises in power as a threat or fear of threat, reinforce the gender hierarchy and patriarchal supremacy. The "authoritarian security paradigm" (Young 2003, 9) validates the arguments of male dominance, and the male protagonist becomes the "master and patriarch where slaves, wives and children are his property" (Mosher and Tomkins 1988, 64). Similarly, in many of the Mammootty and Mohanlal films, the male protagonists are drawn using the help of violence, fear of violence, and the emerging figure of the male patriarch who protects and guards his property including the women and children in his family and community. This calls for a critical analysis of these films which depict masculinity in ways that are misogynous and toxic.

DEPICTION OF MASCULINITY IN
MALAYALAM CINEMA

Sreehari, in his article on Malayalam cinema, writes that masculine hegemony is visible in Malayalam films right from the beginnings of the industry. Even when the films depicted social realism or focused on female centered projects, the perspective was invariably patriarchal and dominated by the male point of view (Sreehari 2008, 1240–1241). The much-lauded art films were no exception. By the 1980s, a celebration of male bodies began which saw its glorious era from the 1990s to the turn of the millennium. "Man is the megastar" (Sreehari 2008, 1241) in the films where the superstars Mammootty and Mohanlal reigned as hegemonic male protagonists. A masculine consciousness, a powerful male identity that seeks to negate all other male selves in Kerala is perpetuated by Malayalam cinema and films where its superstars reiterated the hegemony of the upper-caste misogynous male self.

Malayalam cinema's rich and varied tradition has witnessed the rise of heroes, male protagonists who were predominantly identified as upper caste, since the latter half of twentieth century. Even in films that depicted the lives of the marginalized, the heroes were almost always fair complexioned and visibly belonging to the hegemonic caste categories. For example, Prem Nazir, the earliest male hero from Malayalam cinema, a Mollywood leading man from 1950s to late-1980s, was "gentle and almost feminized" and "constructed an image of the ideal conjugal" (Kumar 2015, 33). Satyan, a male lead mainly known from his 1960s and 1970s work, was "suave and sophisticated" (33), while Madhu, yet another leading man from the 1960s to the 1980s, was "romantic and self-sacrificing" (33). Their masculinity was not defined in muscular physique or flexing muscles. This changed in the 1980s, after the actor Jayan had become celebrated as a new strong male hero who singlehandedly fought his enemies. Jayan's "trademark swagger and temerarious stunts" (33) are iconic even decades after his untimely demise. While Jayan's films had a niche audience, and they rarely found favor among the family audience, a growing number of admirers lauded his skills and made his films highly successful. After the tragic death of Jayan (1980), while shooting a risky stunt, two actors, Mohanlal and Mammootty, emerged as trendsetters. The trajectories of these actors' careers are different, yet they are strikingly similar in how they have portrayed masculine identities since the early 1990s.

Even as Kerala remains distinctly unique with high literacy rates, social development indices on par with developed nations, and communist governments in power several times since independence, the shifts in ideological leanings are visible. The Sabarimala verdict[1] barring the entry of young women into the temple premises and the subsequent agitation, the cultural struggle over women's right to enter religious spaces versus impureness of femininity within the space dedicated to a male deity, clearly illustrates a shift toward the masculine Hindu nationalist agenda in motion across the nation. Even as public spaces have remained immune to the Hindutva agenda in the last decade, the paradigm shift toward a Hindu identity had begun in the 1990s, especially within domestic spaces and the increasing importance given to temples and associated ritualistic religious patterns. Films captured this shift in a nuanced way, as the hypermasculine identities triumphed over the "villains," often depicted as belonging to the marginalized classes.

During the 1980s, Kerala witnessed revolutionary social changes as a response to the increased flow of revenue from the Gulf migration. In the new social order, neoliberalism emerged as the hegemonic normative practice, masquerading as apolitical in social interactions (Hu 2015, 152). "Neoliberal capitalism . . . portends the death of politics by hiding its own ideological underpinnings in the dictates of economic efficiency, in the fetishism of the free market" (Cameroff and Cameroff 2000, 322). With economic liberalization in the 1990s, India's social, political, and economic environments were subject to radical modifications. The shift from feudal social relations and hierarchies to neoliberal consumption patterns were mirrored in cultural practices as well. Increasing commodification and the wholehearted acceptance of a capitalist normative system redefined gender identities and relationships. Neoliberalism enforced greater participation of people in the economy, which reduced gender differences. This resulted in shifts in gender relations, from the "rising non-hegemonic male communities and the dominant women members" to male anxiety (Rowena 2010, 135).

Cinema's response to these changes is perceptible even to a casual filmgoer. With the rise of intimidating and fierce heroes, the perfect representations of hegemonic masculinity, Malayalam cinema became a representation of male anxiety. In the films of the era, the previous decades' revolutionary zeal and an ardent desire for social change toward an egalitarian society is no longer fashionable, being seemingly apolitical is the norm. The individual, especially the male, is believed to be powerful enough to challenge institutions and governments that are corrupt and nepotic. These representations of individuals are carefully nurtured and designed as they emerge as symbolic figures, as tropes to be drawn into narratives repeatedly. These heroes also signaled the emergence of a new male identity, the Hindu male. Apolitical and reactive, the Hindu male is a leader who enjoys huge popularity among the masses and manipulates the public by means of affective politics in films like *Devasuram* (Kailas 1995), *Hitler* (Siddique 1996), *Aaram Thampuran* (Kailas 1997), *Narasimham* (Kailas 2000), *Ravanaprabhu* (Ranjith 2001), *Praja* (Joshiy 2001), *Thandavom* (Kailas 2002), and *Rajamanickam* (Rasheed 2005). To understand the features of this new hero and its political

dimensions within the nation, I look closer at the hero in *Aaram Thampuran,*
Narasimham, and *Ravanaprabhu.*

SHIFTING SOCIAL SENSIBILITY IN INDIA

Hinduism, once celebrated for its plurality, has no single subjective self that
can be proclaimed as the ideal one, because it avoids monolithic structures
familiar from Semitic religions. Hence gender identities also operate within
the intersectionality of caste, class, and other innumerable differences.
Among them, contemporary India has witnessed the evolution of a Hindutva
masculinity (Anand 2007, 9).

Refining Hindu male identity was a concerted effort that began during the
age of imperialism. "British colonial discourse begins with the establishment of the Hindu male as a weak, lazy cowardly slave," and as such Hindu
male was depicted as "a stereotype of effeminacy" (Roy and Hammers 2014,
23–24). Edward Said (1978, 207) recognized that this construction of the
Other, which depicted the Orient as weak, was opposed to the European
self. During the period of cultural renaissance, attempts were made to create alternative depictions. Among others, Swami Vivekananda (1863–1902),
a Hindu monk and a leader, advocated for a physically and intellectually
enlightened Indian society. In the twentieth century, another Hindu leader,
Golwalker (1906–1973) attempted to create a new image of the Hindu to
replace the colonial stereotype. These attempts can be described with Roy
and Hammers's (2014, 20) words: A "perceived loss of manhood and virility
and the compelling desire to overcome such perceived loss lies at the heart
of Hindu nationalist discourse." This was a step toward the remasculinization
of Hindu identity and this agenda was adopted with renewed vigor several
decades later as a response to social changes. Since the 1990s, neoliberal
structures have created the ideal environment for the growth of a right-wing
political power, and notions of a Hindu masculinity that was hypermasculine
in essence grew in strength as well. It continues to present itself through the
process of othering and strives to evolve into the norm. Its claim to hegemonic status is still debatable, yet we see a determined effort to disseminate
its values through cultural practices like cinema's popular narratives where
Hindu masculinity has emerged as a significant political agenda.

With neoliberalism emphasizing identities that effectively satisfy the needs
of the market, the Indian populace has responded to transforming identity
politics in several ways. There is a close link between the economic and political mechanisms of neoliberalism and "its cultural politics of subjectification
and self-regulation" (Giroux 2008, 1). Neoliberalism is, therefore, a "political
project, intent on producing new forms of subjectivity and particular modes

of conduct" (Giroux 2008, 1). When India went into a political crisis post the declaration of Emergency in 1975,[2] it ushered in normative shifts not only in the political sphere but also in other social structures that defined the lives of Indian citizens. Subsequently, like in every other postcolonial nation, there was a general disillusionment that gave way to new paradigms of social behavior. A mistrust of political leaders, lack of transparency in administration, and a frustration in the public sphere culminated in a trend toward being apolitical. This lack of concern for the political sphere was reflected in cultural practices as well. The new media, including the television channels, promised possibilities to converse, to express dissent as part of the democratic machinery, but there was a rampant mistrust in these tools causing political conversations no longer to be in vogue. This space was subsequently occupied by individual celebrities, and attention moved toward a celebration of individuals and their victories. Cinema, like other popular cultural practices, thrived on employing these new methods of representation and contextualization.

A seemingly apolitical Hindu collective, disillusioned with the corrupt political environment, and deeply unsettled by the neoliberal ethos sweeping through the sociopolitical, economic and cultural discourse, demanded new assemblages, new identities. Neoliberalism that celebrated individual achievements and offered illusory hopes of personal growth, created an anxiety that was individualistic, accompanied by a drive to explore and accumulate wealth and power. With a failing political leadership and an individualistic self that has lost faith in institutions and the community, the lacunae got filled fast by the new political Hinduism that sought to function through new paradigms of hegemonic power. Tropes and images were created and circulated, and promises were made, foregrounding the religious identity of the Hindu and assimilating it with concepts of nationhood and patriotism. The growing relevance of the right-wing Hindutva political parties has increased distrust between Hindus and Muslims across the country.[3] Cultural representations aptly identified these molecular patterns forming in Indian societies and responded through a fundamentally altered iconography celebrating the neoliberal Indian self, the male hero who resembled a construct that was claimed to be a Hindu. Responding to the molar formations in the Indian political realm, the sensibilities of the individuals changed accordingly.

In the new millennium India, turbulent and adapting itself to the new realities, the new Hindu identity established itself through political powers like the right-wing Bharatiya Janata Party (BJP). They enticed a society in a state of flux toward a current leader, Narendra Modi, whose identity was carefully conceived and nourished through image building exercises and a cunningly executed public relations program. Ambar Kumar Ghosh (2019) notes: "Armed with tremendous financial clout and technocratic wherewithal, the party assiduously created the Modi personality cult, which enjoys almost habitual reverence from a significant section of Indians." The identity of this new leader, the expressions, the mannerisms, the articulations intended to create affects successfully captured the popular imagination.

For a generation of a middle-class population feeling stymied by the humungous structures of capitalism and the values of neoliberalism that demanded individuals to be selfish, self-centered, and competitive, the desire for a leader who is all-powerful and father-like is a comforting solution and a possible future for the nation and its people. This leader figure's "machismo combines a deeper bullying, masculine set of performances with a paternalistic dominance that claims to protect their 'own' people," as Eksi and Wood (2019, 5) argue. This new male identity is distinctly hypermasculine, arrogant, bellicose and with a body and mind disciplined to perfection. Ghosh (2019) explains further: "The narrative that created the cult of Modi has a four-pronged approach—Modi as a selfless leader with a humble origin; Modi as a decisive and strong leader capable of defending India against its adversaries; Modi as a beacon of hope for development; and, Modi as an indispensable national leader in the absence of any credible alternative." This image of the Hindu male leader was also reinforced through the building of the other, where the Muslim male identity is vilified as the other, and Islamophobia, prevalent in the West, is adopted in order to demonize the community. The binaries in these discourses are aplenty, the Hindu and the other, the male and the other, the upper-caste Brahmanical male and the other, to name a few.

BJP's agenda of molding Indian identities is performed on cultural and political platforms. For example, they have cleverly reimagined the mythical and androgynous hero Ram, who was designated as an avatar of Lord Vishnu in Ramayana, the Sanskrit epic of ancient India. BJP's right-wing religious groups have politicized and embraced Ram to symbolize the idealistic Hindu male. "BJP's reconfiguration of Ram" helped in "creating a masculine discursive space" (Roy and Hammers 2014, 20). A complex Hindu masculinity has been shaped out of these discourses around real and imagined Hindu heroes and cultural representations strive to capture them in multifarious ways in different art forms, of which films are the most popular one.

CINEMATIC REPRESENTATIONS

Performative in nature, constructs of gender identities regenerate through social actions (Butler 1993). Therefore, gender identities are often articulated through tropes in cultural practices. Representations of masculinity and "an exaggerated hypermasculine gender script" can be easily established as popularly performed and accepted (Mosher and Tomkins 1988, 65). The dialectics of social practices and cultural representations emphasize the complexities of social formations. A reading of the politics of representation of masculinities portrayed by Mohanlal and Mammootty, the two male superstars of Malayalam cinema, reveals that the features of hypermasculinity that became established as the hegemonic one also portend the growth of an aggressive Hindu masculine identity. This overwhelming self, aggressively male and patriarchal to the core, has remained the dominant male ego over the last few decades.

During the 1990s, Malayalam films saw a proliferation of hypermasculine characters as the infallible heroes, accompanied by a celebration of toxic male subjectivity and misogyny. There was also decisive change in the nature of masculinity portrayed by Mammootty and Mohanlal. The public conferred superstardom to these actors, and the media enabled the creation of alpha males. The creation of fan clubs accelerated this growth toward a regressive male identity. This celebration of phallocracy has had significant repercussions on social structures.

In Malayalam films, hypermasculine and overtly sexual images validate misogyny. According to Gates (2006, 53), "Masculinism is the ideology that justifies and naturalizes male domination. As such it is the ideology of patriarchy." The misogyny that defines patriarchal relations finds its pride of place in these films. For example, *Aaram Thampuran* (Kailas 1997), starred by Mohanlal, is extremely misogynistic in the depiction of gender relations. Unnimaya, the hero's love is described as disciplined and modest, never leaves the home, and is treated as property. Jagan, the hero, chooses to marry her instead of his old girlfriend, a city-bred, bold, and individualistic woman who arrives at Jagan's village and proposes to marry him. Women are casually referred to as "expensive blankets," and are willing accomplices in the construction of toxic masculine identity. While actions transmit misogyny in *Aaram Thampuran*, in another Mohanlal film, *Praja* (Joshiy 2001), the protagonist gives words to this attitude. In an emotional outburst, he observes that progressive thoughts about a girl's individuality are meaningless. The moment a girl is born, parents have a fire burning in them to marry her off. He also tells his lady love that she is too feisty and has to be kept under lock and key, which is marriage.

Similarly, in Mammootty's films *Kasaba* (Panicker 2016) and *The King* (Kailas 1995), misogyny is rampant. In *The King*, women are infantilized and physically abused. For example, when the hero slaps a woman, the act is justified in the narrative. In the case of *Kasaba*, the film created a heated debate in Kerala for its misogynous content. There is a scene in the film, where Mammootty, in the role of a police officer, pulls a woman police officer by her belt and insults her with sexist references. Following the release of the film, an actor, Parvathy, dared to challenge the making of sexist content and initiated discussions which problematized toxic gender constructs. These films, and many other Malayalam films, normalize misogyny while justifying men's dominating positions.

Hypermasculine heroes played by the two superstars in the turn of the millennium were mostly bachelor leaders with "a vigilante mentality" (Kazmi 1996, 34). In films like *Hitler* (Siddique 1996), the bachelor hero (Mammootty) protects his younger sisters, turns into a ruthless older brother, a "Hitler," when male attention falls on his sisters. In *Aaram Thampuran* (Kailas 1997), the bachelor hero (Mohanlal) turns into a savior and fiercely and violently protects the village, which has crowned him as a *thampuran*, a feudal term used to address the upper-caste male, privileged and powerful by birth. Young (2003, 2) points out that the masculine role of the protector "illuminates the meaning and effective appeal of a security state that wages war abroad and expects obedience and loyalty at home." In this patriarchal logic, "a hierarchy is built wherein women and children are allotted, a subordinate position of dependence and obedience" (Young 2003, 2). Subordination is visible in *Lucifer*, a film released in 2019 (dir. Sukumaran). The hero (Mohanlal) is a protector in every sense, a guardian, a crown prince who turns violent and ruthlessly destroys lives in order to save women and children. All these heroes proclaim themselves the protectors of land, people, habitation, women, and children, even if their gentle protective side is often accompanied with vengeful and destructive actions. Thus, the subservient women's vulnerability is designed to offer moments for the male protagonists to be heroic. Long sermons about gender roles and the "inherent" qualities of the gendered binaries complement these narrative decisions. For example, in *Hitler*, the protagonist Madhavankutty (Mammootty) is the protector, with five younger sisters, who finds it morally viable and socially acceptable to marry off his sister to her rapist professor, much against her will. Similarly, in *Praja* (Joshiy 2001), the elder brother Parameswaran plans the life of his younger sister Padmaja and offers long sermons about women who stray away, by falling in love and marrying against the wishes of the elders. The protector male emerges as a dominating god figure in these films.

Gates (2003, 36) argues that men are expected to "perform masculinity through activities in order to confirm virility, power, and toughness." In films, violence emerges often as the single most evident marker of this kind of manhood. Particularly, the willingness and desire to fight is of importance (Kimmel 2009, 65). Manhood, defined through violent encounters, is equated with power—over women, over other men—which is validated and institutionalized in various ways, including films discussed in this study. The hegemonic male figures, celebrated through their violent actions in these films, be it *Devasuram* (Kailas 1995), *Aaram Thampuran* (Kailas 1997),

Narasimham (Kailas 2000), or *Valliettan* (Kailas 2000), have their manhood defined through incidents that consolidate masculine power. "The political significance of these patriarchal paradigms of violence, ruthlessness and dominance is that the qualities associated with belligerent masculinity are normalized and reinforced" (Kumar 2015, 38).

Violent masculinity is glorified and celebrated in the film *Narasimham* (Kailas 2000), where a member of the hero's coterie narrates a fist fight that took place on-screen between the hero, Induchoodan, and his opponents. The re-telling, which happens a few minutes after the fight, is accompanied by awe-struck expressions on the listeners' faces. In *Aaram Thampuran* (Kailas 1997), the reactions from the mob, cheering and adulating the protagonist, complete the act of violence. The mob's sense of awe and delight in watching Jagan, the protagonist, fight is a significant part of the narrative. In a central and visual scene, Jagan involves himself in a fist fight with several "goons" who had dared to attack his friend. After the scene, the event is narrated again, foregrounding the features of the male identity the film celebrates. Alexander (2003, 538) mentions the ideal of "tough guise" as defined by Media Education Foundation as a "performance in which violent masculinity is the norm."

The violent actions are not only about domination, because in these films, they also offer a social structure for male relationships. In *Rajamanikyam* (Rasheed 2005), the protagonist Bellary Raja (Mammootty) is a boor, with no niceties, uses rustic language, is violently assertive, and is encircled by trustworthy male accomplices. These masculine "men bond with other men in comradely male setting" (Young 2003, 4). Homosocial bonds aim at foregrounding the hero's abilities and virtues also in the film *Devasuram* (Kailas 1995), which has the male protagonist (Mohanlal) occupying exclusively male spaces, and his friendship with other men, equally aggressive, serves to highlight the hypermasculine identity of the protagonist. His downfall begins with the disruptive arrival of a woman into this male space.

As Kirkham and Thumim (1993, 12) suggest, "the filmic construction of being (the body) and of doing (the body in action) are both sites where assumptions about masculinity are made manifest." The corporeal selves of these characters foreground a particular kind of masculinity that manifests itself in various ways, including the actors' bodies and public images. According to Thomas Harris (1991, 40), "the star system is based on the premise that a star is accepted by the public in terms of a certain set of personality traits" that are "catalogued into a series of traits, associations and mannerisms." Malayalam masculine mannerisms meant to thrill the fans are aplenty. The twirling of the moustache is an oft repeated gesture in all of these films, to the point where it becomes "a metaphorical and metonymic indication of the masculine virtue: resolution and invincibility" (Kumar 2015, 41).

Close-up shots of the hands powerful enough to silence huge crowds, or the walk captured in slow motion with low angle shots signal power and significance. Another facet of the performative aspect is the use of the traditional Kerala dress, the *mundu*, which is used to assert an aggressive masculine identity. At the level of dialogue, catch phrases, usually created out of slang, meaning nothing in particular, became trendy. For example, nonsense phrases *savarigirigiri* (*Ravanaprabhu*) or *nee po mone dinesha* (*Aaraam Thampuran*) emerged as character-defining phrases and defined these masculine images. Masculinity is also performed through lengthy monologues using a mix of English and Malayalam, highlighting the elitist and suave masculine selves, even when the protagonists belong to lower classes or communities. In these films, the new hypermasculine Hindu man prospers in male spaces, protects the land and the people, and resorts to violence if required.

HINDU IDENTITY

The hypermasculine images portrayed by the superstars reflect the social sensibilities of the post-1990s era, particularly the apolitical Hindu identity that embraces the Hindutva politics of the right-wing powers in India. In this context, the religious identities of the two actors Mammootty and Mohanlal also demand a discussion. Mohanlal is a Hindu by birth, and his Hindu characters are convincingly placed within the cultural and social structures of the changing Indian religious climate. Mammootty's Muslim background asks for certain negotiations. His characters are often from varied religious identities, identified by characteristic features assigned to these categories. These can be a particular regional dialect, a sartorial taste, or references to local, regional customs and cuisines. Yet, Mammootty has also played several Hindu characters that fall into the category of hypermasculine selves. In an earlier film, *Aavanazhi* (Sasi 1986), and its sequel *Inspector Balram* (Sasi 1991), Mammootty is Balram, a Hindu police officer, with curled up moustache, and patriarchal to the core. Mammootty's characters, especially the Hindu protagonists, share the features of religious nationalist agenda, akin to the roles of Mohanlal. Films like *Dhruvam* (Joshiy 1993), *Pallavoor Devanarayanan* (Vinu 1999), and *Prajapathi* (Ranjith 2000) have Mammootty as the protagonist, his characters being upper caste, either of Brahmin or Kshatriya castes. These are male protagonists who reiterate their commitment to their families and are willing to sacrifice themselves for their loved ones. These glorified relationships are typically portrayed as patriarchal, with emphasis on misogyny and sexism.

As Friedland argues, religious nationalism, unlike capitalism or the democratic state, focuses on the organization of sexuality. Religious nationalists give primacy to the family, not to democracy or the market, as the social space through which society should be conceived and composed. Familial discourse, with its particularistic and sexual logic of love and loyalty, is pervasive (Friedland 2001, 135). In Malayalam films, religious values tie into a celebration of patriarchy. In films like *Vatsalyam* (Haneefa 1993), *Hitler* (Siddique 1996), and *Valliettan* (Kailas 2000) Mammootty's characters are misogynous and patriarchal, with the male protagonist as the protector and warrior. In a Mohanlal film *Ustaad* (Malayil 1999), Parameswaran as the paternalistic brother is the Hindu male, elitist, upper class, and the film ascertains the return of a patriarchal authority that had been challenged during the cultural renaissance movements that had shaped the state and ensured the arrival of modernity. Similarly, in *Madambi* (Unnikrishnan 2006), Gopalakrishna Pillai, the protagonist, is a patriarch, sheltering his family and his village, and the film title can literally be translated as the feudal lord. Families are sacred spaces and gender norms are strictly adhered to in these films, all the while enshrining a religious identity that is patriarchal and feudal in nature.

In films where Mohanlal, a Hindu by birth, dons the role of the protagonist, the Hindu identity is repeatedly established and the hypermasculine hero sits comfortably in the hegemonic position. His earlier film, *Bhoomiyile Rajakkanmar* (Kannanthanam 1987), has the male protagonist Mahindra Varma, who belongs to an aristocratic family, once the rulers of the land. Visuals of the temple and the palace, the feudal hierarchy and the lost powers of the monarchy, are skillfully positioned in these films. Hindu spiritual thought, often in the form of Sanskrit verses, accompanies the arrival of the protagonist. Hindu god names are repeatedly invoked in dramatic moments, and built into the vocabulary of the protagonist. In *Narasimham* (Kailas 2000), Hindu symbols are plentiful: temple spaces, traditional lamps, martial arts, and homes are distinctly from the cultural icons of Hinduism. These films use scenes where the male protagonist arrives in moments of crisis soon after the person in distress calls out to a Hindu god. In *Narasimham*, the title of the film refers to one of the avatars of Lord Vishnu and symbolically represents the film's male protagonist, Induchoodan. The film goes on to repeatedly announce the intimidatingly strong protagonist as an avatar, an incarnation of the omnipotent god. His introduction is preceded by loud proclamations about his glory and undefeatable spirit. He is pictured as emerging from the waters accompanied by a hagiographic song and the visual of a lion (Narasimham literally translates into man-lion). Low angle shots and allusions to the Hindu identity politicize the body of the actor. As Balaji (2014) argues, "the heteronormative and hypersexualized man, embodied by Indian male stars, is a commodity that India exports as both an economic imperative and an ideological one." The spectacle of the Hindu male body that is heterosexual and hypermasculine, with vermilion on the forehead and wearing traditional attire, is glorified as the ideal.

Capitalist socialization "includes not only manpower, but also the production of bodies, intellect and affect" (Lemke 2017, 113). The protagonists and their characterization are designed to evoke sensations which are aimed at shaping social images of populist leaders. The affective politics that right-wing leaders employ in contemporary politics has been widely employed in these films. The body of the protagonist is thus a site for "political, cultural and geographical inscriptions, production or constitution" (Grosz 1990, 23). Globalization, especially of capital and commodities, also marks the bodies of the protagonists. These heroes mention the costly watches and the designer wares, and are placed within urbanized settings, even when the film endorses a Hindu identity rooted in traditions and conventions. They fail to represent the multifarious identities of the other, the Dalit bodies, the socially and economically oppressed identities. The Dalit bodies are presented as the side-kicks or the admirers of these upper-caste male selves who thrive by appearing apolitical, yet are arrogant and aware of their privilege and social capital, and employ othered men to their advantage. Thus, upper-caste selves emerge victorious, adding to their superstar stature their salability as commodities of a neoliberal market. These films celebrate hegemonic masculinities that thrive in the Malayalam film industry, even as a new generation of filmmakers imagine a progressive world and seek to challenge the normative patterns of patriarchal hegemony.

CONCLUSION

The hypermasculine Hindu hero gains traction through several modes of entertainment. One innovation that heralded the increasing presence of these masculine images in the social imagination is the multitude of television channels that sprouted post liberalization of the Indian economy. Multiple channels in the vernacular languages aired programs, mostly entertainment programs, such as *Cinemaala*, which was built around short clips from popular movies and short comic skits. Its success resulted in a burgeoning trend in all the channels, where iconic moments, popular dialogues, action, and melodrama were telecast repeatedly. Hypermasculinity emerged as a norm with the repeated enactment of these scenes, sometimes with comic reenactments, often accompanied by programs where youngsters mimicked these scenes in various reality shows. Construction and dissemination of hypermasculine images in Malayalam cinema through the bodies of two superstars was a project aided and advanced by the newfound culture, in which such images of identities create an environment for commodification of bodies and practices.

These hypermasculine images were characterized by a toxicity, a misogyny accompanied by the creation of an ideal Hindu male, a vicious and regressive image, shaped out of a patriarchal myth, a political construct of right-wing forces. This new trend of a hypermasculine and predominantly Hindu male, deceivingly apolitical and patriarchal, has played a significant role in consolidating the power of this male identity that has been useful not only for cinematic narrations, but to political movements in India.

NOTES

1. Sabarimala verdict is a landmark verdict that was passed in 2019, permitting young women to visit the shrine of god Ayyappa, at Sabarimala, in Kerala. The temple had a ritualistic tradition which prohibited young fecund women from entering the shrine. When the Supreme Court of India, permitted it by law, civil society, including a large number of women emerged on to the streets protesting against the new law, and sought to prevent women from visiting the shrine. The campaign titled #readytowait, trended on social media, with a large number of BJP supporters, the right-wing Hindu party of India leading the campaign against change.

2. India went through a period of political Emergency in the year 1975. It was a period of suppression of dissent where principles of democracy were abandoned. Smt. Indira Gandhi who had assumed complete control over the government suffered a brutal defeat during the ensuing election. It was also a period when Indian citizens learned the value of freedom of speech and expression.

3. The demolition of the Babri Mosque in 1992 and the Ram Janmabhoomi controversy have remained a bone of contention between Hindus and Muslims and resulted in increased distrust between the two communities.

BIBLIOGRAPHY

Alexander, Susan M. 2003. "Stylish Hard Bodies: Branded Masculinity in *Men's Health* Magazine." *Sociological Perspectives* 46 (4): 535–554.

Anand, Dibyesh. 2007. "Anxious Sexualities: Masculinity, Nationalism and Violence." *The British Journal of Politics and International Relations* 9 (2): 257–269.

Balaji, Murali. 2014. "Indian Masculinity." *Technoculture: An Online Journal of Technology in Society* 4. https://tcjournal.org/vol4/balaji.

Bourdieu, Pierre. 1990. *The Logic of Practice*. Translated by Richard Nice. Cambridge: Polity Press.

Bourdieu, Pierre. 2001. *Masculine Domination*. Translated by Richard Nice. Stanford, CA: Stanford University Press. Butler, Judith. 1990. *Gender Trouble: Feminism and the Subversion of Identity*. London: Routledge.

Butler, Judith. 1993. *Bodies that Matter: On the Discursive Limits of Sex*. New York: Routledge.

Cameroff, Jean, and John Cameroff. 2000. "Millennial Capitalism: First Thoughts on a Second Coming." *Public Culture* 12 (2): 291–343. https://doi.org/10.1215/0 8992363-12-2-291.

Connell, R. W. 1987. *Gender and Power: The Society, Person and Sexual Politics.* Oxford: Polity Press.

Eksi, Betul, and Elizabeth Wood. 2019. "Rightwing Populism as Gendered Performance: Janus-faced Masculinity in the Leadership of Vladimir Putin and Recep T Erdogan." *Theory and Society* 48: 733–751. https://doi: 10.1007/s11186-019-09363-3.

Fazil, dir. 1980. *Manjil Virinja Pookkal.* Kerala: Navodaya Studio. DVD.

Friedland, Roger. 2001. "Religious Nationalism and the Problem of Collective Representation." *Annual Review of Sociology* 27: 125–152.

Gates, Philippa. 2006. *Detecting Men: Masculinity and the Hollywood Detective Film.* Albany: State University of New York Press.

Ghosh, Ambar Kumar. 2019. "Decoding the Modi Personality Cult." *Qrius.com*, May 29, 2019. https://qrius.com/decoding-the-modi-personality-cult/.

Giroux, Henry A. 2008. *Against the Terror of Neoliberalism: Politics beyond the Age of Greed.* London & New York: Routledge.

Grosz, Elizabeth. 1990. "Inscriptions and Body Maps: Representations and the Corporeal." In *Feminine, Masculine and Representation*, edited by T. Threadgold and A. Francis Cranny, 62–74. London: Allen and Unwin.

Haneefa, Cochin, dir. 1993. *Vatsalyam.* Kerala: Jubilee Productions. DVD.

Harris, Thomas. 1991. "The Building of Popular Images: Grace Kelly and Marilyn Munroe." In *Stardom: Industry of Desire*, edited by Christine Gledhill, 31–41. London and New York: Routledge.

Hu, Cameron. 2015. "Where Everything is Political: Architecture against Politics in Global Dubai." In *Globalisation: The Crucial Phase*, edited by Brian Spooner, 143–172. Philadelphia: University of Pennsylvania Press.

Joshiy, dir. 1993. *Dhruvam.* Kerala: Sunitha Productions. DVD.

Joshiy, dir. 2001. *Praja.* Kerala: Mukhyadhara. DVD.

Kailas, Shaji, dir. 1995. *Devasuram.* Kerala: MAK Productions. DVD.

Kailas, Shaji, dir. 1995. *The King.* Kerala: MAK Productions. DVD.

Kailas, Shaji, dir. 1997. *Thampuran.* Kerala: Swargachitra Release. DVD.

Kailas, Shaji, dir. 2000. *Narasimham.* Kerala: Aashirvad Cinemas. DVD.

Kailas, Shaji, dir. 2000. *Valliettan.* Kerala: Ambalakkara Films. DVD.

Kailas, Shaji, dir. 2002. *Thandavam.* Kerala: Dickle Cinema. DVD.

Kannanthanam, Thampi, dir. 1986. *Rajavinte Makan.* Kerala: Jubilee Productions. DVD.

Kannanthanam, Thampi, dir. 1987. *Bhoomiyile Rajakkanmar.* Kerala: Jubilee Productions. DVD.

Kazmi, Nikhat. 1996. *Ire in the Soul: Bollywood's Angry Years.* Delhi: HarperCollins Publishers India.

Kimmel, Michael S. 2009. "Masculinity as Homophobia: Fear, Shame and Silence in the Construction of Gender Identity." In *Rethinking Foundations: Theorizing Sex, Gender and Sexuality: The New Basics*, edited by Aby L Ferber, Kimberly Holcomb, and Tre Wentling, 58–70. New York: Oxford University Press.

Kirkham, Pat, and Janet Thumim. 1993. "You Tarzan." In *You Tarzan: Masculinity, Movies and Men*, edited by Pat Kirkham, and Janet Thumim, 11–26. London: Lawrence & Whishart.

Kumar, Preethi. 2015. "Hegemonic Masculinities in two comic Films in Malayalam: *Meesa Madhavan* and *Rajamanikyam*." *ArtCultura* 17 (30): 31–42.

Lemke, Thomas. 2017. "Micheal Hardt and Antonio Negri on Postmodern Biopolitics." In *The Routledge Handbook of Biopolitics*, edited by Sergei Prozorov, and Simona Rentea, 112–122. London and New York: Routledge.

Malayil, Sibi, dir. 1999. *Ustaad*. Kerala: Country Talkies. DVD.

Menon, Neelima. 2019. "Evolution of Superstardom in Malayalam Cinema." *Full Picture.in*, September 15, 2019. http://fullpicture.in/talking-detail/186/evolution -of-superst.html.

Mosher, Donald L., and Silvan S. Tomkins. 1988. "Scripting the Macho Man: Hypermasculine Socialization and Enculturation." *The Journal of Sex Research* 25 (1): 60–84. http://beyondutopia.net/leadership-lectures/tomkins-1.pdf.

Panicker, Nithin Renji, dir. 2016. *Kasaba*. Kerala: Goodwill Entertainments. DVD.

Ranjith, dir. 2001. *Ravanaprabhu*. Kerala: Aashirvad Cinemas. DVD.

Ranjith, dir. 2006. *Prajapathi*. Kerala: S Pictures. DVD.

Rasheed, Anwar, dir. 2005. *Rajamanikyam*. Kerala: Valiyaveettil Movie International. DVD.

Rowena, Jenny. 2010. "The 'Laughter-Films' and the Reconfiguration of Masculinities." In *Women in Malayalam Cinema: Naturalising Gender Hierarchies*, edited by Meena Pillai, 125–153. New Delhi: Orient Blackswan.

Roy, Abhik, and Michele L. Hammers. 2014. "The Recuperation of Hindu Manhood: Echoes of the Past in Present Day Hindu Nationalism." *Comparative Literature: East & West* 21 (1): 19–38. https://doi.org 10.1080/25723618.2014.12015472.

Said, Edward. 1978. *Orientalism*. New York, NY: Pantheon.

Sasi, I. V., dir. 1986. *Aavanazhi*. Kerala: Saj Productions. DVD.

Sasi, I. V., dir. 1991. *Inspector Balram*. Kerala: Liberty Productions. DVD.

Siddique, dir. 1996. *Hitler*. Kerala: Lal Release. DVD.

Sreehari, A. C. 2008. "The Makings of the Man: A History of Eighty Years (1928– 2008) of Malayalam Movies." *Proceedings of the Indian History Congress* 69: 1239–1242. http://www.jstor.com/stable/44147281.

Sukumaran, Prithviraj, dir. 2019. *Lucifer*. Kerala: Aashirvad Cinemas. DVD.

Tosh, John. 1999. *A Man's Place: Masculinity and the Middle-class Home in Victorian England*. London: Yale University Press.

Unnikrishnan, B., dir. 2006. *Madambi*. Kerala: Surya Cinemas. DVD.

Vinu, V. M. dir. 1999. *Pallavoor Devanarayanan*. Kerala: Sunitha Productions. DVD.

Young, Iris Marion. 2003. "The Logic of Masculinist Protection: Reflections on the Current Security State." *Signs: Journal of Women in Culture and Society* 29 (1): 1–25.

Chapter 9

A Prophecy of Bolsonaro

Masculinity and Populism in the **Elite Squad** *Films*

Tatu-Ilari Laukkanen

This chapter provides a critical reading of the two Brazilian *Elite Squad* films in light of the interrelation of masculinity and populism on screen. Particularly, I examine how these elements from the action blockbusters relate to the popularity and politics of the far-right populist Jair Bolsonaro's administration. The film *Elite Squad* (*Tropa de elite*, Padilha 2007) and its sequel *Elite Squad: The Enemy Within* (*Tropa de Elite 2—O Inimigo Agora é Outro*, Padilha 2010) follow a commando unit of the Rio Military Police that fights drug trafficking gangs in Rio de Janeiro's *favelas* (slums). As the sequel's title *O Inimigo Agora é Outro* ("Now the enemy is another") attests to, the villains include corrupt politicians and officials, which aims the critical lens to upper echelons of power and thus arguably takes a more critical stance toward Brazilian society. These films inspired public debates on their direct portrayal of corruption, police brutality and violence in Brazil. Despite, or perhaps because of the controversies over the heroization of the brutal, yet uncorrupted captain Nascimento, these films were the biggest successes in Brazilian film history. For example, the sequel grossed R$ 102 million, with 11 million tickets sold in Brazil alone (Vázquez 2018, 50). Additionally, international crossovers garnered domestic and international critical acclaim. For example, *Elite Squad* took home a Golden Bear from the Berlin Film Festival.

The *Elite Squad* films move in the terrain of crime, corruption, and the masculine world of policing and drug trafficking. The original film is based on a book by former BOPE (Batalhão de Operações Policiais Especiais—the Rio Military Police's SWAT team) officers Rodrigo Pimentel and André Batista, who coauthored it with Luiz Eduardo Soares, an activist/intellectual who served as a national Public Safety Secretary in President Lula da Silva's left-wing cabinet in 2003. Because the *Elite Squad* films are about the police, this analysis pays particular attention to the representations of the state and its organs, such as the justice system, the police, and politicians. Through close textual and narrative analysis, I key in on the representations of men and populism in the context of the socioeconomic conditions of Brazil that led to the Bolsonaro presidency. I utilize the concepts of necropolitics and allegorical nihilism to critically discuss connections between populism, violence, crime, and masculinity.

THE SOCIOPOLITICAL CONTEXT
OF THE *ELITE SQUAD* FILMS

Populism, as Laclau (2005, 32–49) has pointed out, becomes meaningful and defined in the context it is used. Brazil has a long history of masculine populism, Getúlio Vargas "The Father of the Poor" in the 1930s being the first in a long line of populist leaders. Indeed, the advent of Getulism (also known as Varguism) and Peronism in Argentina, similar in several ways, gave birth to populism in Latin America (Fausto 2006, 223, 232). As Grigera (2017) has noted, in Latin America, populism has become a political attribute for both the right and the left-wing administrations, defined by personalization of paternalistic leadership, influencing and mobilizing of the uneducated, poor and the working classes, representation of crisis when allocating resources, and institutionalization of social disputes. In the early twenty-first century, Brazil under the center-leftist PT's (The Worker's Party) tenure was part of the so-called pink tide in Latin America that has many populist components, and at least rhetorically went against the global trends of neoliberalism and rising inequality (even if Brazil remains one of the most unequal countries in the world). PT leaders Lula da Silva (2003–2011) and Dilma Rousseff (2011–2016) started social programs such as the *Fome Zero*/Zero Hunger and the *Bolsa Familia* welfare system to redistribute Brazil's newfound wealth that owed much to a global commodities boom.

An acknowledged growth base for populism has historically been economic upsets, and in 2014 Brazil plunged into a severe economic crisis that peaked with two deep recessions in 2015 and 2016. The crisis resulted from several elements, including the end of the commodity boom and widespread politico-economic precariousness after the *Lava Jato* corruption probe implicated high officials, including the president. The corruption scandal shook the PT government and ended the Rousseff administration. The primary effect of the economic crisis for the common Brazilian was the rise in unemployment (from 6.8 percent in 2014 to 11.9 percent in 2018) (Barros and Santos Silva

2020). A declining economy and disillusionment in politics led to the rise of right-wing populism.

Violent realities of Brazilian society with high homicide numbers and aggressive political protests have also invited "nostalgia for law and order," and increasing the number of citizens (43 percent in 2017) that long for the imagined security and economic growth under the military dictatorship, commemorating the Brazilian Military Government of the 1964–1985 period (Howse 2017, 16). Anger toward the contemporary government erupted in 2013 due to a rise in public transport fares, and soon the protesters added other demands on their list, such as the end of corruption and police violence. Bolsonaro has utilized these emotions and voiced his sympathy for the military regime. The two Brazilian strands of left-wing (Lula and Rousseff) and now the right-wing populism (Bolsonaro) show that the country is deeply divided. Many Brazilian intellectuals lament that neither the left nor the right, nor the media that supports them, cannot find a common ground for debate, consensus, or cooperation (Ortellado and Ribeiro 2018).

There are multiple signs that Brazilian's distrust in liberal democracy has escalated after the initial exhilaration of the post-dictatorship period. A Latinobarómetro poll (2016) that preceded Bolsanaro's campaign demonstrated that support for democratic governance had dropped to a mere 32 percent of the population, and only 9 percent of Brazilians believed that their country was governed for the benefit of the people. Based on these numbers, and on Rousseff's successor Michel Temer's (2016–2018) low approval ratings (14 percent in July 2016), Howse (2017, 3, 16) argues that the constant political scandals damaged the Brazilians' trust and hopes for a democratic political system.

The growing anti-democratic zeitgeist, along with people's concerns with economics and crime/security, were arguably important factors in Bolsonaro's election victory in 2018. His conservative, black and white, and patriarchal rhetoric has similarities with many right-wing populist regimes in Europe and the Trump presidency. Bolsonaro's preelection speeches targeted minorities, women, and particularly the LGBT+ community, yet these increasingly obscene claims have not significantly upset his political career. Instead, this might be a calculated strategy because his core support pillars, angry men, and the evangelical parliamentary bloc whose fundamentalist interests include undermining the expansion of sexual rights, same-sex marriage, and reproductive rights support these gendered views. In an attempt to explain Bolsonaro's victory, economists Barros and Santos Silva (2020), for instance, argue "Bolsonaro's authoritarian and sexist rhetoric may be appealing to men who, due to the economic shock, experience a relative loss in traditional masculine, breadwinner-type social identity." I argue that the sentiments and themes that made Bolsonaro's victory possible were recognizable in Brazilian culture and society long before his campaign started. Several themes outlined above—inequality, violence, patriarchy, and populism—are visible in *Elite Squad* films that, according to their director José Padilha, attempt to make microcosms of the Brazilian society and its discontents (Matheou 2010, 174–185). I use the *Elite Squad* films to show how patriarchal machismo, brutal anti-crime rhetoric, and justifications of using violence against crime are central to both popularity of the *Elite Squad* films and Bolsonaro's political image.

THE *ELITE SQUAD* FILMS, INTERTEXTUALITY AND DEBATES

New Brazilian cinema, or the "new cinema novo," represented by such films as the *Elite Squad*s, which tend to be situated in the megacities and their *favelas*, are occupied with "realist accounts" of Brazil's social problems. Even though art-house filmmakers such as Kleber Mendonça Filho continue to produce artistically ambitious critiques of Brazilian society, many critics have noticed a change from an elitist/utopian intellectual outlook toward a commercial/popular sociological one in mainstream cinema (e.g., Nagib 2004, 239–250; Stam, Vieira, and Xavier 2005, 393–399; Vázquez 2018, 66–67). Consequently, the debates around cinematic populism (making of popular and accessible films) and commodification persist in Brazilian cinema. For example, critics such as Ivana Bentes (2003, 124–125) blamed *City of God* (Meirelles and Lund 2002) for the aestheticization and romanticization of the *favelas* for popularity and profits. The film defenders countered that it drew attention to social problems (Johnson 2005, 13–14). A similar debate surrounded the *Elite Squad* films (Matheou 2010, 184–185).

The *Elite Squad* films can appear populist due to their mass appeal and their attempts to critique the system. The director Padilha has argued that the *Elite Squads* attempt a dissection of Brazilian society with the first part dealing with the drug trade, the second with the media, and the third one (yet to be made) with politics. This ethos is visible in the mission statement of Padilha's production company, according to which Zazen Produções "combines a preoccupation to produce quality films and recruiting the best talent available with a social commitment" (Vázquez 2018, 50). Prior to directing *Elite Squad*, Padilha garnered international acclaim with the documentary *Ônibus 174* (*Bus 174*, 2002). The film is an account of a bus hijacking in Rio, and similarly to *Elite Squad*, the documentary touches on a variety of social problems such as crime, poverty, and police brutality. The incompetent handling of the hijacking by BOPE gained them great infamy. For example, the film shows the police as inept when they accidentally shoot a hostage or execute the subdued and defenseless hijacker. Padilha has said that he wanted to make another documentary of the BOPE, but that proved impossible and even dangerous, so he opted to make fictional *Elite Squad* where the perspective moved from the criminal to the police (Purcell 2008).

Elite Squad caused a huge controversy in the Brazilian media that went in tandem of it becoming a cultural phenomenon with the films dialogue, music and even costumes becoming staples of popular culture. It was widely criticized for glamorizing violence. Because of the militaristic imagery and violent content of the film, the popular magazine, the right-wing weekly *Veja*, and Arnaldo Bloch, a columnist for Rio's primary newspaper *O Globo* accused it of being fascist (Caldas 2008, 3). Indeed, the skull that dominates the BOPE's logo (amply displayed in the posters and the film, see figure 9.1) and the black uniforms resemble the "death's head" logo and SS uniforms of Nazi Germany. However, the film also received critical acclaim for showing the dark side of Brazilian society (Caldas 2008, 7; Riccio 2017, 13–14, 17). While the violent characters disregard the checks and balances of liberal democracy and succumb to a militarized hierarchy, the film refuses to present a black and white moral regime. For example, the police are often corrupt and abuse human rights, and the main character, and narrator, Captain Nascimento (Padilha gave him the same name as the hijacker of *Bus 174*) is troubled and complex. The ambivalence of the reception is testified by Bolsonaro's son, who released a profanity-laced video of his father's anti-crime snippets with militaristic images and the film's theme song, thus appropriating *Elite Squad* to the far-right's populist narrative.

Due to its ambivalence, the *Elite Squad* films appear Lyotardian: they are dismissive of grand narratives such as modernity and the liberal democratic nation-state. In their critique of the Brazilian state, the *Elite Squad* films seem to align with and contribute to the neoliberal and populist discourse on the uselessness of the state and its "corrupt elites" (such as PT administration). This is a familiar strategy from the (right-wing) mainstream media's criticism of the left-of-center government (Kozloff 2008, 207), or the "system" as it is called in *Elite Squad 2*. These films can be characterized by what I call allegorical nihilism, an ideological position, which presents the state as impotent, and yet refuses to offer any solutions. Consequently, the allegorical nihilism of the *Elite Squad* films indirectly buttresses the ideological positions of anti-state and anti-collective powers such as neoliberal capitalism or right-wing populism while appearing "socially conscious" (to use the Brazilian upper-class lingo) in its exposure of society's ills. The concept of allegorical nihilism helps us understand the key ideology of these films by revealing the bankruptcy of the state while withholding alternatives or emancipatory, progressive community-based solutions.

THE DEGRADATION OF THE STATE, THE
GREY ECONOMY, AND THE "SYSTEM"

While *Elite Squad* proposed the theme, *Elite Squad 2* underlines the devaluation of the state that resonates with the Brazilian's wavering faith in democracy. The degradation of the status of the state culminates with the penultimate aerial shot of the administrative Brasília, where the capital was moved from Rio in the 1960s by developmentalist president Jusceliano Kubitchek, and which modernist architecture (designed by the communist architect Oscar Niemeyer) highlights the inseparability of modernity, development, and politics in Brazil. The shot starts from the city's main boulevard, lined by the different ministries of the Brazilian government, moves over the Brazilian parliament, and finally over the *Praça dos Três Poderes* (Square of the Three Powers), where the supreme court and the presidential palace represent the three powers of the republic—executive, legislative, and judicial. The shot concludes with the camera gliding past the huge Brazilian flag while Nascimento's pessimistic monologue castigates the "system." Nascimento's narration begs the question, "What system?" The film does not answer; the camera only directs us to seek the rot in the parliament and the administrative capital. The open ending underlines the *Elite Squads* position of allegorical nihilism; it represents the bankruptcy of industrialization, developmentalism, capitalism, the nation-state, liberal democracy, and even modernity.

Echoing Brazilians widespread disbelief in the judiciary and the state, in *Elite Squad*, the law and police work are separated and at odds from the start. Nascimento, a middle-level ground commander of the BOPE, comments on his protégé Andre Matias's belief in the system (his voice-over commenting on images of Matias's legal studies): "Andre was very naïve. He thought that policemen and lawyers had the same mission, to enforce the law. To be part of my team, he would have to get real" (Padilha 2007). During the films, Matias, indeed, starts to torture and kill suspects with impunity. Nascimento's commentary pinpoints the divorce between law and the state's repressive mechanisms.

BOPE is represented as a highly militarized and masculine organization that fights the gangs of the favelas with surgical strikes. Nascimento encounters and inflicts cruel violence and torture on a regular basis, and his job is extremely hard. In Brazil, police work is a dangerous and low paying job, often done by the underclass of the slums. Nascimento, on the contrary, is middle class, while his colleagues like Mathias echo the voice of "the people." He also frequently lambasts the elite in a language similar to populist politicians where "the pure people" versus "the corrupt elite" discourse "entails a claim against the elites, but the claim is a pluralist, not an antipluralist one" (Howse 2017, 3). In this scenario, incorruptible Nascimento and Matias resemble populist heroes in their disdain for the upper class and vigilantism. In a scene where upper-class students buy drugs from the *favela* where they have started an NGO, Nascimento laments, "how many have to die so that the rich get their joints." Mathias, similarly, castigates his marihuana smoking classmates after his partner and friend is killed: "you bourgeois bastards and potheads!" (Padilha 2007).

In the *Elite Squad* films, all the characters are somehow connected to or affected by the drug trade, and the ensuing grey economy encompasses the whole of society, including the police and government officials. Gina Marchetti, in her analysis of the *Infernal Affairs* series from Hong Kong that also is about corruption in the police and men in crisis, tied the drug trade to colonialism as well as globalization. In her allegorical reading, drugs become commodities that are symbolic of the transnational capitalist economy and its discontents, such as post-colonial exploitation of labor and profitable commodities as well as consequences of substance abuse. She argues that contradictory film images where drugs and the drug trade are both demonized and admired "provide a rare opportunity for filmgoers to indulge in fantasies about the ills of consumer capitalism" (Marchetti 2006, 99–100).

If we read the drug trade as an allegory for global capitalism, as suggested by Marchetti, *Elite Squad* that evolves around drugs and corruption ties into the critical theories of political economy. This allows a provisional glimpse at the Brazilian social entity and its position in the world system. Semi-peripheral Brazil has been and continues to be a producer of commodities that has often been under the influence of more developed nations (Portugal, England, the United States, and China). Brazil suffers from its colonial past, and many of the problems described in the *Elite Squads* corruption, clientelism, poverty, and violence, have post-colonial origins. However, in terms of populist politics, these kinds of informal capitalist activities fuse together with the theme of the receding state and weak governance, which manifests in Nascimento's continuous criticism of the "system." In contemporary Brazilian cinema, the police are often on the take, out of governmental control, or at least loyal to their respective institutions, units, or careers—not to the people, their nation, or the state. Thus, the films' representations align with Brazilians' widespread skepticism, whether the state works for their benefit.

In the case of *Elite Squad*, the informal economy was important not only on screen but in its distribution as well. The first installment was leaked onto the black market, incorrectly rumored to be done by angry police holding a grudge against Padilha because of *Bus 174*. Instead, the police and BOPE sought to limit the distribution of the film through the courts and pressured the producers to cut scenes of police violence. An estimated 10–12 million people (mainly in the *favelas*) saw the pirated version, and as Ramon Lobato (2012, 49–52) notes, the film's plot alternates between the formal and informal economies in a way that all sectors of society from the drug dealing college kids to the compromised police force are enmeshed in the film. The constant foregrounding of the informal economy in the film, as well as the methods by which it was viewed, reflects the polarized nature of informal/ illegal networks of distribution and consumption.

In *Elite Squad*, the police participate in or have to resort to *jeitinho brasileiro*—that is, operating outside the system in an unofficial, illegal way to achieve one's goals. *Jeitinho* and *esquema* being common concepts and ways of achieving one's objectives in Brazil using one's connections and informal networks. For example, in one scene, Matias's friend and partner Neto is assigned to the police station's vehicle pool that is chronically under-supplied to the extent that he and Matias organize a scheme in which they steal a payment made to a corrupt police officer to buy spare parts for the department. In addition to the hapless motor pool, the *Elite Squad* films have countless examples of inefficiency or corruption, including police selling guns to *trafficantes* and robbing a police station and taking its weaponry. In *Elite Squad 2*, the police, after they do not receive protection money from the drug dealers that Nascimento's operations have interrupted, start a militia that collects a "tax" on the provision of utilities in the *favelas*.

While the films show police corruption, the BOPE unit is non-bribable; it is portrayed as a rogue yet selectively chivalrous force. In the first *Elite Squad,* idealistic Neto and Matias, disillusioned by the purchasable and inept regular force, join BOPE and go through its grueling boot camp to be in an uncorrupted unit of gallant warriors. Yet, in terms of official legislation, it is otherwise uncontrolled. Again, the state appears unable to control its own organs. The disregard for law and due process shown by the BOPE operators is foregrounded in the multiple scenes in which they torture and kill suspects. This implicit critique of the state becomes poignant because it problematizes the state monopoly of violence, a central political question.

Nascimento's position as narrator aligns the viewer with him and forms an important ideological component to the film as he obviates the perspectives of favela dwellers and criminals as obscure subaltern entities. Padilha comments on Nascimento's position in an interview that shows his ethos of mixing entertainment with a social message:

I think the great thing that Fernando [*City of God* director Meirelles] did was say, "Let's make a movie that has social content, but it's gonna grab you by the balls." It's gonna be emotive, and we're gonna run with it and you won't have time to think while it goes on. . . . And this is what we do with *Elite Squad*. Engage with Nascimento, my friend and you're going to like the fucking torturer, and you're going to be emotionally in there. (Matheou 2010, 184–185)

Padilha has also embraced his political motives for making the documentary *Bus 174*. He wanted to tell the bus hijacker's story because the hijacker saw himself as a victim of state institutions that converted him from a street kid into a violent individual. The same theme, where the state breeds violence in Brazil, also guides *Elite Squad*. Padilha said that he wanted to explain that "many Brazilian policemen become corrupt and violent" because of the environment created by the state (low wages, insufficient training, dangerous work). Padhila emphasizes that "in *Elite Squad* we are basically saying that a society cannot sustain itself if its police believe in the idea that violence is something you control with violence, which is of course a stupid idea" (Matheou 2010, 174).

Padilha's argument that the state breeds violence would be valid if the state had such powers instead of economic circumstances, mechanisms, and systems that form the state do. In this context, the *Elite Squad* films are about the corporatization of the police force and surviving as an independent entity (corporation) in a decaying community/state. The police become examples of *capitalism a brasileira* (Brazilian style capitalism)—that is, they are making personal gain from the country's social problems. The police become another gang. In *Elite Squad,* a regular police officer's comment on BOPE—"Knife in the skull and an empty wallet," which refers to the impaled skull of the exhaustingly used BOPE logo—illustrates the fragmentation of the police force in the film. Whereas administrative and inter-force turf wars, budget competition, and interpolicial or interstate security apparatus conflicts could explain the fragmentation, these films put the blame on the state, which has reduced police forces into weak, disorganized, and ideologically lacking corporate entities. The supplanted gang-like ideology and criminal adversaries within the police are imprinted on Neto's "gang tattoo." The shadowing of the nation by the BOPE corporation is most forcefully represented in Neto's and Matias's funeral scenes when the BOPE black flag is placed on top of the Brazilian flag on the coffin, signifying loyalty to the unit rather than the nation (figure 9.1).

In terms of the representation of politico-economical aspects of populist politics in *Elite Squad 2*, one scene is particularly poignant. It presents a neighborhood feast and political rally organized by corrupt police and politicians such as legislator Fortunato who also runs a demagogic true crime TV show, to get votes on the streets of a *favela*. The party features samba (appropriated by Vargas as symbolic of the nation), a multiracial community, epicurean abundance, conviviality, and sensuousness. Yet, things that are stereotypically seen as positive Brazilian national attributes are shown in this scene to be a façade of a rotten system. Nascimento's didactic monologue accompanies the travesty of this communal gathering: "In Brazil the elections are a business [*negocio*] and the votes are the most valued commodity in the

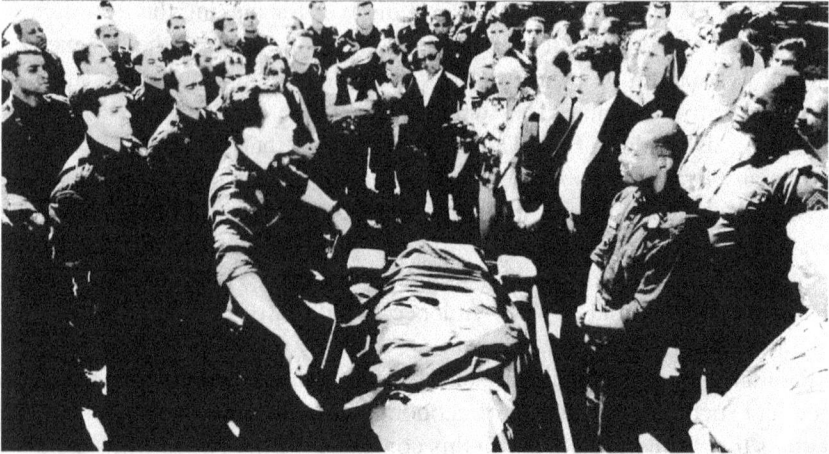

Figure 9.1   Nascimento Covers the Brazilian Flag with the BOPE Flag at Neto's Funeral.
Source: Screenshot from *Tropa de Elite* (*Elite Squad*), directed by José Padilha, 2007.
Brazil: Universal Pictures.

slums." Nascimento's character is voicing another critique of the system and
even liberal democracy. Also, coming from a representative of the security
services just three decades from military dictatorship, the cynical outlook
toward voting raises specters of authoritarianism.

If in the older Brazilian films, the street was a forum, a national public
sphere, and the *favelas* were romanticized, contemporary films demarcate the
private and public space differently: the street has become a location for a
brutal Darwinian struggle (Frey 2014). For example, in the first *Elite Squad*,
BOPE is sent to pacify the *favela* that the Pope slept next to. The story is
based on real-life when Pope John Paul II visited Rio in 1997, and thirty
people were killed when the police brutally neutralized the gangs in the *favela*
near the Pope. At one point, after torturing an informant, the BOPE men kill
him after Nascimento orders to "put him on the tab of the Pope" (Padilha
2007). In the *Elite Squad* films, the streets are deserted by the rule of law and
the state, yet BOPE's intrusions are only short-term interventions with no
long-term reform plan.

The *Elite Squads*' social critique of the "system" of Brazilian society is
ambivalent. It utilizes Hollywood's style and narratives of vigilantism and
competes on the global film market where its critique might be misunder-
stood. After all, little is said of Brazil's colonial history and its position in the
world system, even though the films form a part of "a twenty-first-century
Brazilian cinematic response to the challenges posed by global and national
film industries and the globalization of the Brazilian society and economy as
a whole" (Vázquez 2018, 66). The films' alignment with generic conventions

and its entertaining, sensational, and spectacular components might outflank the social commentary. However, the identity politics presented in the films bring another and perhaps more approachable aspect to the topic.

TORN MASCULINE IDENTITIES

A wave of intellectual work in the early twentieth century tried to conceptualize a Brazilian identity. As part of these attempts, the myth of *Homem Cordial*, or "cordial man," was coined by Sérgio Buarque de Holanda in his book *Raízes do Brasil* (*Roots of Brazil* 1936). Holanda's "cordial man" did not mean someone amiable as it is in common parlance, rather his concept posited that Brazilian men were guided by the heart (classical Latin *cor*) more than rationality. The men at the center of *Elite Squad* films are cordial men in Holanda's sense: they follow their passions (fighting crime), utilize *jeitinho brasileiro*, and circumvent rules or social conventions not unlike populist leaders who promise to bypass the corrupt or inefficient system promising simple solutions.

In terms of aesthetic conventions, these films owe a great debt to *film noir*, which has a gravid history of men in crisis and at the mercy of mechanisms beyond their control. Particularly the first *Elite Squad* foregrounds the *noir* quality of the uncanniness of home life and connects it to the crisis of masculinity, a theme driving many Bolsonaro voters. The femme fatale of *noir*, however, are missing from these Brazilian films. The *Elite Squad* films represent women as inactive and dependents, bystanders, and victims, wives, and relatives. A feminist film theory reading of active men and women without agency or the "bearer of meaning, not maker of meaning" (Mulvey 1975, 7) fits the *Elite Squad* films well: they repeat classic Hollywood narration where men, such as narrator Nascimento, drive the story.

The first words after the opening credits of *Elite Squad* are Nascimento's, who speaks on the phone with his pregnant wife: "I would like to be with you, but I have to work" (Padilha 2007). He listens to the heartbeat of his child-to-be through the phone as he is on a stakeout, watching police sell their weapons to drug dealers. After work, Nascimento returns home to his apartment, where he pours out the ill feelings after a hard day onto his pregnant wife. Nascimento is even on a mission when his wife gives birth, and when he is holding his newborn son, he thinks about work on the soundtrack narration. These scenes are not part of the primary narrative, but they suggest that issues of masculine identity are central to the story.

Habermas's (1989) concept of "Man of the House and Man of the Market" and Lauren Berlant's (2011) instrumentalization of this concept are useful for our analysis here. This "split in the man of modernity" suggests that these two different territories serve as an example of cruel optimism, a common affective state in the era of precarity (Berlant 2011, 33). This relation of cruel optimism exists when something you desire is actually an impediment to your thriving—an example is the affective state in which one strives to manage to be simultaneously a man of the house and a man of the market, despite consciously or unconsciously recognizing that this will be out of reach. Nascimento exhibits this "split" well. At home, he is an emotional "little leader" (Berlant 2011, 33). For example, the sequel shows him practicing Brazilian jiu-jitsu and talking intimately with his (now grown-up) son. However, the sequences of his work outside of the home undermine this familiar imaginary in their ultrabrutality.

These films, according to action genre conventions, show that the public image of Nascimento, and other men of BOPE, such as Matias, is completely hard and hyper-masculine. Still, the films strive to show also the personal side of the BOPE men, and this side is most often in plight. Matias, for example, suffers relationship problems after his girlfriend finds out he is a police officer. And in Nascimento's case, stress causes him psychological problems, and he starts taking antidepressants and seeing a psychiatrist. He takes his frustration out on other people like suspects, informers, and his wife, who later leaves him. The business of policing breaks up Nascimento's family because, ultimately, he cannot function both in the house (family) and in the market (work). The films underscore that one cannot draw brackets around the home and the street—or, in other words, the private and the public. This represents patriarchy in a deep crisis.

The family in Brazil, as in many developing economies, is the prime social unit, and (populist) politicians tend to represent themselves as father figures. Getúlio Vargas, "the father of the poor," was a prime example who, in an extraordinary trajectory, moved from head of the oligarchy to a leader and champion of Brazilian workers (Fausto 2006, 223; Stam 2005, 159). The family is the first form of sociality in developing nations, but it is threatened or broken by intrusions and interruptions from the outside by excessively hard work, violence, and the media. In *Elite Squad 2*, this culminates in an assassination attempt in which Nascimento and his family are embroiled in. In other words, these films have a strong theme of the family in crisis, and with the family in trouble, masculine dilemmas often surface as well. In the sequel, Nascimento is already divorced, his ex-wife married to a human rights activist, his son estranged.

"Machismo," the deep-rooted culture of patriarchy and toxic masculinity that permeates Brazilian culture and life, is by no means easy on men, particularly of the lower strata or even the middle class. As in many other countries in Brazil, men have a shorter life expectancy than women have. Their probability of facing incarceration or a violent death at a young age is higher than in other demographics. Potentially deadly aspects of machismo were written over Bolsonaro's dismissal of Covid-19 as a *gripezinha* (sniffle) and his urge for people to face the virus as "men not kids" (Robinson 2020). The disease, like crime and violence, affects the poorest and non-white segments of the population hardest. The image of the BOPE, and the public persona of Nascimento aligns with machismo ideology.

POLICE FETISHISM AND NECROPOLITICS

In *Elite Squads*, the politico-economical criticism of "the system" and machismo ideologies appear to support right-wing and neoliberal populist values. It is at the core of neoliberal theory that the state maintains the repressive mechanisms that allow the market to function in the best possible manner. As Harvey (2005, 2) notes, the state must set up the repressive apparatuses that include the police, legal structures, and other functions required to guarantee private property rights and to ensure the proper functioning of markets. Thus, crime films and cinematic representations of the police provide fertile ground for studying the representations of the state and politics, including populism and how it is mobilized. The *Elite Squad* films exemplify a shift in the functioning of capitalism from neoliberal politics to what Mark LeVine (2020) has termed "necroliberalism," riffing Mbembé's (2003) concept of necropolitics. Levine notes that neoliberalism needed a fluid and unified world system and even a growing middle class to work. Necroliberalism in turn, demands increased "securitization, (re-)militarization and racketization" to run efficiently. Also, necroliberalism has close ties with (nationalist) populism in conjunction with necropolitics because it marginalizes large swaths of the population:

> What I term necrocapitalism comprises the unprecedentedly racialised, racketised, militarised, revanchist and necropolitical form of capitalism and its attendant politics in the era of Donald Trump, Vladimir Putin, Bashar al-Assad, Jair Bolsonaro, Viktor Orban, Rodrigo Duterte and co. (LeVine 2020)

Here, necropolitics has close ties with what Howse (2017, 3), following Dani Rodrik, calls anti-pluralist "bad populism" that attack minority rights and are hostile to foreign workers.

Durão (2020) also evokes the concept of necropolitics to describe Bolsonaro's ideology and practice, where the use of power, social or political, dictates how some people can live and how some have to perish. Bolsonaro's techniques of marginalization involve ultrabrutality on criminals, the use of macho misogynistic and anti-LGBT+ rhetoric and legislation. There is a racial component to his anti-crime rhetoric. The target of his necropolitics is a disposable population of criminals, who usually are economically and racially marginalized favela dwellers. The *Elite Squad* films represented a nightmarish vision of crime and how it is fought as if showing a Brazil that Bolsonaro wants to realize. In its narrative, the role of the marginalized is to perish and its ideological architectonics concentrate on a middle-class police narrator who holds power over the *favelas*. It is notable that the predecessors of *Elite Squad* that were international crossovers and/or festival successes, such as *City of God* (Meirelles and Lund 2002), *Central Station* (Salles 1998), *Carandiru* (Babenco 2003) or even the older *Pixote* (Babenco 1981), feature *favela* dwellers and the poor as the main protagonists, unlike Nascimento. *Elite Squad* is a microcosm of Brazil and the practice of necropolitics. And, as elections in Brazil have shown, these necropolitical imaginaries are not unfounded as longing for the harsh authority of the military dictatorship is on the rise. Bolsonario has made his appreciation of the military dictatorship clear through commenting, for example, in 2008 that their mistake was to "only torture and not kill" (Jovem Pan 2016).

Inspired by Marx's concept of commodity fetishism, criminologist Robert Reiner (2010) has coined the concept of "police fetishism." This is the *a priori* assumption that chaos would reign in society without police. Reiner has also discussed this concept in relation to fictional representations of the police: "During the 1990s, the peccadilloes attributed to police protagonists threatened at times to make them indistinguishable from criminals. But the constant factor remained the idea that they were needed to defeat even more evil threats to ordinary people—I have called this myth 'police fetishism'" (Reiner 2016, 189). In the *Elite Squad*, the transgressions of the police are not merely small mistakes, "peccadilloes," as the torturing and killing of criminals is common in Brazil. Yet, the power of police fetishism and Nascimento's role as a narrator invite the audience to align with Nascimento's perspective, and as such, the viewers have an option to see Nascimento's brutality as a must. Wagner Moura, who played the role of Nascimento, said he was "shocked" by the heroization and "pop icon" status of his role as he felt he was portraying a violent and inhumane character (Padilha 2011).

When analyzing the ideological roots of Bolsonaro, Susana Durão (2020, 25) uses the concept of police fetishism to scrutinize the status of the police in Brazil. She criticizes Bolsonaro's former justice minister Moro's harsh necropolitical measures to not be motivated by coherent crime reduction policies or by any thoughtful public security strategy. The goal to govern through the moral panic of crime, a familiar strategy from US politics, does not suit Brazil very well because the people see the police as incompetent. This leads to police impunity and populist hard on crime approaches that were a large part of Bolsonaro's campaign. (Durão 2020). These processes are also described in a critical fashion by the *Elite Squad* films that, at times, seem to function as preludes to the Bolsonaro presidency.

Elite Squad 2, for example, is a commentary on the relation between mass media and populist politics that have had a strong linkage since the *Estado Novo* of Vargas. In the film, Falstaffian demagogue and congressional representative Fortunato with his aggressive calls to be tough on crime and the cynical approach of the compromised media, are reminders of both the populist and personalized governments that have been in power in the country. The character of Fortunato is modeled after populist true crime reporters who have gone into politics, with Bolsonaro-style calls to be tough on crime, and with a vigilante slant. For example, São Paulo's governor João Doria, the businessman who gained fame with Brazil's *Apprentice* TV show before his career in politics, similarly to Trump in the United States, has been harsh with his comments on crime. His popular comments, such as "whoever resists arrest goes directly to the cemetery, not to jail" (Durão 2020, 28), are emblematic of the necropolitical stance of many Brazilian elites but also of the ethos of the *Elite Squad*'s BOPE as articulated in the film's slogan: "A good criminal is a dead criminal" (Padilha 2007).

In the Brazilian National Congress, there is a "bullet-coalition," a caucus of ex-military and police force representatives that has soared in recent years. Durão argues that "Retaliation has long been a hallmark of the Brazilian police. Nevertheless, what used to circulate as part of a Brazilian 'cultural intimacy'—for example, that 'the only good bandit is a dead one'—is now politically mandated. Since the transition to democracy starting in 1985, we have not seen such a fetishization of the uniform, nor such social tolerance for lethal force" (Durão 2020, 28). The graphic violence inflicted by the police in *Elite Squad* and its popularity and ambivalence of reception is part of the recent political shifts where masculinity and the military go in tandem. "Masculinity" was even a requirement for Brazilian police until 2018 after pressure from gay rights groups; the requirement of masculinity was changed to "endurance" (Schow 2018). The *Elite Squad* films meticulously represent the battlefield standard of equipment and training of the BOPE, and Nascimento's narration often refers to their mission as war (see figure 9.2), this established already in the opening sequence of *Elite Squad*: "In Rio a cop has to choose between bribes, leaving or going to war."

CONCLUSION

The themes and subtexts of the masculine crisis and political-economy of the *Elite Squad* films bring forward ideological aspects that have created room for populist politics. The problems described are a reality in Brazilian

BOPE soldiers kill guerrillas

Figure 9.2 The BOPE Training Course Brutalizes and Dehumanizes the Trainees, They In Turn Replicate their Training in the Streets in Elite Squad. *Source*: Screenshot from *Tropa de Elite (Elite Squad)*, directed by José Padilha, 2007. Brazil: Universal Pictures.

society, and populist demagogues exploit them. This is not the case only in Brazil; other neoliberal demagogues have often been "tough on crime," good examples being such historical leaders as Ronald Reagan, Margaret Thatcher, and later Rudolph Giuliani. Ample examples of this trend are also to be found in Latin America and Brazil, for instance, the populist president Collor de Mello, Brazil's military dictatorship, and right-wing radical Bolsonaro. The anti-crime bill that Bolsonaro's minister of Justice Moro proposed in 2019, being essentially "combating violent crime through violence itself" (Durão 2020, 28).

The state and its repressive apparatuses, and the police that exemplify them, are represented in the *Elite Squad* films as a clan-like entity in a decaying polity. Postmodern texts tend to favor allegory and reading these films in this manner, one can find signs of the devaluation of the state and its organs and the BOPE men's crisis of masculinity. Representations of police or security entrepreneurs who are out of control and corrupt are a recurring motif in not only Brazilian cinema but in Latin American film in general. These films reiterate the theme of gang mentality and corporatization of security and other state functions in addition to narratives of colonized cities. If not providing for any options for the future, this ideological vista is a growth base for populist politics, not least in its rejection of the state and negative representation of politicians and other elites. The *Elite Squad* films stand out from mainstream and Hollywood cinema in the sense that they foreground various social problems but do not provide simple solutions to them. This ambiguous position correlates with its unsettling action aesthetic that, on the other hand, offers an immersing spectacle. In other words, the films have an open ending that prompts the audience to make up one's own subject/audience position. The election of Bolsonaro and his policies and rhetoric that are closely aligned with the problems pointed out by films suggest that the political response that Padilha called for with the films have as of yet been meagerly developed.

BIBLIOGRAPHY

Babenco, Héctor, dir. 1981. *Pixote: A Lei do Mais Fraco*. Empresa Brasileira de Filmes S.A.
Babenco, Héctor, dir. 2003. *Carandiru*. Columbia TriStar.
Barros, Laura, and Manuel Santos Silva. 2020. "Right-Wing Populism in the Tropics: The Rise of Jair Bolsonaro." *VoxEU*, January 24, 2020. https://voxeu.org/article/right-wing-populism-tropics-rise-jair-bolsonaro.
Bentes. Ivana. 2003. "The *Sertão* and the *Favela* in Contemporary Brazilian film." In *The New Brazilian Cinema*, edited by Lúcia Nagib, 121–137. London: I.B. Tauris.
Berlant, Lauren. 2011. *Cruel Optimism*. Durham: Duke University Press.
Buarque de Holanda, Sérgio. 1936. *Roots of Brazil (Raízes do Brasil)*. Translated by G. Harvey Summ. Notre Dame: The University of Notre Dame, 2012.
Caldas, Pedro. 2008. "O (ab)uso da palavra fascismo a recepcao de *Tropa de Elite*." *Viso: Cadernos de estética aplicada* 2 (4): 46–56. https://doi.org/10.22409/1981-4062/v4i/54.
Durão, Susana. 2020. "Bolsonaro's Brazil and the Police Fetish." Hot Spots, *Fieldsights*, January 28, 2020. https://culanth.org/fieldsights/bolsonaros-brazil-and-the-police-fetish.
Fausto, Boris. 2006. *The Concise History of Brazil*. New York: Cambridge University Press.
Frey, Aline. 2014. "Violence in the Streets of New Brazilian Cinema." In *Brazil In Twenty-First Century Popular Media*, edited by Naomi Wood, 55–71. Lanham MD: Lexington Books.
Grigera, Juan. 2017. "Populism in Latin America: Old and New Populisms in Argentina and Brazil." *International Political Science Review* 38 (4): 441–455.
Habermas, Jurgen. 1989. *The Structural Transformation of the Public Sphere: An Inquiry into a Category of Bourgeois Society*. Polity Press: Cambridge.
Harvey, David. 2005. *A Brief History of Neoliberalism*. Oxford: Oxford University Press.
Howse, Rob. 2017. "Populism and Its Enemies." Presented at Workshop on Public Law and the New Populism, Jean Monnet Center, NYU Law School, September 15–16, 2017.
Johnson, Randal. 2005. "TV Globo, The MPA, and Brazilian Cinema." In *Latin American Cinema; Essays on Modernity, Gender and National Identity*, edited by Lisa Shaw and Stephanie Dennison, 11–38. London: McFarland and Company.
Jovem Pan 2016. "Defensor da Ditadura, Jair Bolsonaro reforç a frase polêmica: 'o erro foi torturar e não matar.'" *Pânico*, July 8, 2016. https://jovempan.com.br/

programas/panico/defensor-da-ditadura-jair-bolsonaro-reforca-frase-polemica-o-erro-foi-torturar-e-nao-matar.html.

Kozloff, Nikolas. 2008. *Revolution! South America and the Rise of the New Left.* New York: Palgrave MacMillan.

Laclau, Ernesto. 2005. "Populism: What's in the Name?" In *Populism and the Mirror of Democracy*, edited by Francisco Panizza, 32–49. London: Verso.

Latinobarómetro. 2016. *Informe Latinobarómetro 2016.* Santiago de Chile: Corporación Latinobarómetro. https://www.latinobarometro.org/latNewsShow.jsp.

LeVine, Mark. 2020. "From Neoliberalism to Necrocapitalism in 20 Years." *Al Jazeera*, July 15, 2020. https://www.aljazeera.com/opinions/2020/7/15/from-neoliberalism-to-necrocapitalism-in-20-years/?gb=true.

Lobato, Ramon. 2012. *Shadow Economies of Cinema, Mapping Informal Film Distribution.* London: Palgrave McMillan.

Marchetti, Gina. 2006. *The Infernal Affairs Trilogy.* Hong Kong: HKU Press.

Matheou. Demetrious. 2010. *The Faber Book of New South American Cinema.* London: Faber and Faber.

Mbembé, Achille. 2003. "Necropolitics." *Public Culture* 15 (1): 11–40. https://doi.org/10.1215/08992363-15-1-11.

Meirelles, Fernando, and Kátia Lund, dir. 2002. *Cidade de Deus* (*City of God*). São Paulo: Imagem Filmes.

Mulvey, Laura. 1975. "Visual Pleasure and Narrative Cinema." *Screen* 16 (3): 6–18.

Nagib, Lúcia. 2004. "Talking Bullets." *Third Text* 18 (3): 239–250.

Ortellado, Pablo, and Marcio Moretti Ribeiro. 2018. "Mapping Brazil's Political Polarization Online." *The Conversation*, August 3, 2018. https://theconversation.com/mapping-brazils-political-polarization-online-96434.

Padilha, José, dir. 2002. *Ônibus 174* (*Bus 174*). Rio de Janeiro: Zazen Produções.

Padilha, José, dir. 2007. *Tropa de Elite* (*Elite Squad*). Universal Pictures (Brasil).

Padilha, José, dir. 2010. *Tropa de Elite 2: O Inimigo Agora é Outro* (*Elite Squad 2: The Enemy Within*). Rio de Janeiro: Rio Filmes.

Padilha, José. 2011. "Interview in 61st Berlinale Press Conference Grand Hyatt Hotel, Berlin." February 11, 2011. https://www.berlinale.de/en/archive/jahresarchive/2011/02_programm_2011/02_filmdatenblatt_2011_20116613.html#tab=video10.

Purcell, Andrew. 2008. "Lionizing the Bad Boys of Brazil." *The Irish Times*, July 26, 2008. https://www.irishtimes.com/news/lionising-the-bad-boys-from-brazil-1.946959.

Reiner, Robert. 2010. *The Politics of the Police.* New York: Oxford University Press.

Reiner, Robert. 2016. *Crime: The Mystery of the Common Sense Project.* Cambridge: Polity.

Riccio, Vicente. 2017. "Crime and the Visual Media in Brazil." *Oxford Research Encyclopedia of Criminology*, July 27, 2017. https://oxfordre.com/criminology/view/10.1093/acrefore/9780190264079.001.0001/acrefore-9780190264079-e-27.

Robinson, Andy. 2020. "Bolsonaro is Bonkers but There is a Method to His Madness." *The Nation*, April 22, 2020. https://www.thenation.com/article/world/coronavirus-brazil-bolsonaro-coup/.

Salles, Walter, dir. 1998. *Central do Brasil (Central Station)*. São Paulo: Europa Filmes.

Schow, Ashe. 2018. "'Masculinity' No Longer a Requirement for Brazilian Cops." *Daily Wire*, August 15, 2018. https://www.dailywire.com/news/masculinity-no -longer-requirement-brazilian-cops-ashe-schow.

Stam, Robert. 2005. "Land in Anguish." In *Brazilian Cinema*, edited by Randal Johnson, and Robert Stam, 149–161. New York: Columbia U. Press.

Stam, Robert, Joao Luiz Vieira, and Ismail Xavier. 2005. "Brazilian Cinema in the Postmodern Age." In *Brazilian Cinema*, edited by Randal Johnson, and Robert Stam, 389–472. New York: Columbia U. Press.

Vázquez Vázquez, Maria Mercedes. 2018. *The Question of Class in Contemporary Latin American Cinema*. Lexington Books: London.

Chapter 10

Send in the Clowns

*Twisted Masculinity, Supergendering,
and the Aesthetics of Populism in
Todd Phillips's JOKER (2019)*

John Quinn

This chapter explores the interplay between the aesthetics of masculinity and populism in Todd Phillips's *JOKER* (2019). Inhabiting "its own universe [and having] no connection to any of the DC films that have come before it" (Phillips and Silver 2018), Phillips's narrative, the first R-Rated production to gross in excess of one billion dollars at the global box office (Hughes, 2019), disregards the already muddled canon of the Batman cinematic franchise to reconceive the origin story of its titular antagonist. At the heart of this reimagining lies a confrontation with problematic masculinities and social inequality. In their prefatory note to the original screenplay, writers Phillips and Silver set out the initial conditions for that conflict. "It's a troubled time. The crime rate in Gotham is at record highs. A garbage strike has crippled the city for the past six weeks. And the divide between the 'haves' and the 'have-nots' is palpable. Dreams are beyond reach, slipping into delusions" (Phillips and Silver 2018).

Set against this backdrop, our protagonist, Arthur Fleck, is presented to us in a fractured, twisted, and dysfunctional mode of masculinity that lies far beyond the supergendered norm of the conventional superhero movie (Behm-Morawitz and Pennell 2013; Pennell and Behm-Morawitz 2015). Arthur is one of the "have-nots" with aspirations of being one of the "haves." Perhaps more so, Arthur is presented as an "othered" (Diamond and Poharec 2017; Sune 2011) form of masculinity, existing in an asymmetrical relationship (Bernasconi 2012) to both the audience and the denizens of Gotham City. To the observer, Arthur's situation looks bleak; his aspirations appear beyond the

187

limits of his resources, the apparatus of social institutions acting upon him seeming more prohibitive than empowering.

It is through this lens of disillusionment and delusion that Phillips encourages the viewer to, at best understand, or at worst empathize with, Arthur's metamorphosis into the inadvertent inspiration for a populist movement. This chapter considers how the societal conditions of Gotham City are presented in such a way as to align with the key concepts of Mudde's ideational approach to populism (2004, 2017), establishing the context from which the Joker arises. Part of this analysis considers how Arthur's othered mode of masculinity, along with the problematic masculinities of those around him and those constructed in opposition to him, function as a key catalyst for Arthur becoming the accidental champion of Gotham's disillusioned men. The chapter also assesses how the actions of Arthur/Joker's followers function as a "thin-cantered ideology" (Mudde and Kaltwasser 2017, 6). Arthur himself draws upon criminality to situate the Joker as contemporary demagogue rather than a populist leader (Patapan 2019), using populism as a discursive form (Aslanidis 2016) to achieve his own self-serving needs.

THE PEOPLE, ARTHUR, AND THE ELITE

A prominent definition of populism in the literature is that of Cas Mudde, who describes the phenomenon as "an ideology that considers society to be ultimately separated into two homogeneous and antagonistic groups, 'the pure people' versus 'the corrupt elite,' and which argues that politics should be an expression of the volonté générale (general will) of the people" (Mudde 2004, 543). This chapter draws upon that definition to demonstrate how the societal conditions of Phillip's Gotham City align with the core concepts of Mudde's ideational approach to populism. Specifically, this chapter explores how Mudde's four core concepts of ideology, the people, the elite and general will (Mudde 2017, 29), function to establish the societal conditions that facilitate the emergence of a populist movement within the movie.

At the heart of Mudde's definition of ideational populism lies the separation of society into two belligerent groups; the people and the elite. For Mudde, the fundamental opposition between these two groups is organized around the loose notion of morality, constructing a pure, homogenous and authentic people, and a corrupt, exploitative and self-serving elite (29). It is through this moral mechanism that the formative conditions of ideational populism highlight and politicize perceived social inequalities in order to condemn the elites in power (Mudde and Kaltwasser 2017, 32), and it is these perceived social inequalities that Phillips is keen to establish from the outset of the movie and, moreover, present to us through the lens of masculinity.

For Mudde, the people is the foremost of the core concepts of ideational populism (2017, 31), and in *JOKER*, we encounter that foremost force of ideational populism as they struggle against rampant social inequality. That encounter is negotiated for the audience in two distinct yet connected ways. First, the people—as corpus of discontent, unease, and oppression—is expressed to us via the central allegory of the garbage strike and the recurring motif of the clown protests. Second, and for the overwhelming majority of the narrative, our interpretation of those people, their situations and the wider societal happenings of Gotham City, is steered via the unreliable, often delusional, lens of Arthur Fleck. This lens constructs a predominantly masculine gaze throughout the movie, while the aesthetics of that gaze construct a specifically othered (Diamond and Poharec 2017; Sune 2011) interpretation of the people, where, like most populist movements, the people and the elite are constructions based on a warped interpretation of reality (Mudde and Kaltwasser 2017, 68). This facilitates a multifaceted process of othering within the diegesis of film, where Arthur is othered by the people, the people are othered by Arthur, and both are othered by the elite, which leaves the audience to negotiate this nexus of otherness from their extra-diegetic location, which, of course, functions as a further form of othering on the macro level. Together, these two modes of encounter construct our understanding of the "have-nots" and set in play the perceived moral dialectic that will drive the conflict between the people and the elite, fabricating, patterns of binary opposition that form, and reinforce the cause and effect logic of the narrative (Stam, Burgoyne and Flitterman-Lewis 2002, 76–79).

To begin with, the garbage strike presents the people as a looming yet intangible threat of social unrest. Just like they have been in life, they are consigned to the background of the narrative, with us learning of their suffering indirectly through media broadcasts, newspaper headlines and snippets of conversation. Indeed, in the opening scene of *JOKER*, we hear on the radio that a state of emergency has been declared, with the commentator suggesting that the garbage strike has an impact on everyone. This assertion soon becomes incongruous with the visual aesthetic of the film, as we see that it is the inner-city streets of the "have-nots" that are strewn with rat-infested garbage, while the "haves" of the suburbs remain garbage free. In this way, the matter of the garbage strike allows the narrative of *JOKER* to establish a baseline binary of morality, where the purity of the people is disrupted by the inability of the Gotham elite to resolve the industrial dispute, and the specificity of their struggle is negated by the false notion of the issue impacting on everyone.

The building undercurrent of tension throughout *JOKER* first permeates to the narrative surface when Arthur interacts with his social worker. During their session, Arthur asks, if the city is getting crazier or if it's just him; his social worker replies that times are tough, pointing to unemployment as a cause of distress and discontent. This exchange establishes the lived experience of the people for the audience and situates Arthur as one of those people: a "have-not" who is struggling and needs the help of social services. However, the exchange also sets Arthur apart from the people via his mental illness and, indeed, Arthur sets himself apart by framing the people as a force external to him. This adds a level of complexity to the layering of binary oppositions within *JOKER*, where the people are drawn in opposition to the elite and Arthur is drawn in opposition to both the elite and the people.

The core masculinities at play in *JOKER* form a striking visualization of this layered and exclusionary process of opposition, where the denizens of the talent agency with which Arthur works, Ha-Ha's Talent Booking, exist far from the traditional hyper-masculine modality of the conventional action movie (Tasker 1993a). Rather than adopting the traditional hard-body aesthetics of action cinema (Jeffords 1994), the clown performers of Ha-Ha's appear as a collection of past-their-prime misfit males, best represented by the middle-aged, balding and overweight Randall, and the often ridiculed and exploited little person Gary. They exist on the fringes of masculinity, forced to scratch out an existence via a mechanism that accentuates their very otherness. Yet even among these masculinities, Arthur is set apart from his fellow performers, who do not feel comfortable around him. Arthur's body is a key location of this extended otherness. Emaciated and twisted through unusual posturing, Arthur's body is presented as a site of spectacle to be read in opposition to that of the conventional action movie body (Tasker 1993b). Rather than represent the traditional masculine ideals of strength, power, resiliency, and heterosexual desirability (Brown 2016), Arthur's slender, bruised and beaten body inverts such coding, constructing a spectacle of the othered among the others.

As such, the narrative of *JOKER* presents to the audience an additional framework of inequality as experienced specifically by Arthur. Arthur believes himself to be pure. Indeed, he self-situates as morally just when he daydreams about appearing on the Live with Murray Franklin show, receiving praise and respect from Franklin and the audience when he tells them that as the man of the house, he takes good care of his mother, with Franklin suggesting that this sacrifice must cause his mother to love him. This forms an opposition in and of itself; while Arthur does indeed live with and care for his sick mother Penny Fleck, Penny devotes the majority of her time writing letters to former employer Thomas Wayne asking him to help her and her son, despite the fact that it is Arthur, not Thomas, who delivers her primary care. Here Arthur is presented as being inadequate in fulfilling the role of the absent masculine provider that Penny yearns for. Penny interprets Arthur's masculinity as less than that of Thomas Wayne, framing Arthur as a child in need of help, rather than a strong masculine provider. The latter is, of course, how Arthur identifies himself and how he would like others to perceive him, yet, in the narrative of *JOKER*, Arthur is only presented as the righteous masculine provider from within the context of his own delusions.

This notion of injustice and unrecognized contribution builds throughout the narrative, constructing a cycle of perceived moral inequality, where Arthur is continually undermined in his activities and aspirations. This undermining continues into Arthur's professional context, where the conditions of his employment at Ha-Ha's Talent Booking are also established as morally unjust, when his boss Hoyt does not believe that Arthur was jumped by a group of kids and asks him to pay for the sign that the kids used to beat him with. As the sign no longer exists, Arthur cannot return it; therefore, with Hoyt unwilling to consider further discussion on the matter, Arthur must accept this injustice. Arthur's reaction to this situation draws directly on the allegory of the garbage strike, with Arthur going to the alleyway outside Ha-Ha's and kicking at the piles of uncollected garbage bags until he eventually collapses amidst them, becoming one with the discarded waste of Gotham City. Here Arthur displays an inverse of what Tasker terms the controlled performance of the hyper-masculine (Tasker 1993a, 233–236), where he beats the garbage rather than fighting his cause with Hoyt.

The conceptualization of Arthur as an unwanted environmental object is extended further when he meets Sophie and her young daughter in their apartment building elevator. When the elevator temporarily stops, Sophie turns to Arthur and makes conversation while they wait for the elevator to resume, telling him that the building is awful. When Sophie's young daughter parrots this line back at her, Sophie playfully mimics shooting herself in the head. Arthur misinterprets this exchange, thinking that Sophie is attempting to bond with him, and attempts to continue their interaction once they are out of the lift by mimicking shooting himself in the head. Out of context, this unsettles Sophie, who becomes wary of Arthur and retreats to the safety of her own apartment. Here, Arthur is presented as a problematic masculinity: much like the piles of rat-infested garbage blighting the city, Arthur is a potential source of danger, further separating Arthur from the rest of the "have-nots." This constructs an oppositional binary around Arthur's self-conceived purity, and the impression of him held by the wider community. At its most bleak, therefore, *JOKER* situates Arthur's mental health condition as another problematic issue for the people, one which, like the garbage strike, has been neglected by the elite. This is visualized in stark terms for the audience via Arthur's journal, where he writes about being expected to hide his mental illness.

Such problematizing of Arthur's conception of his own masculinity continues in his relationship with his mother, when, as he bathes her, she stresses how Thomas Wayne is a good man and if he only knew of their plight that he would help them. Yet when Arthur tells her that she does not need to worry about money as his stand-up comedy is ready for the big clubs, Penny doubts his abilities, asking him why he thinks he could be a stand-up comedian when he is not funny. Penny not only undermines Arthur's ability to be her masculine provider, but also an essential element of Arthur's sense of identity. After this interaction with his mother, Arthur develops an unwanted and unsolicited fixation with Sophie, following her first to school as she drops her daughter off, and then to her place of work, only retreating when he fears she may have seen him. Later, Arthur slips into delusion, imagining that Sophie comes to his door to ask if he was following her. She is not angry that he followed her, instead she is glad, joking that she hoped he'd come to rob the place. Arthur tells her he has a gun and could come by tomorrow. Sophie laughs; she finds him so funny. Arthur invites her to come to his stand-up performance and she agrees.

This further problematizes Arthur's masculinity and his ability to form relationships with the female-identifying characters around him. While his real-life retreat signals that Arthur is, at least to some extent, aware of the inappropriate nature of his relationship with Sophie, his fantasy connects his masculinity and sexual attractiveness with violence and danger. This turns the negative external perception of his personality into a positive by drawing on the wisecracks traditionally used in action cinema as a mechanism for breaking moments of symbolic tension (Tasker 1993b, 29–31).

When Arthur visits Pogo's Comedy Club as a customer he does not fit in there either, his uncontrollable laugh setting him apart from the rest of the audience. Worst still, when Arthur visits Pogo's as a performer, his imagined mastery of comedy doesn't materialize and his stand-up is a disaster, the people unable to engage with him due to his laughing and his material appearing trite and passé. In the real world, Arthur appears out of touch. He is unable to connect with the audience on an emotional level. In the face of this adversity, Arthur attempts to resolve the conflict by once more escaping into delusion. He imagines that the performance is a success, with the audience recognizing his talent; Arthur connects that adulation with his sexual prowess, visualizing Sophie in the audience just as she promised. She is entranced by his performance, allured by his comedic abilities, and afterward, he imagines that the success of his performance facilitates a wonderful date between the two. Arthur's masculine aspirations are again contrasted with the realities of his existence. Arthur wants to be seen as a successful, sexually attractive male, who is respected in his profession and venerated by his new lover. Arthur imagines that he is competent at forming relationships with the female identities around him, and, moreover, he imagines that these relationships are built on appreciation of him as a provider and master of his craft.

Riding the subway home after being fired from Ha-Ha's Talent Booking for taking a gun into a performance at a children's hospital, Arthur encounters three drunk "Wall Street" types harassing a young woman on the train. This is Arthur's first direct interaction with the forces of the elite in the narrative. The Wall Street Three are a representation of the "haves." They are also a representation of the hyper-masculine mode of representation common to action cinema (Jeffords 1994; Lehman 2013; Tasker 1993a, b, 2019). Dressed in suits, they look down their nose at the young woman on the train abusing her for not engaging with their drunken antics. Here, they form a spectacle of the hyper-masculine, where they define and articulate their masculine strength though conflict (Tasker 2019), and draw themselves in opposition to the femininity of the train passenger.

Such articulations of the "hard" body in action cinema have long been deployed to reinforce and disseminate an idealized mode of masculinity that emphasizes strength, toughness, and assertiveness (Jeffords 1994). These deployments have also long facilitated indirect discussion around the contentious issues of gender and sexuality via the medium of cinema (Lehman 2013, 1–2). Functioning as such, the Wall Street Three operate as a marked articulation of the contemporary debates around toxic masculinity (Veissière 2018), speaking to issues such as patriarchal hegemony (Messerschmidt 2018), white male privilege (McIntosh 2018), and heteronormativity (Utamsingh et al. 2016) which, somewhat ironically, provides the injustice to which Arthur's murderous violence first emerges.

The young woman looks to Arthur for help, but Arthur does not help her; instead, he starts to laugh. This attracts the attention of the Wall Street Three, as they think that Arthur is laughing at them. Taking his bag away from him, they mock his appearance as a clown and then start to beat him, constructing a spectacle of their hyper-masculine superiority. Arthur, unable to compete physically with his accosters, retaliates by shooting all three dead. Through this action, Arthur rebalances his internal conflict, fighting his cause rather than avoiding the confrontation as he did earlier with Hoyt.

This transformation is, however, temporary. Escaping from the scene of the murders, much like after his earlier confrontation with Holt, Arthur locates himself amidst the garbage piled streets. Fleeing home past the huddled homeless, the inadequacy of Arthur's masculinity is reinforced as he is surrounded by the symbolism of the unfortunate and dispossessed. This reaffirms Arthur as the antithesis of the symbols of privilege and entitlement with which he just interacted. It is only once Arthur is safe at home that he can again appropriate the behaviors of the hyper-masculine, where he connects his violent actions with sexual desirability and power, aligning himself with the familiar hyper-masculine tropes of action cinema (Brown 2016) by engaging in a fantasy about sleeping with Sophie.

The Wall Street Three notwithstanding, elite proper are most prominently represented by the Wayne Family, which forms an antithesis (Mudde 2017, 32) of the people and Arthur. This moral binary is first made explicit to the audience when Arthur and Penny watch a TV news report detailing Thomas Wayne's reaction to the subway killings. Wayne describes the murdered men, all of whom worked for Wayne Investments as "Good. Decent. Educated. And, although I didn't know them personally, like all Wayne employees, past and present, they're family" (Phillips 2019, 00:37:06). Here, the narrative again draws directly on the incongruity between the actuality of the Wall Street Three as experienced by the audience, and Wayne's interpretation of their character, situating his viewpoint as one that has been corrupted by his position, allowing him to privilege his own "special interests and [the] inauthentic morals of the elite over those of the people" (Mudde 2017, 30).

This notion of privileging the interests of the elite over the people is further exemplified when the discussion turns to the public reaction to the killings:

TV HOST: There appears to be a groundswell of anti-rich sentiment in the city. It's almost as if our less fortunate residents are taking the side of the killer.

WAYNE: Yes, that's a shame. It's one of the reasons why I'm considering running for Mayor. Gotham has lost its way.

TV HOST: What about the eyewitness reports of the suspect being a man in a clown mask?

WAYNE: Well it makes total sense to me. What kind of coward would do something that cold blooded? Someone who hides behind a mask. Someone who is envious of those more fortunate than themselves, yet they're too scared to show their own face. And until those kinds of people change for the better, those of us who made something of our lives will always look at those who haven't as nothing but clowns. (Phillips 2019, 00:37:17–00:37:37)

In responding this way, Wayne clearly articulates a Manichean distinction between the people and the elite assuming "that the people should be conceived as a dangerous mob while depicting the elite as a reduced group of actors who, due to their intellectual and moral superiority, should be in charge of the government" (Hawkins and Kaltwasser 2017, 515). As such, Wayne recodifies the moral binary between the people and elite of Gotham City to a "struggle between the forces of good and the forces of a knowing, diabolical evil" (Hawkins and Kaltwasser 2017, 515), with both sides holding themselves as the former.

This binary opposition is made personal to Arthur through his direct interactions with the Wayne family. After reading one of his mother's letters to Thomas Wayne, Arthur discovers that Penny believes Thomas Wayne to be his father. Arthur is enraged by this but, again, Penny uses this knowledge to situate Arthur's masculinity in opposition to that of Wayne. She tells Arthur that she could not be with Wayne because of how such a relationship would appear; as such, she positions herself as inferior to Wayne. In telling Arthur that she can only imagine what the people would say about him, Penny insinuates that Arthur's inferiority to Wayne is more pronounced than her own, and that this inferiority is so marked that it may bring about shame for Wayne if the information became public knowledge.

Reacting to this discovery, Arthur journeys to the Wayne estate. Travelling by train, as the skyline of Gotham City recedes amidst the emerging greenery of the countryside, Arthur sits in a clean carriage among the "haves," who are all male, white, neatly dressed, and engrossed in reading their broadsheet newspapers, which position Thomas Wayne's campaign as progressive. Arriving at the estate, Arthur entertains Bruce Wayne through the bars of wrought iron gate with magic tricks and flowers before reaching through to mold Bruce's face into a smile, until Alfred arrives and separates Bruce from Arthur, asking Arthur to identify himself. Here, Arthur once more self-identifies as pure, telling Alfred that he is a good person, however, upon learning that Arthur is Penny's son, Alfred becomes hostile toward Arthur, telling him that his mother was delusional and a sick woman, before laughing at the notion that Thomas Wayne might be Arthur's father.

The Alfred Pennyworth of *JOKER* is presented, therefore, in contrast to his other cinematic incarnations. Here Alfred appropriates the behaviors and appearance of the hyper-masculine. Alfred is large and well built. He steps in close to Arthur in order to threaten him. He is not above mocking those whom he perceives as his lesser, and it is this mocking that causes Arthur to reach through the gates and grab Alfred by the throat, choking him before running off. Here, the incongruity of the greenery and the city, as well as Arthur and the other commuters on the train, and the physical partition imposed by the high walls and gate, function to visually manifest for the audience Arthur's "(1) separation from the elite and (2) connection to the people" (Mudde and Kaltwasser 2017, 68).

Arthur eventually confronts Thomas Wayne in the Wayne Hall theatre. Here the binary opposition of the people and the elite is perhaps most marked. Making his way through a raucous and violent clown protest, Arthur sneaks into Wayne Hall dressed as an usher. Outside, the streets are a raging torrent of "have-nots," strewn with litter, angry men, and angry police officers. Inside, there is calm, as "haves" sit in orderly rows, dressed identically in their finest evening wear, amidst the sumptuous décor of the theatre. This constructs the notion of "one homogenous corrupt group that works against the 'general will' of the people" (Mudde and Kaltwasser 2017, 12) and furthermore, situates that group as a "cultural elite" (Mudde and Kaltwasser 2017, 26), who have the time and resources to enjoy an evening at the theatre while the city descends into chaos around them.

Pausing for a moment to watch Charlie Chaplin perform on the screen, Arthur shares in a laugh with the great and good of Gotham City, reminding the audience that by "determining the main opposition to be between the pure people and the corrupt elite, populism presupposes that the elite comes from the same group as the people, but have willingly chosen to betray them" (Mudde 2017, 30). This betrayal is then laid bare, when Arthur comes face to face with his suspected father in the bathroom. Wayne first assumes that Arthur wants an autograph, then once Arthur explains who he is, Wayne denies that he is Arthur's father and tells Arthur that his mother had to be arrested and committed due to her delusions. When Wayne asks Arthur if he wants money, Arthur reacts angrily, telling him he wants some decency, before asking "What is it with you people?" (Phillips 2019, 01:03:48). This reinforces Arthur's construction of the people and the elite as a potentially warped interpretation of reality (Mudde and Kaltwasser 2017, 68), where either Arthur has bought into the delusions of his mother, or Wayne is attempting to gaslight Arthur, manipulating him into insanity (Abramson 2014). Moreover, when Wayne ends the exchange by punching Arthur in the face and threatening to kill him should he ever come near his son again, it is Wayne who appropriates the form of the supergendered ideal, typifying the conventional gender norms associated with action cinema (Rosenberg 2013).

This process of betrayal is then amplified in *JOKER*, becoming a central theme of the narrative that is located specifically on Arthur. Arthur is betrayed when he returns to see his social worker and attempts to discuss his feelings with her. Rather than addressing what Arthur is telling her, his social worker instead informs him that there is no more funding for his programme. The city has shut them down. Arthur tells her that for most of his life, he has doubted his own existence and it is only now that he is being noticed. His social worker simply replies that they don't care about him or her, and doesn't reply when Arthur asks her where he will get his medications now.

The betrayal of Arthur is extended to his mother when Arthur travels to Arkham State Hospital to investigate Wayne's claims that his mother is mentally ill. There, a clerk reads from Penny's file, telling Arthur that Penny was clinically diagnosed as suffering from delusional psychosis and narcissistic personality disorder, and found guilty of endangering the welfare of her own child. When the clerk refuses to give Arthur the file, Arthur steals the file and reads that Penny was frequently and involuntarily admitted to Arkham, lobotomized and that he had been abandoned by his natural parents and adopted by Penny. Arthur slips into delusion, imagining himself at Penny's interrogation, listening as Penny asserts that Thomas Wayne had the papers made up to hide the truth, and Dr. Stoner explains that she let her then boyfriend harm her and Arthur, leading to Arthur suffering severe trauma to his head. This functions as an inverse for the devoted care that Arthur has provided to his mother, constructing a moral binary where Arthur's actions and sacrifices have been pure, motivated by a selfless duty of care toward his mother, while his mother has exploited him since early childhood, beholden to men laden with hyper-masculine tendencies.

This revelation causes Arthur's delusions to collapse. Returning home, Arthur visits Sophie for real, sneaking into her apartment and sitting on her couch. When Sophie finds him there, reality intrudes on Arthur's imagined relationship, as she reacts with fear and revulsion. Here Arthur realizes that he is not an incarnation of the traditional masculine ideals of strength, power, and heterosexual desirability (Brown 2016, 134). This again forms a binary of betrayal from Arthur's perspective, where his loving relationship is not reciprocated by Sophie, who, fearing for her child, asks him to leave. As such, the intrusion of Arthur into Sophie's home situates Arthur as a potential analogue for his own abuser, and when Sophie suggests that she could call Arthur's mother for help, Arthur once more simulates shooting himself in the head, leaving the fate of Sophie and her daughter unclear, while heading back to the hospital to kill his mother rather than seek her help.

The final betrayal of the elite perpetrated on Arthur is that of Murray Franklin. After footage of Arthur performing at Pogo's is screened on Live with Murray Franklin for comic effect, Arthur is invited to come onto the show as a guest. As Arthur rehearses for this appearance, it is insinuated that he plans to kill himself live on air, hoping that his "death makes more cents than my life" (Phillips 2019, 01:36:14). Events transpire somewhat differently during his appearance, however. After Franklin makes fun of Arthur, causing the studio audience to laugh at him, and Dr. Sally chastises him for making an inappropriate joke, Arthur reveals that he killed the Wall Street Three. Franklin, Dr. Sally and the audience react to this information with disgust, and it is here then, in response to that repulsion, that Arthur presents himself as a reluctant and nonpolitical vox populi, expressing the general will of the people (Mudde 2017, 33) to Franklin and his television audience:

Oh, why is everybody so upset about these guys? If it was me dying on the sidewalk, you'd walk right over me! I pass you every day and you don't notice me. But these guys, what, because Thomas Wayne went and cried about them on TV? . . . Have you seen what it's like out there, Murray? Do you ever actually leave the studio? Everybody just yells and screams at each other. Nobody is civil anymore. Nobody thinks what it's like to be the other guy. You think men like Thomas Wayne ever think what it's like to be someone like me? To be somebody but themselves? They don't. They think that we'll just sit there and take it, like good little boys! That we won't werewolf and go wild! (Phillips 2019, 01:39:00–01:39:49)

In this way, Arthur publicly foregrounds a set of ideas that symbolize a widespread antagonism between the downtrodden people like him, and the exploitative elite like Thomas Wayne. This emphasizes the "primacy of popular sovereignty, whereby the virtuous general will is placed in opposition to the moral corruption of elite actors" (Gidron and Bonikowski 2013, 6). Furthermore, his discourse conceptualizes that vox populi and its associated general will as masculine, describing the people holistically as "good little boys" while anchoring the Manichean binary around two male identities—his, and Thomas Wayne's—thereby constructing a masculine context (Mudde and Kaltwasser 2015) for the populist clown protests of Gotham City.

Ultimately, Franklin reinforces Arthur's role as the vox populi by affirming the "anti-populist rhetoric of the establishment" (Mudde and Kaltwasser 2017, 68), which solidifies Arthur as the inadvertent champion disillusioned males in Gotham City, as he enacts that perceived general will of the people by executing Franklin live on his television show:

FRANKLIN: You finished? I mean it's so much self-pity, Arthur. You sound like you're making excuses for killing those young men. Not everybody, and I'll tell you this, not everyone is awful.

JOKER: You're awful, Murray.

FRANKLIN: Me? I'm awful? Oh yeah, how am I awful?

JOKER: Playing my video. Inviting me on this show. You just wanted to make fun of me. You're just like the rest of them.

Franklin: You don't know the first thing about me, pal. Look what happened, because of what you did. What it led to. There are riots out there. Two policemen are in critical condition [*Joker laughs*]—and you're laughing. You're laughing. Someone was killed today, because of what you did.

JOKER: I know. How about another joke, Murray?

Franklin: No, I think we've had enough of your jokes-

JOKER: –What do you get

FRANKLIN: –I don't think so.

JOKER: when you cross a mentally-ill loner with a society that abandons him and treats him like trash? . . . You get what you fucking deserve! [*Joker shoots the side of Murray's head off*]. (Phillips 2019, 01:39:00–01:40:51)

In *JOKER*, therefore, Arthur is presented as the antithesis of the super-gendered superhero ideal (Behm-Morawitz and Pennell 2013; Pennell and Behm-Morawitz 2015). He is the othered masculinity that will take on the hyper-masculine elite. He is the expression of the subaltern masculine position. He is the "have not" who will disrupt the "haves." He is the othered strongman who has "to be more creative" (Mudde and Kaltwasser 2017, 68) in his articulation, and does so by weaponizing his otherness and proclivity to violence.

GENERAL WILL, THIN IDEOLOGY, AND THE ACCIDENTAL DEMAGOGUE

Arthur's self-conceptualization as the vox populi of Gotham City notwithstanding, the presentation of the general will of the people in *JOKER* is detached from Arthur. The people take Arthur as their champion, rather than Arthur recruiting them to his cause. Indeed, it is the people who, by appropriating Arthur's image, empower Arthur in his transformation into the titular Joker. This demonstrates that "charismatic leadership is about a specific bond between leader and followers, which is defined at least as much by the expectations and perceptions of the followers as by the individual characteristics of the leader" (Mudde and Kaltwasser 2017, 66). In *JOKER*, as is always the case with Arthur, this bond is one of detachment. Arthur is apart from the populist movement he "leads." As such, the general will expressed in the narrative aesthetics of *JOKER* "refers to the capacity of the people to join together into a community" (Mudde and Kaltwasser 2017, 16) and struggle toward a "popular sovereignty" (Gidron and Bonikowski 2013, 6) independently from Arthur.

In the early stages of the narrative, that expression appears to haunt Gotham City through the mass media, manifesting in a dumbed-down modality (Crick 2005) via newspaper headlines and TV sound bites. After Arthur has committed the subway murders and is on his imaginary date with Sophie, we see a newsstand with the headlines covering killer clowns and vigilantes. After this, Arthur makes contact with a passenger in a taxi wearing a clown mask, signifying the start of his influence on the disenfranchised. Later, after Arthur's mother has been taken to hospital, Arthur lies on his bed in apparent depression while on the floor beside him, the headline of a discarded newspaper discuses a new movement focused on killing the rich.

Arthur perks up as a TV news bulletin details how this looming spectre of potential civil unrest has now boiled over into organized demonstrations, where many of the protestors have come dressed as clowns. Here again, the emergent movement is unintentionally reinforced by Wayne's "rhetoric of the establishment" (Mudde and Kaltwasser 2017, 68), as it is Wayne's derision of the struggling people as "clowns" that has inspired them to appropriate Arthur's image as the emblem of their movement, demonstrating that "depending on the political culture of the country in which the populist leader mobilizes, her or his 'extraordinary' nature lies on very specific and different features" (Mudde and Kaltwasser 2017, 62).

In this way, Arthur can be perceived as appealing to the people "on the basis of a 'cult of the leader,' which portrays him as a masculine and potentially violent figure" (Mudde and Kaltwasser 2017, 63). Arthur, however, does not rule. He has no control over the actions of his cult and is not involved in the organization of their movement. He is a cult leader detached. This notion of disconnection is made evident in the latter stages of the narrative, where Arthur, now transformed into the Joker, mingles anonymously with the protestors on the train as he makes his way to the Live with Murray Franklin show, then laughs at their rioting from the window of a police car as he is led away from the scene of Franklin's murder. Only for a brief moment are the people and Arthur seen as one, when the police car containing Arthur is rammed by a van, and three clown protestors pull Arthur from the wreckage and leave him on the hood. As Arthur starts to come round, his "followers" urge him to get up, giving him the adulation he has been seeking as he rises. In return, Arthur dances for his people, painting a smile on his face with his own blood (see figure 10.1). After that, Arthur is once more separated from his movement, stripped of his Joker attire, and incarcerated, like his mother before him, in Arkham State Hospital.

Given that the narrative of *JOKER* does not reveal a clear outcome for the clown protests or Arthur, other than the killing of Thomas and Martha Wayne, which of course functions as the origin story for Batman, the central thrust of populism mobilized in *JOKER* could, therefore, be seen as a "thin-centered ideology based on a Manichean, anti-elitist logic and a desire to reclaim political institutions on behalf of 'the people'" (Gidron and

Figure 10.1   Arthur/JOKER Paints a Smile on His Face. *Source*: Screenshot from *JOKER*, directed by Todd Phillips, 2019. United States: Warner Bros. Pictures.

Bonikowski 2013, 23) which "lacks the capacity to put forward a wide-ranging and coherent programme for the solution to crucial political questions" (Stanley 2008, 95) asked within the narrative. Indeed, this lack of solutions to fundamental problems is a theme often present in the wider DC Universe. Batman, in most of his cinematic incarnations, explores the difficulties of masculinity, inhabiting a mode of manhood that is divided and troubled. Conceptualized as such, Batman enacts hyper-masculine violence against an array of villains in an effort to protect the people, while never resolving the crime-ridden social order of Gotham City or restoring the disintegration of his family that brought about his hyper-masculinity in the first place (Jeffords 1994, 95–100). Ultimately, as the last images provided to the audience of the Gotham City of *JOKER* are those of the city burning, and the last images provided of Arthur are those of incarceration, violence and chaos, the "morphological structure" (Stanley 2008, 99) appropriated by the people from Arthur to form the expression of their populist movement can be seen as defective, just like Arthur himself. As such, where the Gotham City of the wider DC Universe looks for its savior in Batman, the Gotham City of *JOKER* finds instead only Arthur Fleck.

This failure of the popular movement to achieve ideological coherence (Aslanidis 2016, 89), realized for the audience by the failure of the narrative to provide a comprehensive conclusion, could, therefore, also be caused by Arthur's lack of a true ideological drive. When Arthur as the Joker first meets Franklin in the green room prior to his appearance on his show, Franklin asks Arthur if his painted face means he is a part of the protests. In response, Arthur tells him that he does not believe in the protests; he paints his face for his act. Later, on the show, Franklin asks Arthur to confirm that his look is not political, which Arthur does, telling Franklin that he just wants to be funny. Once Arthur has declared that he killed the Wall Street Three, Franklin asks him if he started this movement to gain notoriety, to which Arthur replies, "Come on, Murray. Do I look like the kind of clown that could start a movement? I killed those guys because they were awful" (Phillips 2019, 01:38:36).

In this light, Arthur's actions can be seen to have been misinterpreted by the people who, having framed an aspect of their social life that is problematic and developed an "urgency to take corrective action" (Aslanidis 2016, 99), organized their movement around Arthur's empty discourse that "contains ideational elements that have been mistaken for constituting ideology" (99).

For Arthur, the movement around him is enjoyable but incidental to him. What is important to Arthur is pursuing his own goals. He wants to make the people laugh. He wants to make people see the world the way he does, and he wants to do so using violence and criminality. Arthur is, thus, not a populist leader in the modern conception. Arthur is not constrained "by the success of liberal aspects of modernity, specifically the principle of the rule of law and the institutions shaped by it in modern constitutionalism" (Patapan 2019, 754). Arthur is more akin to the traditional demagogue. Arthur seeks "personal, rather than common advantage via unscrupulous appeals to the desires and passions of the many" (Patapan 2019, 754).

As such, in *JOKER*, the confused aesthetics of populism can be seen to correlate with the contested nature of populism as a concept (Mudde 2017, 27), constructing a narrative where the hopes and dreams of the people appear to be "beyond reach, slipping into delusions" (Phillips and Silver 2018).

CONCLUSION

This chapter set out to explore the complex interplay between the aesthetics of masculinity and populism in Todd Phillips's *JOKER* (2019). In doing so, it considered how the societal conditions of Gotham City are presented in such a way as to align with the key concepts of Mudde's ideational approach to populism (2004, 2017). Specifically, the chapter demonstrated how the fundamental opposition between the people and the elite of Gotham City is organized around the notion of perceived social inequality, and how that inequality is expressed via the general will of the people, as represented by the clown protests that grow and spread throughout the narrative, as well as via the self-assumed vox populi of Arthur Fleck as the Joker. Moreover, this suggests that the general will of the people—and its articulation by that vox populi—exists within a masculine context, constructing an overtly masculine phenomenon, realized by, and anchored around, a Manichean binary of masculinity.

Central to this articulation of populism is the othering of masculinity, where the people and Arthur are presented as an authentic inverse of the inauthentic hyper-masculine elite and supergendered Wayne family. Furthermore, the actions of the inadvertent followers of Arthur as the Joker function as a thin-centered ideology which, when formed loosely around the notion of the disenfranchised male rising up in anger against perceived social injustice, provided little in the way of meaningful solutions, and indeed resulted in no meaningful social resolution being demonstrated in the narrative. Finally, rather than being an ideologically driven populist leader, Arthur himself draws upon criminality to become a modern-day demagogue who, in the end, used the discursive form of populism to achieve his own self-serving needs rather than those of the people. Together, and ultimately, these analyses demonstrate how Phillips encourages the viewer to understand and perhaps even empathize with Arthur's metamorphosis into the Joker. It does this by constructing an othered lens of social inequality, disillusionment and delusion.

BIBLIOGRAPHY

Abramson, Kate. 2014. "Turning Up the Lights on Gaslighting." *Philosophical Perspectives* 28: 1–30. https://doi.org/10.2307/26614542.

Aslanidis, Paris. 2016. "Is Populism an Ideology? A Refutation and a New Perspective." *Political Studies* 64 (1, Suppl April): 88–104. https://doi.org/10.1111/1467-9248.12224.

Behm-Morawitz, Elizabeth, and Hillary Pennell. 2013. "The Effects of Superhero Sagas on Our Gendered Selves." In *Our Superheroes, Ourselves*, edited by Robin S. Rosenberg, 73–98. Oxford: New York NY: Oxford University Press.

Bernasconi, Robert. 2012. "Othering." In *Critical Communities and Aesthetic Practices: Dialogues with Tony O'Connor on Society, Art, and Friendship*, edited by Francis Halsall, Julia Jansen and Sinead Murphy, 151–157. Dordrecht: Springer Netherlands.

Brown, Jeffrey A. 2016. "The Superhero Film Parody and Hegemonic Masculinity." *Quarterly Review of Film and Video* 33 (2): 131–150. https://doi.org/10.1080/10509208.2015.1094361.

Crick, Bernard. 2005. "Populism, Politics and Democracy." *Democratization* 12 (5): 625–632. https://doi.org/10.1080/13510340500321985.

Diamond, Aidan, and Lauranne Poharec. 2017. "Introduction: Freaked and Othered Bodies in Comics." *Journal of Graphic Novels and Comics* 8 (5): 402–416. https://10.1080/21504857.2017.1355833.

Gidron, Noam, and Bart Bonikowski. 2013. *Varieties of Populism: Literature Review and Research Agenda*. Working Paper Series, Weatherhead Center for International Affairs, Harvard University, no. 13–0004. http://dx.doi.org/10.2139/ssrn.2459387.

Hawkins, Kirk A., and Cristóbal Rovira Kaltwasser. 2017. "The Ideational Approach to Populism." *Latin American Research Review* 52 (4): 513–528. http://doi.org/10.25222/larr.85.

Hughes, Mark. 2019. "How 'Joker' Is First R-Rated Film Topping Huge $1 Billion Box Office." *Forbes*, November 4, 2019. https://www.forbes.com/sites/markhughes/2019/11/04/how-joker-is-first-r-rated-film-topping-huge-1-billion-box-office/#456a94a731bb.

Jeffords, Susan. 1994. *Hard Bodies: Hollywood Masculinity in the Reagan Era*. New Brunswick NJ: Rutgers University Press.

Lehman, Peter. 2013. *Masculinity: Bodies, Movies, Culture*. New York, NY: Routledge.

McIntosh, Peggy. 2018. "White Privilege and Male Privilege." In *Privilege: A Reader*, edited by Michael S. Kimmel, 28–40. New York NY: Routledge.

Messerschmidt, James W. 2018. *Hegemonic Masculinity: Formulation, Reformulation, and Amplification*. London: Rowman & Littlefield.

Mudde, Cas. 2004. "The Populist Zeitgeist" *Government and Opposition* 39 (4): 542–563. https://doi.org/10.1111/j.1477-7053.2004.00135.x.

Mudde, Cas. 2017. "Populism: An Ideational Approach." In *The Oxford Handbook of Populism*, edited by Cristóbal Rovira Kaltwasser, Paul Taggart, Paulina Ochoa Espejo, and Pierre Ostiguy, 27–47. Oxford: Oxford University Press.

Mudde, Cas, and Cristóbal Rovira Kaltwasser. 2015. "Vox Populi or Vox Masculini? Populism and Gender in Northern Europe and South America." *Patterns of Prejudice* 49 (1–2): 16–36. https://doi.org/10.1080/0031322X.2015.1014197.

Mudde, Cas, and Cristóbal Rovira Kaltwasser. 2017. *Populism: A Very Short Introduction.* Oxford: Oxford University Press.

Patapan, Haig. 2019. "On Populists and Demagogues." *Canadian Journal of Political Science* 52 (4): 743–759. https://doi.org/10.1017/S0008423918001099.

Pennell, Hillary, and Elizabeth Behm-Morawitz. 2015. "The Empowering (Super) Heroine? The Effects of Sexualized Female Characters in Superhero Films on Women." *Sex Roles* 72 (5): 211–220. https://doi.org/10.1007/s11199-015-0455-3.

Phillips, Todd, dir. 2019. *"JOKER".* United States: Warner Bros. Pictures.

Phillips, Todd, and Scot Silver, dir. 2018. *"JOKER" An Origin.* Warner Bros. Pictures.

Rosenberg, Robin S. 2013. *Our Superheroes, Ourselves.* Oxford: Oxford University Press.

Stam, Robert, Robert Burgoyne, and Sandy Flitterman-Lewis. 2002. *New Vocabularies in Film Semiotics: Structuralism, Post-Structuralism, and Beyond.* London: Routledge.

Stanley, Ben. 2008. "The Thin Ideology of Populism." *Journal of Political Ideologies* 13 (1): 95–110. https://doi.org/10.1080/13569310701822289.

Sune, Jensen. 2011. "Othering, Identity Formation and Agency." *Qualitative Studies* 2 (2): 63–78. https://doi.org/10.7146/qs.v2i2.5510.

Tasker, Yvonne. 1993a. "Dumb Movies for Dumb People: Masculinity, the Body and the Voice Incontemporary Action Cinema." In *Screening the Male: Exploring Masculinities in Hollywood Cinema*, edited by Steven Cohan, and Ina Rae Hark, 230–244. London & New York NY: Routledge.

Tasker, Yvonne. 1993b. *Spectacular Bodies: Gender, Genre and the Action Cinema.* London and New York, NY: Routledge.

Tasker, Yvonne. 2019. "X-Men/Action Men: Performing Masculinities in Superhero and Science Fiction Cinema." In *A Companion to the Action Film*, edited by James Kendrick, 381–397. Hoboken, NJ: John Wiley & Sons, Inc.

Utamsingh, Pooja Dushyant, Laura Smart Richman, Julie L Martin, Micah R Lattanner, and Jeremy Ross Chaikind. 2016. "Heteronormativity and Practitioner–Patient Interaction." *Health Communication* 31 (5): 566–574. https://doi.org/10.1080/10410236.2014.979975.

Veissière, Louis Samuel Paul. 2018. "'Toxic Masculinity' in the Age of #MeToo: Ritual, Morality and Gender Archetypes Across Cultures." *Society and Business Review* 13 (3): 274–286. https://doi.org/10.1108/SBR-07-2018-0070.

Chapter 11

Crisis of Masculinity in Disney Era *Star Wars* Sequel Trilogy

Janne Salminen

In recent years, the *Star Wars* film franchise has reemerged as a heatedly contested piece of popular culture. A loose assemblage of angry viewers, who have some overlapping values with the Alt-right, claim that the franchise has betrayed its past and is now pushing a socially liberal agenda, at the expense of white male representations. This type of attention is not unique for a contemporary film series. Other well-known franchises, like *Mad Max* and the Marvel films, have been targeted by Men's Rights Activists (MRAs) on a regular basis since the mid-2010s, especially if they view these franchises as catering to a more diverse audience (Johnson 2018, 91–92). Even though white male characters were at the center of *Star Wars* films before 2015, they were not exclusively about them and their heroics. Fans have debated, reinterpreted, and negotiated the franchise's gendered aspects since the first film premiered in 1977 (Bruin–Molé 2018). Still, it seems that during the last decade, these debates have garnered mainstream attention. The resurgence of interest toward the franchise began when news of Disney purchasing Lucasfilm became public in October of 2012, which also sparked fan concerns over the possible "Disneyfication" of the franchise (Proctor 2013, 198–204). Two prominent themes that emerged from the Disney produced *Star Wars* sequel trilogy are female heroism (and by extension, the fluidity of gender categories) and failure of masculinity. These themes were seen by the Alt-right and the MRAs as a threat to white masculinity, which is already in their perception in a state of crisis (Koulouris 2018). Gender populism, which is sometimes framed as "sex realism," is strongly present in the MRAs' responses. Sex realism is an anti-feminist tactic utilized when gender boundaries are challenged or traditional forms of masculinity are problematized (Shaw 2018).

Even though Disney has produced five *Star Wars* films so far, this chapter's focus will be on the sequel trilogy: its central character arcs and what kind of gender narratives they construe. Perception of these narratives is likely shaped by the fact the person most responsible for the production of these films is a woman, producer Kathleen Kennedy (Ellison 2016). The sequel trilogy comprises of *Force Awakens* (Abrams 2015), *The Last Jedi* (Johnson 2017), and *The Rise of the Skywalker* (Abrams 2019). For clarity, I divide the *Star Wars* film franchise into three different trilogies; the original trilogy (1977–1983), the prequel trilogy (1999–2005), and the sequel trilogy (2015–2019).[1]

The sequel trilogy starts out by conveying a sense that white male-centric heroism has run its course, and it is time for other types of heroes to step up to the plate. Even if the films do not make gendered systems of oppression explicit, they are a clear departure from what critics and academics have perceived action-adventure films to be in the past. While Hollywood films have historically featured narratives that resist hegemonies, they have tended to be mostly ideologically vague and multidimensional to avoid alienating audiences (Nelson 2013, 1038–1039). The two major themes present particularly in the first two parts of the trilogy are the failure of traditional masculinity (or the crisis of masculinity) and the emergence of significant female heroism, converging in the potential of rejecting a rigid hierarchical gender binary. However, the last episode of the trilogy does not follow through with those elements that were interpreted as feminist and ends on a middle ground that tries to appeal to everyone by sanding out the more provocative elements.

Star Wars films are at the center of a curious phenomenon emerging in the field of blockbusters. Several films consistently feature gender representations that are renegotiable rather than unchangeable. Gender becomes an unstable category if seen as fluid, as in this chapter, allowing for a multiplicity of identities, resistant to rigid binary coding of gender positioning (Fontanella et al. 2013, 2554–2555). In the context of cinematic representations, gender fluidity would then entail that characters are not defined purely based on gender stereotyping but rather move between masculine and feminine identities. As a result, transgressions between masculinity and femininity read as disruptions to the gender binary (Butler 2004, 42–43), which is at the core of the angst toward female heroes becoming more prevalent (White and Baldwin 2018). From 2015 onward, *Star Wars* films have become rife with female heroes, a turn that for some has become symbolic of a larger shift in which straight white men are no longer at the center of culture.

In 1977, *A New Hope* was a phenomenally successful action-adventure movie that blended science fiction and fantasy with archetypical characters, plus a hint of counter-culture attitude. The film told the story of young Luke Skywalker (Mark Hamill), who leaves his home planet to join a rebellion against an evil empire. This story of a young man finding his destiny has become, for some, a defining element of the franchise. *A New Hope* and the rest of the original trilogy follow a "hero's journey" (Campbell 1949, 12). In that story arc, a hero travels from humdrum surroundings to a world of adventure and fabulous forces. After winning a decisive victory, they return from their travels with newfound skills and abilities. In Luke's case, these abilities revolve mostly around the magical energy called "the force," an element that introduced mysticism to the series' science fiction setting. With each sequel, the *Star Wars* galaxy grew larger, the mythology denser, and audiences' expectations more unreasonable. Despite what Director George Lucas later claimed, he never had a detailed plan laying out a saga with nine parts (Kaminski 2008, 212–213). Since George Lucas is not producing the *Star Wars* films of the 2010s, they are open to dismissals of "not being canon," including criticism for progressive gender representations. While many viewers welcomed the updated gender representations and increased diversity, some saw it as irreverent treatment of the franchise's legacy. The criticism of the sequel trilogy's gender representations seems to stem, or at least resonate with right-wing populism and its assumed crisis of masculinity that is caused by feminism and other progressive forces.

NOSTALGIA AND PERCEPTION OF *STAR WARS* AS A CONSERVATIVE FILM SERIES

Frederic Jameson (1998, 8–9) argues that the first *Star Wars* film, *A New Hope*, evoked a sense of nostalgia without referencing or reimagining any particular historical era. Jameson notes that the film replicates aesthetic elements from the Saturday afternoon serials from the 1930–1950s, which trigger nostalgic emotions. Since it has been over forty years since the release of *A New Hope*, the franchise itself and its aesthetics have become a source of nostalgia. It is also likely that this sense of nostalgia has motivated some parts of the fandom and audiences to react aggressively toward the series' new, more inclusive nature, and even critical elements toward masculine strategies. The Disney films look different from the previous films when it comes to the central characters. When *A New Hope* arrived in 1977, an emerging wave of nostalgia for the 1950s brought along the regressive gender attitudes that dominated the cultural landscape of the 1980s (Dwyer 2015, 54). Even if the film itself was not fully informed by of those attitudes, the *Star Wars* brand might evoke nostalgic feelings toward the retrograde gender ideals of the late 1970s and early 1980s (when Lucasfilm released the original trilogy), rather than the content of the films themselves.

The original trilogy featured a strong female character, Princess Leia Organa (Carrie Fisher). She is introduced as a damsel in distress and rescuing her from captivity is the main impetus for Luke to begin his adventure. Leia turns out to be at least as capable as the male heroes and is consistently unimpressed by the heroics of both Luke and Han Solo (Harrison Ford). Han is a smuggler who joins Luke's quest, and later the Rebellion, initially only for financial reasons. Leia's agency diminished as the series progressed. By the third film, *Return of the Jedi* (1983), she seemed to have no say in her own romantic life. The love triangle developed between her, Luke, and Han evaporated when Luke reveals to her that he is her brother. Leia is more informed by the feminist movement than most female characters of the mainstream cinema of the 1970s, but academic writings see her narrative trajectory as disappointing or disempowering (Merlock and Merlock Jackson 2012, 80–84).

In the prequel trilogy, Padme Amidala (Natalie Portman) had a similar trajectory as Leia: initially active and independent, but eventually limited by the films' narrative choices. Padme is a young queen of a planet, who becomes a significant player in intergalactic politics, but later on, her primary function is to be the love interest and wife of Anakin Skywalker (Hayden Christensen), a Jedi knight who eventually becomes the evil Darth Vader, the Emperor Palpatine's (Ian McDiarmid) right-hand man. Both Leia and Padme subvert gender binary expectations but are nevertheless sexualized, unlike the male characters (Cocca 2016, 87–88). Mara Wood (2016, 64–66) remarks that while the first two trilogies of *Star Wars* films focused on narratives of male exceptionalism, ancillary texts like tie-in novels, comic books, and video games featured more fleshed-out female characters with meaningful narrative arcs. Scarcity of female characters and lack of diversity have fueled criticism from both film critics and academics.

Save for the voice work of Black actor James Earl Jones *A New Hope* featured an all-white cast. Some film critics even called the film racist during its initial theatrical run, a comment that reportedly upset Lucas (Jones 2016, 249–250). Lucas saw the Galactic Empire as a twisted futuristic version of the United States and was veiling his liberal leanings under science fiction metaphors (Jones 2016, 180). As a response to the accusations of racism, Lucas cast Black actor Billy Dee Williams as Lando Calrissian in *The Empire Strikes Back* (1980). A small but deliberate step toward a more diverse cast.

A considerable amount of contemporary scholarly criticism argues that *Star Wars* is one of the key conservative film series of the 1980s (Britton 1986; Jewett and Lawrence 1988; Wood 1985). Despite Lucas's reactions to contemporary criticisms, Douglas Kellner (2010, 174) sees the original trilogy propping up the era's conservative hegemony and subduing the countercultural elements it contained to suit the ethos of the 1980s. Even though there is little evidence to support that audiences agreed with that assessment

(Lyden 2018), the perception of *Star Wars* as a conservative franchise is strong. Yvonne Tasker (1993, 59–61) argues that while critics and scholars were eager to label *Star Wars* films and similar films as "Reaganite entertainment," it is possible that the basis for this approach is the presumption that meanings of popular cinema are obvious and contradictory meanings are left unexamined. The difficulty of labeling the original *Star Wars* films as either conservative or liberal suggests that perhaps they are rather vague in their ideological messaging.

BOYCOTTS AND OUTRAGES

Even before Disney released their first *Star Wars* film, *The Force Awakens* (2015), it was generating malaise among some potential viewers. A Men's Rights Activist blog, *Return of Kings*, demanded their readers to boycott *The Force Awakens*. They saw the film promoting a social justice agenda and later claimed having made a 4.2-million-dollar dent in the film's box office (Denham 2013). The film made over two billion dollars worldwide, so the boycott was hardly successful (Box Office Mojo 2015).

   Rogue One: A Star Wars Story (Edwards 2016), a self-contained spinoff film released around the same time, also faced a boycott. This time from the Alt-right movement (Ellis 2016). George Hawley (2017, 16) describes the Alt-right as a racist political movement that supports white-supremacy, promoting what they call "sex realism." They see that men face more discrimination than women and that societal roles are determined by biological differences (Hawley 2017, 17). Even though there is significant overlap between MRAs and the Alt-right (Johnson 2018, 85), the boycott was motivated by Alt-right perceptions of *Star Wars* being now anti-Trump than by specific representation issues. *Rogue One* has a female protagonist, Jyn Erso (Felicity Jones), who is fighting alongside men of color against an empire dominated by selfish, power-hungry white men. The type of gender hierarchy that Donald Trump has promoted valorizes aggressive masculine behavior, especially when performed by white cis men (Carian and Sobotka 2018). Playing to the perception that contemporary masculinity is in a state of crisis, Trump had implicitly promised to restore those gender and race-based privileges that white men enjoyed before deindustrialization and increased social mobility of marginalized groups (Ashwin and Utrata 2020). *Star Wars* was a part of a movement to resist the project of restoring patriarchal masculinity that Trump and others like him were supporting at least in the mind of those boycotting it. In November 2016, only a few days before the presidential election, the official *Star Wars* account tweeted a picture of Jyn, with the question "are you with her?" Since Hillary Clinton's unofficial campaign slogan was "I'm with her," the tweet and its implications caused outrage among the Alt-right (Ellis 2016). *Rogue One* earned a little over one billion dollars globally (Box Office Mojo 2016), leaving the boycott's impact minimal. Nevertheless, this controversy further underlined the undercurrent of sexism present in the negative discourse surrounding the Disney films.

The Last Jedi (2017) was not targeted by a boycott specifically but sparked perhaps more outrage among MRA-minded viewers than any of the previous films. A small, loud group managed to create a public perception of 50/50 division among audiences when, in reality, most audiences found the movie enjoyable.[2] Critics also viewed the film extremely favorably, 91 percent of them gave it a positive review (Rotten Tomatoes 2017), and it has a Metacritic score of 85/100, signaling "universal acclaim" (Metacritic 2017). The polarized reaction from some fans' reactions inspired Mark White (2019, 1–3) to survey *Star Wars* fans. The survey revealed correlations between those fans who viewed the Disney era films unfavorably and their conservative social attitudes. While White's findings are tied to the fan community specifically, they suggest that fans view the sequel trilogy as promoting progressive values, such as gender fluidity and ethnic diversity. Mortem Bay (2018, 8) makes a compelling argument that Russian bots and trolls saw an opportunity to spread discord in the United States by amplifying negative reactions that also utilized rhetoric associated with the Alt-right. This does not make *The Last Jedi* some kind of acid test for a viewer's ideological leanings, rather it illustrates the polarized discussion around the film.

A subset of *Star Wars* fans, presumably some of them engaged in the online discourse attacking *The Last Jedi*, called for a boycott against all future installments of the series as means of voicing their displeasure of the series' direction (Lowry 2018). The implication was that the new entries into the saga had failed to live up to certain fans' expectations, and their dislike of these films would force Disney to fire Kathleen Kennedy as the head of Lucasfilm (Lowry 2018). The fact that the president of Lucasfilm is a woman gives these fantasies of pushing her out misogynistic undertones, especially considering Kennedy's success as a producer of commercially and critically acclaimed films (Ellison 2016).

Out of the three films, *The Last Jedi* received the strongest reactions against it and its assumed feminist messaging. An example of the bitter reaction toward it was the release of a fan edit of the film. This edit had all of the female characters removed, resulting in a nonsensical 46-minute version of the originally 152-minute movie. As with most things on the internet, it is difficult to discern if the creator was ironic or sincere, but they described their version of the film as "basically *The Last Jedi* minus Girlz Powah and other silly stuff" (Tsjeng 2018). Also, 13,000 "fans" signed an online petition to have the film removed from the *Star Wars* canon (Sharf 2017). Presumably, the same section of fans launched a remake campaign, demanding a reshoot of the entire movie, but this time following their demands and expectations (Heritage 2018).

When 2019 saw the release of *The Rise of the Skywalker*, conclusion to the sequel trilogy, it caused significantly less of a stir. While critics were less than enthusiastic about the film, fans seemed to be generally satisfied with it (Tassi 2019). No boycotts or public outrages emerged during or after *The Rise of the Skywalker*'s theatrical run, which would indicate that either the film managed to appease the most fervent haters of the new movies or that enthusiasm for protesting against changes in representation had subdued.

PASSING THE TORCH

The sequel trilogy takes place some thirty years after the events of the original. It features a cast of new characters with enough old ones to connect the films to previous installments. The first film of the new trilogy, *Force Awakens*, tells a story very similar to Luke's, but with a female character: Rey (Daisy Ridley), who has grown up with stories about the Rebellion, the Jedi, and, especially adventures of Luke Skywalker. The film features a scene where she re-enacts events from the previous films with toys that appear self-made. The scene appears as an obvious allusion to the enormous impact that the first waves of *Star Wars* action figures had in the toy stores. These figures arrived between 1977–1985 and illustrated a change in how toys represented female characters and how children were ready to accept the malleability of gender roles (Inness 2004, 83–84). This scene sets up later events in the film when Rey is given Luke's old lightsaber, metaphorically passing the torch to a new generation. She eventually runs into Han Solo, who now has a similar purpose in the story as Obi-Wan Kenobi (Alec Guinness) had in the original film, to help the protagonist on their journey toward becoming a hero. Just like Obi-Wan, Han joins the younger protagonists on one last adventure that ends in his demise.

Since the Empire's defeat, things have not improved dramatically in the galaxy, or at least conditions have deteriorated to the same level that they were in the original trilogy. The Empire is gone, but an equally nefarious group, The First Order, has risen from its ruins. Leia is once again leading the Rebellion, now rebranded as the Resistance, to reinstate freedom to the galaxy. From the original band of heroes, she is the only one who has kept on fighting. Luke has become a recluse whom no one has seen in years, and Han and his copilot Chewbacca (Peter Mayhew)[3] have returned to the smuggling business. Leia is the only character who seems to have a continuing interest in implementing permanent societal change.

The plot points of *The Force Awakens* are so similar to *A New Hope* that it is essentially a palimpsest of the 1977 original. Palimpsest is perhaps best understood as a text written over the original text so that the original text is partially visible (Dillon 2007, 4). *The Force Awakens* tells the new story over the original in a manner that informs older viewers that this story is now told with different types of characters and allows those not familiar with the original film to enjoy a traditional hero's journey plot. These types of plotlines centering around girl- or woman-identified characters remain scarce. A major movie like the *Force Awakens* can influence cultural attitudes when they feature female characters interacting with narratives traditionally reserved for male characters (Larabee 2016, 7–9). The palimpsestuous nature of the sequel trilogy continued in the two later films as well. Just like *Empire Strikes Back*, *The Last Jedi* features the heroes at their lowest, introduces some complexity into the story, and has the force-sensitive hero (Luke in 1980 and Rey in 2017) train with a reclusive Jedi master, while the rest of the heroes are trying to escape the villains. *The Rise of the Skywalker* similarly retreads the pattern of *The Return of the Jedi* as the trilogy once again concludes in the redemption of the main antagonist and thus culminating the hero's journey.

The sequel trilogy is informed by the context of a crisis of hegemony that Hollywood started to experience during the 2010s. Isabel Molina-Guzmán (2016, 442) notes that technological, economic, and social changes are affecting the status quo of the US film industry, leading to improved representations of diversity. These improvements happen at a glacial pace, but since certain popular culture phenomena receive more public attention than others, a significant change in one or two of them might seem like a larger cultural shift is taking place. The destabilization of Hollywood hegemony appears to coincide with a larger cultural shift happening in the United States. Pippa Norris and Ronald Inglehart (2019, 331–338) argue that the slow disintegration of the conservative hegemony of traditional values in America has reached a critical point. The backlash against this tectonic shift has been prominent, but those who, for instance, oppose LGBTQ+ rights and significant efforts to stop the climate crisis are in an ever-shrinking minority. The *Star Wars* films of the 2010s appear to be going along with this shift rather than trying to hold it back.

The people making *Star Wars* films in the 2010s appear to understand that gender stereotyping can severely limit the potential of individuals and, by extension, any group of which they are a member. In *The Force Awakens*, Han Solo is initially skeptical of Rey's capabilities, as is Finn (John Boyega), a former First Order stormtrooper who joins the Resistance. Finn treats Rey as a damsel in distress, but he quickly realizes that she does not need him to hold her hand, which Rey says explicitly to him. Han develops a paternal relationship with Rey during the course of the film, eventually acknowledging that she "knows her stuff." In *The Last Jedi*, as well as in *The Rise of the Skywalker*, Rey's abilities are no longer questioned based on her gender but rather on the basis of her origins.

Hollywood films have a problematic history of treating female heroes as de-feminized women who must shed all markers of femininity to be taken seriously as heroes, or at least this is what the critical discussion on female heroes often centers around. Tasker (1993, 132–139) notes that female heroes who are masculine have the potential to transgress and to secure a gender binary in which the terms "masculinity" and "male" are interlinked, as are "femininity" and "female." Tasker refers to muscular female heroes and female heroes who transgress the borders of femininity and masculinity. Whether a viewer sees these characters as transgressive celebrations of gender fluidity or reinforcing existing gender relations by making female characters symbolically male depends on the point of view and, to some extent, at least if they see certain genres as inherently "male," such as mainstream action-adventure films. Tasker's evaluations on how female heroes are perceived underline the complexity of understanding cinema as a terrain of gender negotiations. However, Nicola Rehling (2009, 102–103) argues that masculinized female heroes destabilize ontological discourses of the body in a way that also impacts how male bodies are understood. Both Tasker and Rehling refer to films that featured scenes that display the female characters' muscular physique (*Aliens* from 1986 and *Terminator 2: Judgement Day* from 1991). Considering that the sequel trilogy does not feature scenes that focus on Rey or any other character's body or musculature, these films sever the link between traditional signifiers of masculine power and heroism. The sequel trilogy has a recurring theme of presenting women as consistently competent defenders of freedom, perhaps not despite of their gender but because of it. Simultaneously, it shows men being more erratic in their efforts if they are not openly trying to instate space-fascism. Masculinity, it seems, is in a state of crisis even in the galaxy far far away.

GALACTIC CRISIS OF MASCULINITY

Failure of masculinity is present in the sequel trilogy, especially in *Force Awakens* and *The Last Jedi*. In *Force Awakens*, the complex father-son-relationship between Han and Kylo Ren (Adam Driver) serves as the platform for this failure. Between the original trilogy and the sequel trilogy, Han and Leia have had a son, Ben Solo, with whom Han has an estranged relationship. The details are left haze, but Han has been absent for a significant portion of his life. Ben has taken the name Kylo Ren and has become so disillusioned with the Rebellion's achievements that he has turned to the dark side. Kylo serves as the main antagonist for two-thirds of the sequel trilogy. In *The Force Awakens*, he kills father Han; in *The Last Jedi*, he almost kills his mother. Finally, in *The Rise of the Skywalker*, after being mortally wounded by Rey who then uses to the force to heal him, Kylo is confronted by his father's "memory ghost." Han then explains that Kylo might be dead, but Ben is still alive, putting him on the path to the side of good.

Hannah Hamad (2011, 250–251) notes Hollywood films tend to feature redemptive narratives of fatherhood. An absent father will redeem himself to preserve the patriarchal notion of fathers having the most crucial role in the project of parenthood. The popular Hollywood cinema of the 1980s, which the original trilogy is associated with, had a tendency to emphasize the importance of paternal relationships and suggesting that the absence of a strong, decisive father(figure) results in societal turmoil (Jeffords 1994, 63–72). Parenting and issues of fatherhood have always been present in *Star Wars*. The original trilogy focused on Luke discovering his father's legacy and the prequel trilogy explored how the Skywalker family came to be. Han's death in the sequel trilogy comes at a point when Rey has accepted him as a type of father figure, but Kylo's redemption seems unlikely. The sequel trilogy initially seems to avoid the conventional paternal arc described by Hamad and Jeffords but eventually settles back into a familiar pattern of fathers being at the center of parenting.

In *The Last Jedi*, this failure of masculinity becomes more of a crisis. Luke has failed profoundly as a Jedi master that he has become a cranky recluse living in self-imposed exile. *The Last Jedi* also features subplots that undermine male characters' risky strategies, but Luke's unheroic turn is at the film's front and center. Hollywood films typically have arcs that recuperate hegemonic forms of masculinity through crisis narratives that reinforce aggressive and violent behavior as remedies for stabilizing personal and societal problems (Donnar 2020, 7). The sequel trilogy begins by going a different route but eventually concludes in a more traditional story of redemption as *The Rise of the Skywalker* jettisons most of the more subversive story elements through retroactive continuity.

In the original trilogy, Luke's arc of discovering his Jedi heritage had thematic similarities with the Mythopoetic Men's movement of the 1980s and early 1990s. The movement attempted to solve the "crisis" of masculinity by spiritual means (Kimmel 2006, 211). Generating a sense of an ongoing crisis is often present in populist performances of political speech that tries to appeal to "common sense" and the "people" (Moffitt and Tormey 2014, 387–389). *The Last Jedi* does not frame Luke's crisis as something that can be resolved by retrieving masculine strategies that worked in the past, but as something that needs to be confronted and accepted. The crisis of masculinity is not universal, but rather the experience of some men who see a connection between their own masculinity and sense of powerlessness, meaninglessness, or uncertainty (Edwards 2006, 17). John Fox (2004, 105–106) notes that the Mythopoetic Men's movement contextualized the "crisis" of (white) masculinity resulting from overexposure to female role models. Fox also adds that the movement ran out of steam by the late 1990s as it had no real vision of social change or social justice. The sequel trilogy places Han and Luke in similar positions. The Rebellion initially coalesced around a white male savior. It could not create permanent social and structural change, leaving those who started the Rebellion to pick up the pieces, particularly Leia and later Rey.

The premise of the sequel trilogy suggests that overreliance on outdated masculine strategies is what prevented the Rebellion in the original trilogy to enact long-term change. Neither Han nor Luke could reimagine themselves in the post-imperial context that followed after their successful escapades. Two leading male-figures in the Rebellion failed to live up to their expectations, and the situation has once again deteriorated. *The Last Jedi* makes it explicit that the risky heroics that saved them in the past provided only short-term success. Actor Mark Hamill himself acknowledged that he believed that his generation (Hamill was born in 1951) would bring an end to racial discrimination and wars once they gained political power and that Luke's arc as a failure mirrors the failure to do so (Skrebels 2018). Film critic Dave Schilling (2017) made similar observations about *The Last Jedi* being metaphorically about baby boomers passing the torch to a new generation. *The Last Jedi* addresses the past events without a celebratory tone and perhaps failed to meet some viewers' nostalgic expectations. Those fans who felt betrayed by the film described it as "too political" and the new characters as "tools to push an agenda of masculine inferiority" (Miller 2018).

In *The Last Jedi*, Luke gives his life to help the Resistance, distracting Kylo long enough to allow the heroes to escape once more. For a few brief minutes, it seems as if Luke has miraculously arrived to intervene in the final battle to do what he mockingly suggested everyone thinks he should do,[4] only to reveal that Luke never even left the remote corner of the galaxy where he had exiled himself. By making Luke's triumphant return mere subterfuge, the film distances itself from the more traditional heroic narratives. *The Force Awakens* concluded with Rey finding Luke and offering him his lightsaber. The cliffhanger ending built up expectations of Luke making a triumphant return, wielding the weapon he lost long ago. *The Last Jedi* began with Luke examining the saber and then tossing it unceremoniously away. While this scene set the pace for the rest of the film, it encapsulates how the middle part of the sequel trilogy was a potential point of reexamination of the franchise's entire premise.

Luke subverts the expectations set for him and the narrative departs from the traditional "hero's journey." The force projection gimmick allows the film to both embrace and resist "the call to adventure." Even if his choice eventually lands on the side of resisting. Kevin Alexander Boon (2005, 308) argues that men are still valorized in contemporary US society for bravery and violence, despite major changes in gender discourse. This valorization happens both in the field of popular culture and in real life. Luke's decision not to engage in the fight against the First Order is not depicted as lack of bravery but rather as a realization that he and his style of masculine heroics have outrun their use. He is also less sure of the force's absolute nature, the dark side versus the light side, a theme that was central to all previous *Star Wars* films. Boon (2005, 307) contends that threatened (real or imagined threat) groups that see absolutes as an appealing way to view the world are also more likely to believe in heroes who are god-like in their purity and, on at least some abstract level, immortal. Humanizing elements are almost offensive in heroic narratives to these groups, and they see heroes as hyperbolic extensions of masculine characteristics. The reveal that Luke, the central hero of the *Star Wars* saga, is not only very human with his fears and mistakes, has also denounced violence and eventually dies somewhat unceremoniously from exhaustion, provoking fans already anxious of losing ground.

The original trilogy valorized both the indifferent brashness of Han and Luke's mythopoetic search for a deep masculine identity. The narrative arcs of Han and Luke both revolved around failing to resolve personal (or societal) problems in a sustainable manner, resulting in exiling themselves from emotional labor required by their roles: Luke failing to train a new generation of Jedi, Han abandoning his family. Both characters are redeemed in the end as they try their best to undo mistakes of the past.

Kylo, on the other hand, is more interested in recreating the past by trying to emulate his grandfather, Darth Vader. He holds a similar position in the First Order as Vader did, later rising to be their supreme leader. Despite his best efforts, Kylo is unable to assume the stoic and ominous masculine presence of Vader. He attempts to restore the fascist regime of the Empire and reinstating himself, a white male, at the center of galactic power. These attempts link him to a pernicious form of nostalgia associated with gender populism. Tuija Saresma (2018, 181–182) noted that gender populism is present in online-based MRA texts and evokes nostalgic and imaginary images of a traditional gender order. As mentioned earlier, the Alt-right and MRAs see a need to reinstate white men as the sole custodians of positions of power in society. Such a mindset would respond positively to fantasies of returning to mythic and "original" modes of masculinity. The sequel trilogy begins by framing Kylo as the clear villain, the first two films vilify endeavors of remasculinization of political power and deflate notions of white men being at a disadvantage in contemporary society.

In this context, *The Rise of the Skywalker* mitigates the feminist themes that the trilogy was now seemingly embracing by giving Luke and Han a chance, albeit from beyond the grave, to tell the heroes to do the right thing. The Emperor, who had been previously absent in the sequel trilogy, returns to tie everything conveniently together. The resurrected Emperor displaces Kylo as the main antagonist and becomes a thematically vague threat to the galaxy's freedom. Kylo is reimagined as a tragic hero, resulting in the more critical gender narratives of the new trilogy to fade in favor of his new storyline. The trilogy concludes on a note of improved diversity and a rushed attempt to rehabilitate those inflicted by harmful modes of masculinity. As the ending negotiates a less polarized future of gender co-operation, it fails to reevaluate the central gendered strategies of the series in favor of a clear good versus evil battle.

CONCLUSIONS

The *Star Wars* sequel trilogy has the promise of genuinely upsetting the gendered narratives of the franchise but this promise is only half-fulfilled. Characters like Leia and Rey hold positions of power in the narrative, but these films' fundamental structure remains the same. The sequel trilogy ends up following the monomyth of a hero's journey, lessening the impact of the more subversive and potentially feminist story choices. The issue of how *The Last Jedi* or *The Force Awakens* were seen as feminist by MRAs and other similar groups is more about how those groups denounce feminism rather than how feminist these films are. Anti-feminism runs rampant among right-wing populists in the United States. They see feminism being disruptive to the "natural order" of society and demand usurping social, political, and economic power from women as a way to reclaim their masculine identity (Dignam and Rohlinger 2019). Narratives that place women in central heroic roles are likely to enrage groups who agree with these values.

The sequel trilogy initially coupled female heroism with failing masculine strategies and identities in a constant state of crisis, suggesting a need for a profound reexamination of how gender identities are constructed and understood. While female characters that disrupt the gender order are not unique to the 2010s, combining them with failing masculinities is novel, at least in the context of *Star Wars* films. The narrative in *The Force Awakens* tiptoed around this concept but left it unrealized. *The Last Jedi* took some steps toward more complex gender narratives. In that film, Luke, the central hero of the series, was portrayed as an embittered broken hermit, unwilling to fulfill the expectations that the galaxy (and the audience) had for him. At this point, the sequel trilogy seemed to be creating a narrative in which men who rely on traditional forms of masculinity are incapable of solving contemporary social problems. Leaving Rey with the task of constructing her own heroic identity without depending on masculine performances. *The Rise of the Skywalker* mitigated much of *The Last Jedi*'s impact by turning Kylo from a quasi men's rights activist villain to a tragic hero. Kylo's redemption happens after a talk with his deceased father, which has implications of underlining the importance of paternal relationships. The perception of the new *Star Wars* trilogy being particularly feminist might be less about the franchise making a drastic turn ideologically but rather about how the series stayed primarily on the same course it has been on since its inception with some improvements of diversity and representation. The hostile discussion around the films tells us less about the content of the sequel trilogy but more about how popular culture is discussed and understood in the 2010s and 2020s.

NOTES

1. All the *Star Wars* films are addressed with their distinctive titles, a title like *Star Wars: Episode IV—A New Hope* (1977) is called *A New Hope*. The original trilogy: *A New Hope* (Lucas 1977), *The Empire Strikes Back* (Kershner 1980), and *Return of the Jedi* (Marquand 1983), the prequel trilogy: *The Phantom Menace* (Lucas 1999), *Attack of the Clones* (Lucas 2002), and *Revenge of the Sith* (Lucas 2005). The individual spinoff films produced by Disney *Rogue One: A Star Wars Story* (Edwards 2016) and *Solo: A Star Wars Story* (Howard 2018) are not included in the character analysis.

2. Audiences gave the film an A on a scale of A+ being the best and F being the worst. CinemaScore is a market research firm that surveys audiences on their viewing experiences. Their site currently does provide a direct link to the score of a film, and films need to be searched manually from their site, https://www.cinemascore.com/.

3. Peter Mayhew reprised his role as Chewbacca in *The Force Awakens* with Joonas Suotamo acting as his body double. Suotamo has since inherited the role of Chewie (Robinson 2018).

4. "You don't need Luke Skywalker. You think what? I'm gonna walk out with a laser sword and face down the whole First Order?" Luke Skywalker to Rey in *The Last Jedi* (Johnson 2017).

BIBLIOGRAPHY

Abrams, J.J. dir. 2015. *Star Wars: Episode VII—The Force Awakens*. Burbank, CA: Disney/Buena Vista Home Video. UHD Blu-ray.

Abrams, J.J. dir. 2019. *Star Wars: Episode IX—The Rise of the Skywalker*. Burbank, CA: Disney Buena Vista Home Video. UHD Blu-ray.

Ashwin, Sarah and Jennifer Utrata. "Masculinity Restored? Putin's Russia and Trump's America." *Contexts* 19 (2): 16–21.

Bay, Morten. 2018. "Weaponizing the Haters: *The Last Jedi* and the Strategic Politicization of Pop Culture through Social Media Manipulation." *First Monday* 23 (11): 1–37.

Boon, Kevin Alexander. 2005. "Heroes, Metanarratives, and the Paradox of Masculinity in Contemporary Western Culture." *The Journal of Men's Studies* 13 (3): 301–312.

Box Office Mojo. 2015. "Star Wars: Episode VII—The Force Awakens." https://www.boxofficemojo.com/title/tt2488496/?ref_=bo_se_r_1.

Box Office Mojo. 2016. "Rogue One: A Star Wars Story (2016)." https://www.boxofficemojo.com/release/rl2557707777/.

Britton, Andrew. 1986. "Blissing Out: The Politics of Reaganite Entertainment." *Movie* 31/32: 1–42.

Bruin-Molé, Megen de. 2018. "Does it Come with a Spear?" Commodity Activism, Plastic Representation, and Transmedia Story Strategies in Disney's Star Wars: Forces of Destiny." *Film and Merchandise* 42 (2). https://doi.org/10.3998/fc.137 61232.0042.205.

Butler, Judith. 2004. *Undoing Gender*. New York: Routledge.

Campbell, Joseph. 1949. *The Hero with a Thousand Faces*. Princeton: Princeton University Press.

Carian, Emily K., and Tagart Cain Sobotka. 2018. "Playing the Trump Card: Masculinity Threat and the US 2016 Presidential Election." *Socious: Sociological Research for a Dynamic World* 4: 1–6. https://doi.org/10.1177/2378023117740699.

Cinemascore. 2020. "Cinemascore." May 2, 2020. https://www.cinemascore.com/.

Cocca, Carolyn. 2016. *Superwomen: Gender, Power, and Representation*. London: Bloomsbury.

Denham, Jess. 2016. "Men's Rights Activists Actually Think Their Boycott Cost Star Wars: The Force Awakens Millions." *The Independent*, January 4, 2016. https://www.independent.co.uk/arts-entertainment/films/news/star-wars-mens-rights-activists-claim-boycott-cost-the-force-awakens-42m-a6796146.html.

Dignam, Pierce Alexander, and Deana A. Rohlinger. 2019. "Misogynist Men Online: How the Red Pill Helped Elect Trump." *Signs: Journal of Women in Culture and Society* 44 (3): 589–612.

Dillon, Sarah. 2007. *The Palimpsest: Literature, Criticism, and Theory*. New York: Continuum.

Donnar, Glen. 2020. *Troubling Masculinities: Terror, Gender, and Monstrous Others in American Film Post-9/11*. Jackson: University of Mississippi Press.

Dwyer, Michael D. 2015. *Back to the Fifties: Nostalgia, Hollywood, Film, & Popular Music of the Seventies and Eighties*. Oxford: Oxford University Press.

Edwards, Gareth dir. 2016. *Rogue One: A Star Wars Story*. Burbank, CA: Disney Buena Vista Home Video. UHD Blu-ray.

Edwards, Tim. 2006. *Cultures of Masculinity*. London: Routledge.

Ellis, Emma Grey. 2016. "The Alt-Right Hates' Rogue One,' Because Of Course It Does." *Wired*, December 14, 2016. https://www.wired.com/2016/12/rogue-one-alt-right-boycott/.

Ellison, Sarah. 2016. "Meet the Most Powerful Woman in Hollywood." *Vanity Fair*, February 8, 2016. https://www.vanityfair.com/hollywood/2016/02/kathleen-kennedy-hollywood-producer.

Fontanella, Lara, Mara Maretti, and Annalina Sarra. 2013. "Gender Fluidity Across the World: A Multilevel Item Response Theory Approach." *Qual Quant* 48 (3): 2553–2568.

Fox, John. 2004. "How Men's Movement Participants View Each Other." *The Journal of Men's Studies* 12 (2): 103–118.

Hamad, Hannah. 2011. "Extreme Parenting: Recuperating Fatherhood in Steven Spielberg's *War of the Worlds*." In *Feminism at the Movies: Understanding Gender in Contemporary Popular Cinema*, edited by Hilary Radner, and Rebecca Stringer, 241–251. New York: Routledge.

Heritage, Stuart. 2018. "The Last Jedi: What Would the $200m Fan-Funded Remake Look Like?" *The Guardian*, June 25, 2018. https://www.theguardian.com/film/2018/jun/25/the-last-jedi-what-would-the-200m-fan-funded-remake-look-like.

Howard, Ron dir. 2018. *Solo: A Star Wars Story*. Burbank, CA: Disney / Buena Vista Home Video. UHD Blu-ray.

Inness, Sherrie. A. 2004. "It's a Girl Thing: Tough Female Action Figures in the Toy Store," In *Action Chicks: New Images of Tough Women in Popular Culture*, edited by Sherrie A. Inness, 75–94. New York: Palgrave Macmillan.

Jameson, Fredric. 1998. *The Cultural Turn: Selected Writings on the Postmodern, 1983–1998*. New York: Verso.

Jeffords, Susan. 1994. *Hard Bodies: Hollywood Masculinity in the Reagan Era*. New Brunswick, NJ: Rutgers University Press.

Jewett, Robert, and John Shelton Lawrence. 1988. *The American Monomyth: Second Edition*. Lanham, MD: University Press of America.

Johnson, Derek. 2018. "From the Ruins: Neomasculinity, Media Franchising, and Struggles Over Industrial Reproduction of Culture." *Communication Culture & Critique* 11 (1): 85–99.

Johnson, Rian, dir. 2017. *Star Wars: Episode VIII—The Last Jedi*. Burbank, CA: Disney / Buena Vista Home Video. UHD Blu-ray.

Jones, Brian Jay. 2016. *George Lucas: A Life*. New York: Little, Brown and Company.

Kaminski, Michael. 2008. *The Secret History of Star Wars: The Art of Storytelling and Making of a Modern Myth*. Kingston, ON: Legacy Books Press.

Kellner, Douglas M. 2010. *Cinema Wars: Hollywood Film and Politics in the Bush-Chaney Era*. West Sussex, UK: Wiley-Blackwell.

Kershner, Irvin, dir. 1980. *Star Wars: Episode V—The Empire Strikes Back*. Burbank, CA: Disney / Buena Vista Home Video. UHD Blu-ray.

Kimmel, Michael. 2006. *Manhood in America: A Cultural History*. Oxford: Oxford University Press.

Koulouris, Theodore. 2018. "Online misogyny and the alternative right: debating the undebatable." *Feminist Media Studies* 18 (4): 750–761.

Larabee, Ann. 2016. "Editorial: Star Wars and the Girl Hero." *Journal of Popular Culture* 49 (1): 7–9.

Lowry, Brian. 2018. "Star Wars Should Resist Bowing to the Force of its Most Vocal Fans." *CNN*, June 4, 2018. https://edition.cnn.com/2018/06/04/entertainment/star-wars-fans-analysis/index.html.

Lucas, George, dir. 1977. *Star Wars: Episode IV—A New Hope*. Burbank, CA: Disney / Buena Vista Home Video. UHD Blu-ray.

Lucas, George, dir. 1999. *Star Wars: Episode I—The Phantom Menace*. Burbank, CA: Disney / Buena Vista Home Video. UHD Blu-ray.

Lucas, George, dir. 2002. *Star Wars: Episode II—Attack of the Clones*. Burbank, CA: Disney / Buena Vista Home Video. UHD Blu-ray.

Lucas, George, dir. 2005. *Star Wars: Episode III—Revenge of the Sith*. Burbank, CA: Disney / Buena Vista Home Video. UHD Blu-ray.

Lyden, John C. 2018. "The More Things Change: Historical Political Context and The Force Awakens." In Th*e Myth Awakens: Canon, Conservativism, and Fan Reception*, edited by Ken Derry, and John C. Lyden. Eugene, Chapter 1. OR: Cascade Books. Kindle e-book.

Marquand, Richard, dir. 1983. *Star Wars Episode VI: Return of the Jedi*. Burbank, CA: Disney / Buena Vista Home Video. UHD Blu-ray.

Merlock, Ray, and Kathy Merlock Jackson. 2012. "Lightsabers, Political Arenas, and Marriages for Princess Leia and Queen Amidala." In *Sex, Politics, and Religion in Star Wars: An Anthology*, edited by Douglas Brode, and Leah Deyneka, 8–84. Toronto: The Scarecrow Press, Inc.

Metacritic. 2017. "Star Wars: Episode VIII - The Last Jedi." December 15, 2017. https://www.metacritic.com/movie/star-wars-episode-viii---the-last-jedi.

Miller, Matt. 2018. "The Year *Star Wars* Fans Finally Ruined *Star Wars*." *Esquire*, December 13, 2018. https://www.esquire.com/entertainment/movies/a25560063/how-fans-ruined-star-wars-the-last-jedi-2018/.

Moffitt, Benjamin, and Simon Tormey. 2014. "Rethinking Populism: Politics, Mediatisation and Political Style." *Political Studies* 62 (2): 381–397.

Molina-Guzmán, Isabel. 2016. "#OscarsSoWhite: How Stuart Hall Explains Why Nothing Changes in Hollywood and Everything is Changing." *Critical Studies in Media Communications* 33 (5): 438–454.

Nelson, Elissa. 2013. "Beneath the Surface and the Excess: An Examination of Critical and Aesthetic Attacks on Films of the 1980s." *The Journal of Popular Culture* 46 (5): 1029–1050.

Norris, Pippa and Ronald Inglehart. 2019. *Cultural Backlash: Trump, Brexit, and Authoritarian Populism*. Cambridge: Cambridge University Press.

Proctor, William. 2013. "'Holy Crap, More *Star Wars*! More *Star Wars*? What If They're Crap?': Disney, Lucasfilm and *Star Wars*." *Participations: Journal of Audience & Reception Studies* 10 (1): 198–224.

Rehling, Nicola. 2009. *Extra-Ordinary Men: White Heterosexual Masculinity in Contemporary Popular Cinema*. Lanham, MD: Lexington Books.

Robinson, Tasha. 2018. "Chewbacca Actor Joonas Suotamo Explains the Wookiee Mask, Movement, and Mentality." *The Verge*, May 24, 2018. https://www.theverge

.com/2018/5/24/17387164/chewbacca-actor-joonas-suotamo-interview-wookiee
-mask-behind-the-scenes-solo-star-wars-story.

Rotten Tomatoes. 2017. "Star Wars: The Last Jedi (2017)." https://www.rottentomatoes.
com/m/star_wars_the_last_jedi.

Saresma, Tuija. 2018. "Gender Populism: Three Cases of Finns Party Actors'
Traditionalist Anti-Feminism." In *Populism on the Loose*, edited by Urpo Kovala,
Emilia Palonen, Maria Ruotsalainen, and Tuija Saresma, 177–200. Jyväskylä:
Jyväskylän yliopisto.

Schilling, Dave. 2017. "Star Wars: The Last Jedi Review: The Star Wars Film That
Finally Lives Up to Empire Strikes Back." *Birth. Movies. Death*, December 12,
2017. https://birthmoviesdeath.com/2017/12/12/star-wars-the-last-jedi-review-the-
star-wars-film-that-finally-lives-up-to.

Sharf, Zack. 2017. "Petition to Remove 'Star Wars: The Last Jedi' From Official
Canon Has Over 13,000 Signatures." *IndieWire*, December 2017. https://www
.indiewire.com/2017/12/petition-star-wars-last-jedi-remove-canon-signatures-120
1909099/.

Shaw, Daniel Odin. 2018. "The New Language of Hate: Misogyny and the Alt-
Right." In *Identities in Flux Globalisation, Trauma, and Reconciliation*, edited by
Dagmar Kusá, 186–198. Bratislava: Kritika & Kontext.

Skrebels, Joe. 2018. "Mark Hamill on the Weirdly Tragic Trajectory of Luke
Skywalker." *IGN*, June 26, 2018. https://nordic.ign.com/star-wars-episode-v-the
-empire-strikes-back/16345/feature/mark-hamill-on-the-weirdly-tragic-trajectory
-of-luke-skywalker.

Tasker, Yvonne. 1993. *Spectacular Bodies Gender, Genre and the Action Cinema*.
Abingdon: Routledge.

Tassi, Paul. 2019. "Why Has *Star Wars: Rise of Skywalker*" Divided Critics and Fand
So Sharply?" *Forbes*, December 29, 2019. https://www.forbes.com/sites/paultassi/
2020/12/29/why-has-star-wars-rise-of-skywalker-divided-critics-and-fans-so-
sharply/#52cad1824799.

Tsjeng, Zing. 2018. "An MRA Edited the Women Out of 'The Last Jedi' and It's as
Bad as You Think." *Vice*, January 17, 2018. https://www.vice.com/en_us/article/
paqw3y/mra-edit-women-out-star-wars-last-jedi-review.

White, Mark H. 2019. "Star Wars Fandom Survey, Part 3: Sexism and Political
Attitudes." *Mark H. White II*, May 31, 2019. https://www.markhw.com/blog/sw
-survey-pt3.

White, Mark H., and Matthew Baldwin. 2018. "The Force is *Too* Strong with This One?
Sexism, *Star Wars*, and Female Heroes." *The Inquisitive Mind*, January 4, 2018.
https://www.in-mind.org/blog/post/the-force-is-too-strong-with-this-one-sexism-
star-wars-and-female-heroes.

Wood, Mara. 2016. "Feminist Icons Wanted: Damsels in Distress Need Not Apply,"
In *A Galaxy Here and Now: Historical and Cultural Readings of Star Wars*, edited
by Peter W. Lee, 62–83. Jefferson, NC: McFarland & Company, Inc.

Wood, Robin. 1985. "'80s Hollywood: Dominant Tendencies." *CineAction!* 1 (1):
2–5.

Index

About the Contributors

Outi Hakola is a senior researcher at the Department of Cultures, University of Helsinki. She is also the principal investigator of the project focusing on populism and masculinity. Her background is in media studies, and her research concentrates on questions of emotions and affects in films, television, and social media.

Janne Salminen is a doctoral candidate at the Doctoral Programme in Gender, Culture and Society, University of Helsinki, Finland. His research focuses on deconstructing masculinity and femininity in Hollywood mainstream cinema. He has published on gender politics and political ideologies of Hollywood films.

Juho Turpeinen is a doctoral student in the Doctoral Programme in Political, Societal and Regional Change at the University of Helsinki. His research focuses on the relationship between culture and democracy, drawing on political theory and cultural studies. His current work centers on an analysis social media discourses related to land disputes in the American West.

Oscar Winberg is a doctoral candidate at the History Department of Åbo Akademi University, working on modern political history. His research focuses on the intersections of media, especially television, and politics in the United States. He has published on both news and entertainment media in American political history.

Nicholas Blower holds a PhD in American Studies from the University of Kent, where he has taught since 2014. His research focuses on conservative resistance to environmentalism, with a focus on Utah and the wider American Southwest.

Swapna Gopinath is a Fulbright fellow at the Department of Art and Art History, University of Rochester, New York. She is an associate professor of English Literature from Kerala, India. She has a PhD in English Literature, and has completed postdoctoral research in media and cultural studies. Her areas of research include cultural studies, film studies and gender studies.

Christian Jimenez has taught at various colleges. His research topics include social movements, cultural politics, and representation in the mass media. He has published dozens of essays and/or encyclopedia articles on race, gender, conspiracy theory, and religious extremism.

Tatu-Ilari Laukkanen is a postdoctoral researcher at the Faculty of Information Technology and Communication Sciences at the Tampere University. He received his PhD in 2017 from the Department of Comparative Literature at Hong Kong University. A film scholar and industry professional, his research interests include gangster film, geopolitics and the cinema of the BRICS.

Katinka Linnamäki is a doctoral candidate at the Doctoral programme in Gender, Culture and Society, University of Helsinki, affiliated with the Helsinki Research Hub on Emotions, Populism and Polarisation (HEPP). Her doctoral thesis focuses on the concept of hegemony in CEE and the questions of gender in hegemony building and its interwovenness with nationalism and populism.

Nicholas Manganas is a lecturer in International Studies at the University of Technology Sydney. Manganas has published widely in the disciplinary areas of Spanish studies, queer studies and popular culture studies. His current research explores manifestations of "crisis cultures" where he explores what occurs in the cultural sphere when crisis becomes a prolonged phenomenon.

Joshua D. Martin is an assistant professor of Spanish at the University of North Georgia. He holds a PhD in Hispanic Studies from the University of Kentucky and specializes in the representation of masculinity construction and space (particularly borders) in literature and political discourse.

John Quinn is a lecturer in Screen and Performance at the University of the West of Scotland. Working within the division of Arts & Media, Quinn's research explores the narratives and cultural politics of popular culture, particularly film and television.

Didem Unal is a postdoctoral researcher at the Religion, Conflict and Dialogue Research Center at the University of Helsinki. She received her PhD from Bilkent University, Ankara. Her research interests focus on gender politics in contemporary Turkey, feminist subaltern publics, Muslim identities in Western migration regimes, and Islamic feminism.

www.ingramcontent.com/pod-product-compliance
Lightning Source LLC
Chambersburg PA
CBHW050639280326
41932CB00015B/2710